Freedom's Orphans

NEW FORUM BOOKS

Robert P. George, Series Editor

Freedom's Orphans

CONTEMPORARY LIBERALISM AND
THE FATE OF AMERICAN CHILDREN

David L. Tubbs

PRINCETON UNIVERSITY PRESS

PRINCETON AND OXFORD

Copyright © 2007 by Princeton University Press

Published by Princeton University Press, 41 William Street, Princeton, New Jersey 08540

In the United Kingdom: Princeton University Press, 3 Market Place, Woodstock, Oxfordshire OX20 1SY

All Rights Reserved

Library of Congress Cataloging-in-Publication Data
Tubbs, David Lewis, date.
Freedom's orphans : contemporary liberalism and the fate of American children / David L. Tubbs.
p.   cm.
Includes bibliographical references and index.
ISBN-13: 978-0-691-12298-4 (hard cover : alk. paper)
ISBN-13: 978-0-691-13470-3 (pbk. : alk. paper)
1. Child welfare—United States.   2. Liberalism—United States.   I. Title.
HV741.T83 2007
362.7—dc22   2007001484

British Library Cataloging-in-Publication Data is available

This book has been composed in Sabon

Printed on acid-free paper. ∞

pup.princeton.edu

Printed in the United States of America

10 9 8 7 6 5 4 3 2 1

To my mother and father

Contents

Acknowledgments

For comments on different chapters, including drafts, I thank James Wood Bailey, Sotirios Barber, Sammy Basu, Aurelian Craiutu, Patrick Deneen, Caryl Emerson, John Finnis, Michael Frank, David Innes, Edward Keynes, Andrew Koppelman, Yvan Lengwiler, Shannon Masterson, Jacqueline Pfeffer Merrill, Thomas Merrill, Randall Miller, Jack Nowlin, Hilary Persky, Daniel Robinson, Martha Whitfield, Peter Wood, and Michael Zuckert. An anonymous reader for Princeton University Press also read the manuscript and made many valuable suggestions.

For discussing different themes and answering questions for me, I am grateful to Gerard Bradley, Paolo Carozza, Ilene Cohen, Norman Fost, Mary Ann Glendon, Kim Hendrickson, M. Cathleen Kaveny, John Keown, Olga Keyes, Stanley Kurtz, Christopher Levenick, David Novak, Stan Oakes, David Oakley, and A. A. Sharogradskaya.

I received much help in locating sources for Chapter Four from Mr. Dwight King, a superb law librarian. Laura Leslie also provided research assistance with that chapter and others.

My biggest debts are to three former professors, each of whom influenced this project in different ways.

George Kateb is an extraordinary teacher. Despite our disagreements about the matters explored in this book, he was characteristically generous with his comments in response to my arguments here. Those comments often forced me to rethink matters large and small, and whatever the book's shortcomings, it is much better as a result of his engagement with it.

I owe a special thanks to George Downs for so much encouragement and good counsel, without which it is unlikely that I ever would have finished the book. He read multiple drafts of each chapter, and he was always ready to converse (or spar) with me about any point. The breadth of his knowledge of the social sciences amazes me, and I often availed myself of it.

I am flattered that Robert George wanted this book to be part of his series at Princeton University Press, and I hope that his confidence is justified. I thank Robby for his enthusiasm about this project and for providing guidance at the beginning. Thereafter, I benefited at every stage from his formidable knowledge of constitutional law and legal theory.

I have received institutional support from several sources. Having spent a year at the American Enterprise Institute as the W. H. Brady Visiting Fellow in Social and Political Studies, I wish to thank Chris DeMuth, the President of AEI, the sponsors of the fellowship, and Sam Thern-strom, who directs the Brady Program on Culture and Freedom. After my year at AEI, I received a faculty research grant from the Earhart Founda-tion. I thank Ingrid Gregg, its president, and Kim Dennis, who first told me about the research grants. Finally, I am grateful to Luis Tellez and the other officers of the Witherspoon Institute for their continuing support.

An earlier version of Chapter Four appeared in *Pepperdine Law Re-view* 30, no. 1 (2002): 1–78, © 2002 by the Pepperdine University School of Law. I gratefully acknowledge permission to reprint this here.

Freedom's Orphans

CHILDREN DEPEND on adults for many things, and this dependence encompasses more than material needs. Certain intangible goods—education, for example—are just as crucial to their well-being. These observations are hardly provocative, and any sustained commentary on human society that wants to be taken seriously is unlikely to deny this dependence.

In this connection, consider the second of Ralph Waldo Emerson's two epigraphs to his essay "Self-Reliance" (1841):

> Cast the bantling on the rocks,
> Suckle him with the she-wolf's teat;
> Wintered with the hawk and fox,
> Power and speed be hands and feet.

The irony of these lines serves several purposes. It points to the limits of self-reliance, perhaps as a way of tempering the enthusiasm of those readers well disposed to the essay. At the same time, the epigraph forestalls possible criticisms. Without it, some readers might complain that Emerson has forgotten about children and family life, an otherwise startling omission in a disquisition about the individual's relationship to society.

Besides being dependent on adults, children are impressionable. By definition, a child is underdeveloped in several ways: physically, mentally, morally, and emotionally. To say that an adult is mentally, morally, or emotionally underdeveloped often implies that he or she is also impressionable. In adults, such impressionability is considered regrettable (and sometimes a grave misfortune), but with respect to children, it is deemed unexceptional or natural.

These two themes are not unrelated. For good and for bad, a child's impressionability is in some ways linked to his or her dependence on adults.

Nearly two hundred years before Emerson's "Self-Reliance," the Dutch artist Jan Steen (1626–1679) completed a semihumorous painting, *The Way You Hear It Is the Way You Sing It*. Like many Dutch works of the seventeenth century, it is rich in symbolism, though what the painting says about moral education, human appetites, and the impressionability of the young is clear.

The painting depicts a family of three generations gathered for the festival of Twelfth Night. The grandfather of the family, a rotund man who has been crowned king of the festival, sits at the head of a small table set with holiday fare. Above the grandfather, an uncaged parrot, symbolizing mimicry, rests on its perch. The grandfather's wife sits across from him at the table and reads a nursery rhyme of the same title as the painting. Two younger women, perhaps the couple's daughters, sit between the grandfather and grandmother. The younger woman in the background has a baby in her lap. The younger woman in the foreground, only slightly less corpulent than the grandfather, holds a large goblet, being filled with the same liquid that seemingly caused her drunkenness. A beaker of this liquid stands on the windowsill.

Away from the table, on the right side of the painting, an apparently tipsy man stands near two boys and an adolescent playing the bagpipes. Thought by some scholars to be Steen, the man is showing the older of the two boys how to smoke a long and slender pipe; the younger boy awaits instruction. Behind him, the adolescent with the bagpipes plays a tune. His face appears flush, a detail whose meaning can be appreciated in light of the sexual innuendo associated with the Dutch word for "pipe."[1]

Despite the passage of many years, Emerson's epigraph and Steen's painting still provide two useful points of departure for discussing the welfare of children in the modern world. Children are dependent, Emerson (indirectly) concedes, and some persons must care for them. Steen's painting reminds us that young persons, more than any others, do not on bread alone subsist.

These two points may be uncontroversial, but controversy can quickly arise when we discuss what the dependence and impressionability of children should mean for public policy. Consider the following accounts, far removed from Steen's playful wit and Emerson's delicate irony.

In the mid-1990s, three horrific crimes in England and Wales were widely believed to have been influenced by the depiction of similar crimes in American movies, then available on videocassette in Great Britain. Benedict Nightingale, chief theater critic for *The Times* (London), described the crimes and the grounds for his country's anxiety:

> In Liverpool . . . two-year-old Jamie Bulger was abducted from a shopping mall . . . by two ten-year-old boys [Robert Thompson and Jon Venables], led to a railroad line, hammered to death with an iron bar, then cut in half by a train. There were suggestions that a horror film about a demonic doll, *Child's Play 3*, helped inspire the crime. No evidence was presented that either boy had seen it, but the father of one had rented it shortly before.
>
> A gang in Manchester tortured a sixteen-year-old girl, set her afire, and left her dying. [She later died.] One of the sadists repeated the menacing *Child's Play 3* catch phrase "I'm Chucky—wanna play?"

---

[1] My interpretation of Steen's painting is based in part on my reading of Mariët Westermann, *The Amusements of Jan Steen* (Zwolle: Waanders, 1997), and the discussion of the painting in Michael Wood, Bruce Cole, and Adelheid Gealt, *Art of the Western World: From Ancient Greece to Post-Modernism* (New York: Touchstone, 1991), 182–183.

Four hooligans in Cardiff turned on a middle-aged man who had remonstrated with them for vandalizing a traffic barrier, and stomped him to death. As they did so, one repeatedly yelled a line, "I've got the juice," from the movie *Juice,* in which a shopkeeper is murdered for trying to enforce law and order.[2]

Of these three crimes, the murder of Jamie Bulger was the most notorious. In the words of one journalist, Bulger's death caused "much heartsearching," especially on the part of the thirty-eight witnesses who saw Bulger, a large gash on his forehead, being escorted to his death at midday along busy Liverpool roads. The reflectiveness or introspection of the witnesses seems natural and appropriate, but two to three months after Bulger's abductors were convicted of murder, the recriminations had begun:

> Each boy blames the other boy. Each boy's defense counsel blames the other boy. Each boy's mother blames the other boy, though Robert Thompson's mother also blames teachers and social services. Others have blamed videos, single mothers, absent fathers, original sin, and the church.[3]

How did public officials in Great Britain respond? Prime Minister John Major urged parents to pay closer attention to their children's viewing habits. The Independent Television Commission, which regulates the country's commercial networks, issued new (though apparently nonbinding) guidelines to television producers. And roughly 220 members of Parliament expressed support for a proposed law banning the sale of any video with "degrading or gratuitously violent scenes liable to cause psychological damage to a child."[4]

Educated Americans are familiar with these matters. From one perspective, these issues raise perennial questions about individual freedom, moral responsibility, and the common good of society, including the welfare of children. From another perspective, the issues raise novel questions about the power of media, the fragility of families, and the sundry agents that now "socialize" the young.

Regardless of how the issues are framed, the actions of Prime Minister Major and the Independent Television Commission are intelligible in the context of American politics. In response to many complaints about the content of popular entertainment (movies, television, music), public figures

---

[2] Benedict Nightingale, "Yankee Cinema, Please Go Home," *The New York Times,* 10 July 1994, sec. 2, p. 9.

[3] Blake Morrison, "Children of Circumstance," *The New Yorker* (14 February 1994): 48. Most people would say that Robert Thompson and Jon Venables grew up in desperate conditions. Both lived in poverty, neither had a father at home, and Thompson may have been sexually abused. See ibid., 60.

[4] Nightingale, "Yankee Cinema, Please Go Home."

in this country have criticized the entertainment industry, while exploring the feasibility of different types of legislation.

One aspect of the situation in Britain, however, stands out. In the United States, Congress would not consider legislation like that proposed in Parliament without asking whether it conflicts with the Free Speech Clause of the First Amendment, as interpreted by the Supreme Court of the United States. Many Americans would quickly (and correctly) conclude that the British legislation would be unconstitutional in the United States. But because Great Britain does not have a formal charter of rights, members of Parliament may assess the free-speech interests alongside other social interests, such as the possible effects of these movies on impressionable viewers.

Given the interests at stake, which political arrangements are preferable? To pose the question in the United States is probably an invitation to ridicule. To anyone with such thoughts, let me say that the question strikes me as legitimate, it is not inspired by treachery or Anglophilism, and its answer is by no means obvious to me.

In view of the commonalities of the British and American political systems—especially the common influence of the liberal tradition—the difference here is striking. Before making policy, American legislators routinely take account of the codified or enumerated rights of individuals. By contrast, British politicians are at least theoretically freer to consider the full range of interests that conduce to the public welfare.[5]

Most citizens in the United States revere the nation's political institutions, and many would resent the idea that those institutions—specifically, the Bill of Rights and the judiciary—might hinder our responses to problems like the one described here. Whatever the risk of causing such resentment, I want to go further in this direction. Although it may be unpleasant to consider, we should ask whether the exercise of certain freedoms by adults—including some freedoms having the status of constitutionally protected rights—may adversely affect children.

The title of this book provides my answer to that question. The book documents a worrisome development: a growing indifference to what

---

[5] In light of recent policy, some might say that this point needs to be modified slightly. The Human Rights Act (1998) introduced the European Convention on Human Rights into British law, making it unlawful for public authorities to act in ways that are "incompatible" with the rights listed in the Convention. But the European Convention on Human Rights functions differently in British politics than does the Bill of Rights in American politics. In enacting the legislation, Parliament presumably believed that it was advancing the public welfare, and it retains the right to modify or even jettison the Human Rights Act. Furthermore, most of the rights in the European Convention mention competing social interests and duties linked to the relevant freedoms. (See, for instance, Article 10, "Freedom of Expression.")

were long considered important elements of the welfare of children. The analysis focuses on developments in the United States, where the indifference can be seen at the highest levels of law and academic political theory.

The indifference should be described carefully. It typically manifests itself as a tendency to regard certain freedoms of adults as indisputably more important than the competing interests of children. One sign of this tendency is the recurring failure on the part of some jurists and political theorists to consider the interests of children in even a perfunctory way.

The specific interests referred to here are more fully described in the chapters ahead. For now, let me say that these interests are hardly obscure: other jurists and political theorists have described them, and long before the current indifference took root. Large questions remain. How did so many scholars and jurists lose sight of these interests? What caused them to be so rapidly—and so radically—devalued? The full story has many elements, and it resists any quick summary. Hence my decision to write this book.

At this point, I should pause and comment on a few terms found throughout the forthcoming chapters. Let me begin with the most salient.

As used here, the word "children" generally refers to persons aged seventeen and under. In a few places, I distinguish between younger children (i.e., preteens) and adolescents. In other places, I use the term "minors."

Some might object to the use of "children" to cover all persons seventeen and under. They might say that this group should always be divided into subgroups such as infants, very young children, preteens, and adolescents. I appreciate the point. Still, my use of "children" to refer to persons seventeen and under underscores the impressionability and dependence of all persons in this group, including teenagers approaching adulthood (even though these teenagers are generally less impressionable and dependent than both preteens and the very young).[6]

In discussing different needs of children, I often use the word "interest" (or "interests") to refer to those needs. Notice, however, that the words "interest" and "need" are not always synonymous. Children may have an interest in something (e.g., the development of certain abilities or talents), though it would not normally be designated a need. Yet most of the interests canvassed here are sufficiently important to be designated needs. Furthermore, those interests and needs can be described as "basic" or "universal" because they apply to all children and are core elements of their well-being. (Besides having basic needs, some children have special

---

[6] The usage I prefer has been accepted by others. See, for example, David Archard, "Philosophical Perspectives on Childhood," in *Legal Concepts of Childhood*, ed. Julia Fionda (Oxford: Hart Publishing, 2001), 47.

needs—"special" because they are shared by a relatively small number of their peers—and some have unique needs.)

The developments examined here tell us something important about the evolution of the liberal political tradition. What is meant by the liberal tradition? Depending on the context, the word "liberalism" may have strongly positive or strongly negative connotations. I use the word to refer to an identifiable intellectual tradition in both Europe and North America. Prominent modern thinkers associated with this tradition (sometimes called "classical liberalism") include John Locke, Immanuel Kant, Benjamin Constant, James Madison, Abraham Lincoln, John Stuart Mill, and T. H. Green.[7]

Identifying the central values or goods of the liberal tradition can be difficult, but Stephen Holmes provides a useful starting point:

> Liberalism's four core norms or values are *personal security* (the monopolization of legitimate violence by agents of the state who are themselves monitored and regulated by law), *impartiality* (a single system of law applied equally to all), *individual liberty* (a broad sphere of freedom from collective or governmental supervision, including freedom of conscience, the right to be different, the right to pursue ideals one's neighbor thinks wrong, the freedom to travel and emigrate, and so forth), and *democracy* or the right to participate in lawmaking by means of elections and public discussion through a free press.[8]

Although this passage by Holmes does not suggest as much, these four values or norms or goods might be ordered in a rough hierarchy, and their ranking might sometimes change. To my mind, such a "re-ordering" of values has occurred within American liberalism, because liberal theorists and jurists now give personal freedom (for adults) a special or preferred status.

Yet in view of the longevity of the liberal tradition, we should hesitate before making any sweeping judgments about its record in promoting the welfare of children. Clearly, the tradition can claim some successes in advancing their welfare—think, for example, of nineteenth-century legislation in Britain and the United States leading to the abolition of child labor—but this book does not offer a comprehensive assessment.

My goals are narrower. As the reader may have surmised, I assess the status of children in *contemporary* American liberalism—meaning liberalism since the end of the Second World War. More specifically, I want to

---

[7] Leading contemporary liberal theorists are identified and discussed in Chapters One, Two, and Five.

[8] Stephen Holmes, *The Anatomy of Antiliberalism* (Cambridge, Mass.: Harvard University Press, 1993), 4. Other prominent liberal theorists have offered similar lists, and I look at some of them in Chapter Five.

know the position that children have occupied in the minds of contemporary liberal theorists and jurists. Have they taken sufficient account of the dependence and impressionability of children? If not, what explains the lack of solicitude?

As the book's title indicates, the analysis here amounts to a lengthy critique. I stand by the criticisms, despite being broadly sympathetic to classical liberalism. Because of that sympathy, one aim in writing the book has been to encourage American liberals to become more historically sensitive. Greater historical sensitivity might lead them to give more attention to the problems I describe.

Still, I expect that many liberals will be more than a bit defensive about the matters I raise. To prepare the reader, let me share an anecdote.

After reading an earlier version of the manuscript, one friendly (and liberal) critic likened the book to a "syllabus of errors." This was an allusion to an encyclical written in 1864 by Pope Pius IX, in which the pope wrote that no one should expect the leader of the Roman Catholic Church to reconcile himself with liberalism and modern civilization. (Later popes modified this view in significant ways.) Even if made in jest, the friendly critic's remark suggests that some persons might suppose that this book was inspired by religious conviction.

That would be a mistake, and despite being likened to a papal encyclical, this book contains no religious "agenda." None of the arguments here require the reader to accept the tenets of any particular faith, or even a vaguely "spiritual" outlook. In fact, the real inspiration for this book was personal experience. To explain, let me digress briefly.

At one stage in my adult life I worked in state government as a child-support investigator. This work can be both immensely satisfying and extremely frustrating. It is satisfying when a support order is established and executed, frustrating when an absent parent evades such an obligation.

The most discouraging aspect of this work is parental indifference. Such indifference is not rare; an investigator sees it every day. It occurs when an absent parent tries to prevent a support order from being established or manages to avoid complying with an existing order.

I cannot say which type of indifference is worse, but both were common enough to raise questions. How could so many adults be so indifferent to their own children? What explained it? The indifference seemed contrary to long-standing social norms and to everything most people hope to find in a parent.

Another aspect of a child-support investigator's work merits comment. Some parents—the great majority of them being fathers—display much bitterness about the duty to pay child support. They often direct this bitterness at the investigator, as if the latter's work impinged on the father's freedom—specifically, his economic or sexual freedom, or some combination thereof.

Even after leaving this job, I reflected on these experiences, and I had occasion to think about them again a few years later in graduate school. A long-standing criticism of liberalism holds that it is insufficiently attentive to social institutions such as the family. Renowned political thinkers such as Hegel formulated elements of this criticism as early as the first half of the nineteenth century. Having encountered this criticism in a seminar on modern political theory, I tried to extend it to more recent developments in liberal thought and jurisprudence. At a certain point, I saw that contemporary liberal thinkers were minimizing or denying the importance of what were previously considered essential elements of children's welfare.

This tendency was apparent in several developments, such as the weakening of family life in the United States. Now, I scarcely wish to say that contemporary liberal theory caused or "created" the parental indifference described above. (Political and legal theories rarely have such a direct influence.) Yet contemporary liberal theory and jurisprudence have contributed to the problem. Moreover, if we take account of the main currents of liberal thought over the last fifty to sixty years, we could say that it lacks the resources to criticize—in a truly cogent way—such parental indifference. The lack of such theoretical resources would seem to be a serious problem.

These assertions may surprise some readers, so I must ask those who find them implausible to be patient. Perhaps upon finishing the book, readers will find them more intelligible—and more defensible.

I have digressed to explain the origins of this study. I now wish to comment briefly on other aspects of the book, including its relative dearth of solutions to the problems it identifies.

If I am correct in arguing that liberal theorists and jurists have been neglecting or discounting some vital interests of children, some readers might quickly propose a remedy. They might say that the best way to advance the welfare of children is to assign more rights to them. This approach may have some merit, but I cannot embrace it, and for two reasons.

First, I have many misgivings about the federal judiciary's promulgation of various new rights in recent decades. For the reasons put forth below, I regret the declaration of new rights that lack a solid basis in the Constitution. I therefore oppose this project of declaring new rights, even if it purports to help children.[9]

---

[9] By "rights that lack a solid basis in the Constitution," I mean rights that cannot be fairly derived from the text, logic, or original understanding of the document. I am indebted to Robert P. George for this formulation, which he and I have used in several articles. As an

Second, if a reader accepts the main assumptions of this study—namely, that children are impressionable, dependent, and, broadly speaking, "underdeveloped"—then he or she should see that assigning certain rights to children may lead to a rash of problems. We ought to be wary of regarding children as the bearers of a large number of rights, especially "liberty rights." Precisely because they are underdeveloped humans, children normally lack the intelligence and judgment needed to exercise many freedoms responsibly. Accordingly, every decent society criminalizes pornography involving children and prohibits sexual relations between adults and young persons.[10]

A critic might say that my second response is off the mark, because the best way to improve the lives of many children today is not through liberty rights, but through "welfare rights." One scholar defines this term as allowing the holders of such rights "to claim protection or promotion of the constitutive elements of their well-being—such as health, personal security, [and] education."[11] Among academic liberals, this might be the preferred approach for advancing different interests of children. So why do I avoid it?

Apart from my worries about the judiciary's role in formulating such rights, I would suggest that this might be little more than a rhetorical exercise. Assigning a large number of rights to children is easy, and in some circles it can help to establish one's credentials as a "progressive." But if such rights are going to be meaningful, we must be prepared to assess their implications. This is rarely done.

Consider the putative welfare right of "personal security." If assigned to children, could it be invoked on their behalf to restrict the freedom of adults to produce, distribute, or view violent programming? If it cannot be invoked in this manner, we are entitled to ask why. (To those who might say that the "plain words" of the First Amendment preclude such restrictions, I would note that for most of American history, such a reading

---

example, see Robert P. George and David L. Tubbs, "Why We Need a Marriage Amendment," *City Journal* 14 (Autumn 2004): 48.

[10] On the basis of these comments, readers ought to understand why I do not feel obliged to explore the theory of "child liberation" at length here. This theory and a corresponding social movement acquired a certain vogue in the 1970s, with proponents seeking to eliminate many (and perhaps most) of the legal boundaries separating adults from children. They would permit children to exercise a wide range of freedoms because of what they regard as the weakness of the justifications long offered to restrict certain freedoms to adults. The theory of child liberation has disturbing links to child pornography, and however appalling the notion is to others, many consumers of child pornography believe that even children as young as five years old can meaningfully consent to appear in it. See Philip Jenkins, *Beyond Tolerance: Child Pornography on the Internet* (New York and London: New York University Press, 2001).

[11] Archard, "Philosophical Perspectives on Childhood," 50.

of the Free Speech and Free Press Clauses had very few defenders.) Especially in the United States, welfare rights permit theorists to tell themselves that they are attentive to children, but without asking whether interests crucial to their well-being should take precedence over the competing claims of freedom for adults.[12]

A related point should be made. Contrary to what some liberals might now suppose, much of Western political theory and American political history shows that we *can* discuss the well-being of children in a liberal democracy without using the language of rights. But such a discussion requires a willingness to talk about various *duties* adults have toward the young. Unfortunately, contemporary liberalism seems to be characterized by its unwillingness to tackle that subject.

While considering possible responses to my main arguments, I should mention another broad criticism. We live in an age where many things are said to be "socially constructed." Unsurprisingly, since the 1960s, historians in both Europe and the United States have argued that the concept of "childhood" is more fluid or malleable than commonly supposed.[13] Some even say that childhood has no permanent features. On that basis, others predict that childhood may vanish altogether.[14] If these findings are correct, they would undermine a key premise of this book, namely, that all children share some basic needs across time.

What is my response? First, I grant that childhood is in some respects a fluid concept. Even a cursory knowledge of American or European social history bears this out. (If you grew up in the United States or United Kingdom around 1950, your childhood and adolescence had little in common with that of most persons in these countries a century before.)

I also agree with Neil Postman, who believes that the public understanding of childhood in the West changed with the rise of literacy and a "book culture" after the Protestant Reformation.[15] Postman's thesis on the historical contingency of childhood deserves attention, and it may be summarized as follows.

---

[12] I return to this theme at different points in the book, though I do not generally use the term "welfare rights." Clashes between "welfare rights" for children and personal freedoms (or "liberty rights") for adults are unsurprising, since the theory of welfare rights seems to have emerged in response to some persistent problems of national economies in the West (e.g., periodic recessions, "structural" unemployment). Extending the theory to children occurred later, and one might ask whether it ever made good sense.

[13] The pioneering work was written by Philippe Ariès. See his *Centuries of Childhood*, trans. Robert Baldick (New York: Vintage, 1962).

[14] See, for instance, James Fallows, "The Web in Your Future," *New York Review of Books*, 14 March 2002, 4.

[15] Neil Postman, *The Disappearance of Childhood* (New York: Vintage, 1994). This book was originally published in 1982.

During the Middle Ages, the percentage of literate persons in the West was small, especially outside the clergy. Some traits that help to distinguish adults from children were also less pronounced in the Middle Ages than in the modern age, owing to factors that became apparent later. With the invention of the printing press and the spread of certain ideas of the Protestant Reformation, literacy became more widespread. Literacy, however, requires years of training. Schools provide such training, and as schools became more common in Europe, the social categories of childhood and adulthood changed. An adult was understood as a person who had achieved full literacy, whereas a child was *becoming* fully literate.[16]

Adults were distinguishable in another way. Through the printed word, adults had access to knowledge that children generally lacked. This knowledge, especially of matters relating to life, death, and human sexuality, was only gradually revealed to children. Thus, childhood could be characterized as the lengthy period in which a person acquired literacy and the special knowledge or secrets of the adult world.

For Postman, childhood has depended crucially on the transmission of such secrets through the printed word. Before widespread literacy and a "book" culture, many persons were "grown up" by the age of seven or so. Today, in comparison, literacy rates are high, but childhood is imperiled by visual modes of communicating the special knowledge of the adult world. The growth of these modes of communication (e.g., film, television, the Internet) helps to explain why Postman believes that childhood is "disappearing."

When knowledge of the adult world was mainly transmitted through reading, adults could share this knowledge with children by disclosing it through speech or pictures. But such disclosures were long considered shameful, and they were typically stigmatized. In some places, they were also prohibited by law. Postman concludes that "without a well developed idea of shame, childhood cannot exist."[17]

Despite being persuaded by much of what Postman writes, I disagree with him about the malleability of childhood. Plainly, however, much depends on definitions. When Postman writes of the modern understanding of childhood, he refers to a period roughly between the ages of seven and seventeen.[18] By contrast, my use of the term is broader, as noted above.

This difference is significant. In the end, I am sure that Postman would say that very young children (in all places, at all times) have many of the

---

[16] See ibid., ch. 2. A period of several hundred years separates the beginning of the Protestant Reformation and the start of universal schooling in Europe. Yet many persons endorsed compulsory education long before it became a reality. See Postman's remarks on this topic in ibid., chs. 2 and 3.

[17] Ibid., 9.

[18] Ibid., "Introduction," xi.

same needs. Furthermore, he would accept that even older adolescents in the United States still depend heavily on adults for many things.

This brings us back to the central question of this study: What has led contemporary liberalism to disregard so many interests of children? What is the best explanation? In my judgment, our current predicament has multiple sources.

I noted above that in recent decades we have seen a "re-ordering" of the core values of liberalism. Today, most persons in the United States who identify themselves as liberals still want to increase personal freedom for adults and give it a special status among the basic goods of our political life. These liberals tend to be intensely concerned about adult rights, and contemporary liberal theory has affinities with the jurisprudential views of some justices on the Supreme Court of the United States, including William J. Brennan Jr., Thurgood Marshall, David Souter, and Ruth Bader Ginsburg.

If we reflect on European and U.S. history in the twentieth century, the current liberal preoccupation with rights is easy to understand. Many American liberals connect this concern to their opposition to fascism and communism and their support for the civil-rights movement. The same liberals often endorse social movements that claim to be inspired by the civil-rights movement, including feminism and the recent attempts to re-define marriage to include same-sex couples. With respect to institutions, American liberals give most of the credit for the growth of individual freedoms during and after the civil-rights era to the federal judiciary.

The loyalties of most American liberals are thus clear. But notice this: As those loyalties were being established, liberal theorists and jurists gradually lost sight of children. A preoccupation with rights for adults led prominent liberals to play down or forget the importance of competing social interests, including some that are fundamental to children's welfare. In time, this tendency became more pronounced, and liberalism became indifferent to what were previously considered crucial elements of the welfare of children.

Today, because of the development just described, the links between adult freedoms and various interests of children may not be readily apparent. The links therefore need to be explicated, and that is an overriding goal of this book. To give the reader a sense of them now, let me summarize the main arguments of each chapter.

Chapter One looks at an important debate in Anglophone political philosophy after World War II, a debate closely associated with the publication of Isaiah Berlin's famous essay "Two Concepts of Liberty" in 1958. The title of Berlin's essay refers to two different ideas of freedom: the idea of freedom as unhindered choice (or "negative" freedom), and the idea of freedom as self-control or self-government (also known as "positive" freedom). Today, largely because of the abuse of different conceptions of free-dom under totalitarianism, most American liberals accept Berlin's judg-ment that the idea of freedom in the negative sense is, on balance, more humane or dignified than the idea of positive freedom. But few liberals have thought about what the preferred status of negative freedom means for children. That is regrettable, because the idea of negative freedom is not—and cannot be—the only morally valid idea of freedom.

Although the point is seldom acknowledged, freedom in the negative sense has limited relevance for many matters relating to children. Fur-thermore, with respect to public policy, relying exclusively on this idea of freedom leads to some morally intolerable outcomes. At the same time, the idea of positive freedom is highly relevant for understanding children's welfare. Berlin was mindful of these matters. His defense of negative free-dom is historically intelligible, but the defense helped to shape a moral outlook that discounts key elements of the welfare of children.

Chapter Two examines recent efforts, notably by political theorist Susan Moller Okin, to incorporate elements of feminist thought into liberalism, in an attempt to effect change in American family life and improve the life prospects of women and children. Okin criticizes contemporary liberal-ism for its failure to rid itself of patriarchal biases that predate the twen-tieth century. To Okin, such biases are still consequential for women and children, and she proposes far-reaching legislation to eliminate the biases and promote equal opportunity.

Okin's scholarly interest in families and children merits praise—and it distinguishes her from most contemporary liberals—but her work is characterized by an insufficiently critical posture toward different puta-tive rights. Presenting herself as deeply concerned about the well-being of women *and* children, Okin fails to anticipate how certain freedoms, when exercised, will affect the latter. A further weakness in Okin's work is the absence of a cogent normative account of the family as a social institution.

Chapter Three reviews several decisions by the Supreme Court of the United States establishing the "right to privacy" in reproductive matters and considers the significance of this doctrine for the welfare of children. Before the Court's decisions in *Griswold v. Connecticut* (1965), *Eisen-stadt v. Baird* (1972), and *Carey v. Population Services International* (1977), most states regulated the sale and distribution of contraceptives. Despite many views to the contrary today, those laws were meant to ad-vance important interests of children. Specifically, they were meant to discourage sexual promiscuity and promote the traditional two-parent family as a social norm and as the family structure most conducive to the welfare of children. But when the Supreme Court invalidated the statutes and formulated the right to privacy in *Griswold* and *Eisenstadt*, it said scarcely a word about these competing social interests. The Court failed to anticipate the possible ramifications of the new right, such as a greater sexual permissiveness in society, a corresponding rise in out-of-wedlock births, and diminished welfare for children.

Chapter Four evaluates a peculiar inconsistency in the Supreme Court's First Amendment jurisprudence. In some cases, the Court characterizes children as morally impressionable, whereas it elsewhere ascribes the moral capacities of adults to them. More specifically, when children are present at a state-sponsored religious exercise, the Court usually describes them as morally and psychologically frail and incapable of deciding whether they truly wish to participate in the exercise. Yet when children are exposed to various "adult" stimuli (such as hard-core pornography), the Court is apt to characterize them as morally sturdy and resilient beings. Besides documenting this strange inconsistency, this chapter tries to explain its origins.

The inconsistency is significant for two reasons. First, in all likelihood, it helps to explain the decisions in some cases. Second, the inconsistency further entrenches the idea that personal rights for adults associated with the idea of negative freedom should have a preferred status in constitutional jurisprudence. (The point holds even though the Supreme Court does not use the terms "negative" and "positive" freedom.)

Chapter Five assesses recent arguments by liberal legal theorist Ronald Dworkin to justify the sweeping changes in the Court's civil-liberties jurisprudence since the 1950s. Dworkin resourcefully defends the "right to privacy" and a liberal reading of the Free Speech and Free Press Clauses of the First Amendment, but his theory relies almost exclusively on the idea of freedom in the negative sense. Dworkin can also be criticized for neglecting to discuss important interests of children, since his theory requires that government treat all citizens with "equal concern and respect." That requirement should have led Dworkin to discuss the likely effects of different policies on children, who are strangely absent from his theory.

On the basis of this summary, readers should understand the tendencies of liberal thinkers described above. As they engaged different controversies, liberal political theorists and jurists may not have been thinking about children, but the resolution of those controversies implicated different interests of children. Each chapter in this book might therefore be described as a case study in liberal neglect. The neglect may have been unintentional, but its importance cannot be denied, especially since many liberal theorists and jurists do not want to revisit these matters and consider them "settled."

An unpleasant irony must therefore be noted. American liberals tend to pride themselves on being sensitive to the position of vulnerable persons, especially different minorities in society (e.g., European Jews in the 1930s, black Americans living under Jim Crow, and different groups in the contemporary United States). But if sensitivity to vulnerable groups is a source of pride among liberals, they should feel some humility for having so often disregarded the interests of this highly vulnerable group.

Perhaps some liberals will say that children are less vulnerable than I suppose. That is, if a child has loving and responsive parents, there may be little vulnerability in the child's life. But this reply presupposes too much. We cannot assume such favorable circumstances, in part because of cultural and legal changes favored by most liberals. Among such changes, I would cite "no-fault" divorce and the prevailing "nonjudgmental" outlook on sexuality and sexual behavior. One-third of American children grow up in single-parent families, and although such parents often deserve admiration for their efforts and achievements, the children in such families usually face diminished life prospects. We cannot pretend otherwise.

Before concluding this Introduction, I want to make a few more remarks about my goals in writing this book, to avoid some possible misunderstandings.

The first point should be underscored. The book is offered as a contribution to the academic disciplines of political theory and constitutional law; it is not a treatise on child-rearing, adolescent psychology, or family life. Throughout the book, I analyze developments in liberal political theory and jurisprudence and explain how those developments implicated different interests of children. As noted, I aim to document a long pattern of indifference. My account of the welfare of children is primarily based on older sources in political theory and American law. That is, I do not "import" a theory of children's welfare from psychology or another academic discipline. I expect that most readers will say that the account of children's welfare presented here accords with the moral convictions of many ordinary citizens. This does not mean that the account is infallible or beyond criticism, but it does attest to the strength and influence of certain ideas.

Second, although the book focuses on some interests basic to children's well-being, it obviously does not discuss *every* interest related to their welfare. As an example, I scarcely enter into the current debate about the competing claims of parental and state authority to determine the content of a child's education. This is an important debate, and it may end up affecting millions. Thus, anyone interested in the welfare of American children should pay attention. I did not enter the debate here because of considerations of time, space, and "fit."[19]

[19] For three contributions to the debate, see Stephen Macedo, *Diversity and Distrust: Civic Education in a Multicultural Democracy* (Cambridge, Mass.: Harvard University Press, 2000); James G. Dwyer, *Religious Schools v. Children's Rights* (Ithaca, N.Y.: Cornell University Press, 1998); and Stephen G. Gilles, "On Educating Children: A Parentalist Manifesto," *University of Chicago Law Review* 63 (1996): 937. For an assessment of contemporary

Third, simply because I have written a critique of contemporary American liberalism, readers should not assume that I broadly endorse political conservatism as the solution to all of the problems identified here. On a number of issues, I see little difference between the liberalism being criticized in this book and the libertarian current in American conservatism. So if I were to endorse any form of conservatism as an alternative, it is a moral or cultural conservatism that recognizes that children's welfare can all too easily be sacrificed to the ideology of the market.[20]

Finally, I know that some readers might disagree with my assessment of the various interests of children examined here. They might say that the interests never were valid or that they (somehow) lost their validity. Others might say that the interests remain valid but the traditional ideas about how to promote them were wrong.

Such comments would not surprise me. But it would be desirable for persons who hold any or all of these views to state them forthrightly and defend them, instead of merely assuming that every intelligent person shares them.

I say this for the following reasons. As noted, in recent decades liberal political theorists and jurists have gone about their work as though the personal freedom of adults is a political value that outweighs all competing interests, including some closely associated with the welfare of children. This viewpoint has been taken as an article of faith, or as if the correct course of action is self-evident. The result is a number of large gaps in liberal thought, raising many questions about the coherence of contemporary liberal theory and jurisprudence. Those gaps are identified throughout this book, but even someone who points them out can hope that liberals will try to fill them in, instead of maintaining this apparent attitude of indifference toward them.

---

theories of child-rearing (and their relevance to education), see Kay S. Hymowitz, *Ready or Not: Why Treating Children as Small Adults Endangers Their Future—and Ours* (New York: The Free Press, 1999).

The debate about primary and secondary education speaks to an important part of children's welfare. But it would be a mistake to suppose that a high level of welfare for children can be assured simply by providing them with a first-rate education. What happens before and after the school day is just as important as what occurs during the school day. Indeed, what happens to children outside a school often crucially affects what takes place inside it.

[20] I recognize the important role of free markets in helping societies to allocate goods and services efficiently and in responding to consumer preferences. But just as adult civil liberties must sometimes be restricted to protect certain interests of children, free markets need to be regulated. Furthermore, promoting the welfare of children is almost universally recognized as a legitimate principle for market regulation, as evidenced, for example, in prohibitions on child labor and child pornography.

Can any liberal thinker explain why the personal freedom of adults should routinely outweigh the competing interests of children? Can any liberal jurist justify this recurring presumption? If a cogent justification can be produced, I expect that many persons—and not only critics of contemporary liberalism—would like to see it.

CHAPTER ONE

How the "Moral Reticence" of Contemporary Liberalism Affects Children

MOST REFLECTIVE PERSONS would admit that the welfare of children in a country greatly depends on the social conditions and intellectual currents within it. It is easy to imagine some societies being highly sensitive to the needs of children and others being far less responsive. In a dialogue from the first century C.E., the Stoic philosopher Epictetus asked his interlocutor whether it was possible to imagine "a city of Epicureans":

> Where will your citizens come from? Who will educate them? . . . Who will manage the Gymnasia? Yes, and what will be their education? . . . Take me a young man and bring him up in accordance with your judgments. The judgments are bad, subversive of the city, ruinous to family life. . . . Man, leave these principles alone.[1]

This passage raises several questions, and it should prompt us to ask whether the political theory undergirding our way of life is sufficiently sensitive to different interests of children. In view of the importance of the question, this chapter aims to characterize contemporary liberal thought. Today, few persons would dispute Michael Sandel's view that liberalism has been the dominant public philosophy in the United States since 1945.[2] This period has seen an extension of the franchise because of the civil-rights movement and a remarkable expansion of civil liberties.

Yet during the same period, some critics have charged that liberalism has become a radically subjectivist doctrine, masking an ethos of nihilism. This idea is expressed either directly or indirectly in the work of Leo Strauss, Alasdair MacIntyre, and Allan Bloom.[3]

---

[1] *The Discourses of Epictetus,* in *The Stoic and Epicurean Philosophers,* ed. Whitney J. Oates (New York: The Modern Library, 1940), 356–357.

[2] Michael J. Sandel, *Democracy's Discontent: America in Search of a Public Philosophy* (Cambridge, Mass.: The Belknap Press of Harvard University Press, 1996), ch. 1.

[3] See, for example, the opening pages of Strauss's *Natural Right and History* (Chicago: The University of Chicago Press, 1953); Alasdair MacIntyre, *After Virtue,* 2d ed. (Notre Dame, Ind.: University of Notre Dame Press, 1987); Allan Bloom, *The Closing of the American Mind* (New York: Simon and Schuster, 1987). Strauss speaks of the problem of "unlimited tolerance," MacIntyre of a regnant "emotivism," and Bloom of a widespread "moral relativism." In places, it can be difficult to determine whether these statements refer to ex-

This is a provocative thesis, but it goes too far. My view is that contemporary liberalism differs in at least one important respect from the liberalism of nineteenth-century thinkers such as Benjamin Constant, Alexis de Tocqueville, and John Stuart Mill, and that difference is highly consequential for children. Before describing that difference, let me explain why the more radical criticism is wrong.

Any dispassionate observer should admit that most citizens in the United States regard some moral propositions as universally binding. The evidence is substantial. Regularly contested elections for public office and the freedoms listed in the first eight amendments to the Constitution are elements of a political morality that commands almost universal assent. Frequent disagreements about the meaning of broadly defined rights and the legitimacy of certain public demands vis-à-vis the individual do not invalidate this point.

In recent years, some liberal theorists have tried to rebut the charge of radical subjectivity by documenting the readiness of American citizens to champion the rights of others on principled grounds. These liberals cite nineteenth-century abolitionism, Thoreau's civil disobedience, and "freedom marches" in the South during the 1960s. What do these events signify? At a minimum, there are categorical moral precepts within liberalism. In George Kateb's pithy phrase: "The rights anyone has, others must have."[4]

As a rebuttal to the accusation (or intimation) of radical subjectivity, this response is to the point. There *is* a liberal public morality. Subjective satisfaction may count a great deal in liberalism, but liberalism is not reducible to subjective satisfaction.[5] If Strauss, MacIntyre, and Bloom accurately described life in our liberal society, we could say that citizens here really do not care whether their neighbors spend their days poisoning the weeds in their lawns and gardens or poisoning their spouses and families. The example may seem a bit silly, but it should remind us of basic political and social realities.

How, then, should we characterize contemporary American liberalism? Rather than describe it as radically subjectivist, I would describe it as "morally reticent." The meaning of this idea can be grasped if we compare some leading liberal texts of the nineteenth century with those of the

---

isting conditions in the United States or are projections about the future. Certain passages support both readings.

[4] George Kateb, "Democratic Individuality and the Meaning of Rights," in *Liberalism and the Moral Life*, ed. Nancy Rosenblum (Cambridge, Mass.: Harvard University Press, 1989), 193.

[5] On the place of "subjective satisfaction" in contemporary liberalism, consider, for example, John Rawls, "The Priority of Right and Ideas of the Good," in *Political Liberalism* (New York: Columbia University Press, 1993), 177.

post–World War II era. The moral reticence of contemporary liberalism refers to the reluctance of some theorists to distinguish between the good and the bad use of legally protected freedoms. This reluctance has helped to obscure the difference between the responsible and the irresponsible exercise of freedom. By contrast, leading nineteenth-century liberals stressed personal responsibility as a concomitant of freedom. As a result of moral reticence, liberalism has become a much more permissive ethos.

The term "moral reticence" describes a notable feature in the worldview of contemporary liberalism. In saying that liberal theorists are reluctant to distinguish between the good and the bad use of legally protected freedoms, I mean that they are loath to admit that we can question the morality or desirability of many actions protected by rights. If pressed, these liberals would probably concede this point. But they might do so grudgingly. Hence the notion of "reticence."

The danger of moral reticence becomes evident when we consider the impressionability of children. In their capacity as teachers, parents and other adults routinely distinguish different kinds of conduct (e.g., conduct that promotes self-discipline and self-development versus conduct that might lead to sloth or self-destructiveness). Making such distinctions is meant to help the young, so it is odd for political theorists to eschew them. Since the 1990s, many pundits and public figures across the political spectrum have recognized something like moral reticence as a problem, so we might think that this chapter in the history of liberalism is finished. That conclusion may be unwarranted, because there are also signs that the morally reticent outlook persists within liberal thought.

To understand moral reticence, we should review an essay that has shaped the views of many Anglophone liberals, especially in the United States. I refer to Isaiah Berlin's "Two Concepts of Liberty," which legal philosopher Ronald Dworkin described as the most famous twentieth-century essay on liberty.[6] As a statement of liberal anxiety in the wake of totalitarianism, this essay's value to future historians will be high. But accepting certain ideas in the text may engender a different set of worries.

The next two sections explore the connections between moral reticence, Berlin's essay, and the welfare of children. I begin by identifying one matter in "Two Concepts of Liberty" that has received little scholarly attention. I then explain how that matter relates to the moral reticence of contemporary liberalism. I conclude the chapter by showing the connections between moral reticence and liberalism's tendency to disregard or play down important interests of children.

[6] Ronald Dworkin, "What Rights Do We Have?" in *Taking Rights Seriously* (Cambridge, Mass.: Harvard University Press, 1978), 267.

MORAL RETICENCE IN HISTORICAL PERSPECTIVE

Delivered in 1958 at Oxford University, Berlin's essay tells a story about the dangerous casuistry associated with an idea older than the Christian faith. An erudite piece of scholarship, the essay is a historical and philosophical synthesis. Its basic themes are found in Benjamin Constant's speech at the Athénée Royal in 1821.

Yet one section of "Two Concepts of Liberty" stands out in comparison with leading liberal tracts of the nineteenth century. Looking at this passage and writings by Constant, Alexis de Tocqueville, and John Stuart Mill, we might think that the common theoretical understanding of liberalism has changed.

In section 5 of his essay, Berlin summarizes the central goals of modern liberalism:

> Most modern liberals, at their most consistent, want a situation in which as many individuals as possible can realize as many of their ends as possible, without assessment of the value of these ends as such, save in so far as they may frustrate the purposes of others. They wish the frontiers between individuals or groups of men to be drawn solely with a view to preventing collisions between human purposes, all of which must be considered to be equally ultimate, uncriticizable ends in themselves.[7]

Who are the "modern liberals" mentioned here? Presumably, all of the post-sixteenth-century thinkers cited as liberals in the text, including Constant, Tocqueville, and Mill.

If this reading is correct, however, we must challenge Berlin's interpretation. He ascribes to these three theorists a view that none of them embraced. Consider Constant's "Liberty of the Ancients Compared with that of the Moderns," Tocqueville's *Democracy in America,* and Mill's *On Liberty.* Each theorist made strong arguments in defense of basic freedoms, but Berlin is wrong in saying that each considered all human purposes or ends "equally ultimate." In fact, Constant, Tocqueville, and Mill had different worries about the ways in which their contemporaries exercised their freedom. Let me document this.

Of the three, Constant probably comes closest to Berlin's archetypal liberal. In the Athénée Royal speech, he distinguished ancient liberty from modern liberty and defined the major political objectives of both worlds. Sharing social power with his compatriots in the republic was both the raison d'être for the ancient citizen and the essence of his freedom. Modern

---

[7] Isaiah Berlin, "Two Concepts of Liberty," in *Four Essays on Liberty* (New York: Oxford University Press, 1969), 153.

man, by contrast, derives his greatest satisfaction not from the life of the polis, but from "private pleasures." For modern citizens, liberty now has a different meaning: it refers to those institutional safeguards that make the pursuit of private happiness possible.[8]

Asserting that "individual independence" is the "first need of the moderns," Constant defines modern liberty as

> the right to be subjected only to the laws, and to be neither arrested, detained, put to death, or maltreated in any way by the arbitrary will of one or more individuals. It is the right of everyone to express their opinion, choose a profession and practise it, to dispose of property, and even to abuse it; to come and go without permission, and without having to account for their motives or undertakings. It is everyone's right to associate with other individuals, either to discuss their interests, or to profess the religion which they and their associates prefer. . . . Finally, it is everyone's right to exercise some influence on the administration of government, either by electing all or particular officials, or through representations, petitions, demands to which the authorities are more or less compelled to heed.[9]

This notion of modern freedom should be compared with ancient liberty. The latter consisted in the collective and direct exercise of the "complete sovereignty," including public deliberation over war and peace, foreign alliances, voting laws, and the competence of the magistrates. Constant then adds the following qualification:

> But if this is what the ancients called liberty, they admitted as compatible with this collective freedom the complete subjection of the individual to the authority of the community. You find among them almost none of the enjoyments which we have just seen form part of the liberty of the moderns. All private actions were submitted to a severe surveillance. No importance was given to individual independence, neither in relation to opinions, nor to labour, nor, above all, to religion.[10]

Modern freedom, by contrast, allows men to develop their faculties as they choose, so long as they do not harm others in the process. Thus, in at least one important sense, Constant's liberalism approaches Berlin's. But new dangers reside in this new idea of freedom. Private life is seductive. Since modern man relishes its pleasures, he is tempted to ignore politics or even to relinquish his share of political power. For uncomplicated reasons, leaders are ready to relieve him of the burden of political participation.

---

[8] Benjamin Constant, "The Liberty of the Ancients Compared with that of the Moderns," in *Political Writings*, trans. and ed. Biancamaria Fontana (Cambridge: Cambridge University Press, 1988), 317.
[9] Ibid., 310–311.
[10] Ibid.

Accordingly, Constant urges his listeners to moderate their pursuit of happiness and develop important faculties by discharging political duties. The exercise of political liberty is intrinsically less rewarding in the modern world than in the ancient world, but it should not be neglected. In sum, modern man is wrong if he believes that the new concept of liberty has wholly superseded the old: the challenge is to combine the two in a way that avoids the extremes of collective suffocation and individual self-absorption.[11]

Tocqueville's critique of individualism in democracies has much in common with Constant's assessment of ancient and modern freedom, and, like Constant's address, it undermines Berlin's thesis. Individualism—"that calm and considered feeling which disposes each citizen to isolate himself from the mass of his fellows"—is a sentiment peculiar to democracy.[12] It arises from the rough equality of conditions that destroys the "great chain" linking people together in an aristocracy. Individualism also makes democracies vulnerable to despotism, a form of government that further isolates men. Only by participating in civic life can democratic citizens ward off the dangers that individualism breeds. Tocqueville's pessimism was tempered by the existence of many forms of philanthropic, religious, and civic associations in the United States. Instead of relying on the government to undertake projects such as building hospitals and schools, nineteenth-century Americans were ready to break ground themselves. This willingness to promote the public weal at their own expense—Tocqueville called it "self-interest properly understood"—denied government the power that would accrue to it if it were solely responsible for these initiatives.[13] Yet Tocqueville's worries were never put to rest. On a cautious note, he concluded that the "art of association" must develop at the same rate as equality of conditions spread if human societies are to remain civilized.[14]

Finally, there is Mill. A superficial reading of *On Liberty* might seem to support Berlin's assertion that Mill wanted to dispense with judgment about the ways in which citizens exercise their liberty. A close reading of the text, however, leads to a different conclusion.

Wary of majoritarian impulses, reluctant to defer to any societal consensus, and skeptical of the notion of "fixed" or "immutable" truth, Mill challenges those who want to suppress any opinion, even one that is demonstrably false. His controversial claim is that every idea may benefit humanity by helping to illuminate the truth. When truth collides with

[11] Ibid., 326–328.

[12] Alexis de Tocqueville, *Democracy in America*, ed. J. P. Mayer, trans. George Lawrence (New York: Harper and Row, 1966), 506.

[13] Ibid., 526–527.

[14] Ibid., 517.

error, the former will be perceived more clearly and fully than if such a collision had never taken place.[15]

A corollary of this view might be formulated in a way consistent with Berlin's characterization of liberalism: No matter how offensive, absurd, or puerile my self-regarding conduct may seem to others, it will always in some way prove valuable because it aids other persons in distinguishing rightful from wrongheaded conduct. Mill, of course, does not draw this corollary. Despite writing of the desirability of "experiments in living," he never says that shortsighted or "dimwitted" actions perform an epistemological function analogous to benighted or erroneous opinions. The realm of action and deeds is different from the realm of opinion and ideas.[16]

In the realm of action, the "harm principle" permits interference with another person's liberty only to protect other human beings. Yet Mill notes that as private citizens, we may be warranted in "remonstrating with . . . or persuading . . . or entreating" another person when he is acting contrary to what we think is right or advantageous for him.[17] In the chapter "Of the Limits to the Authority of Society over the Individual," Mill even says that we owe one another help in our attempts to distinguish the good from the bad. What resources do we have for this? Among others, our rationality, our knowledge of human history, and our critical faculties, both aesthetic and moral.[18]

Mill's "anthropology" also provides criteria for judging many activities and endeavors. His distinction between the higher and lower faculties and the corresponding distinction between higher and lower human pursuits may sound archaic (and Aristotelian), but they capture important qualities peculiar to the human species. For this reason, the distinctions should be retained. Their most satisfactory formulation appears in chapter 2 of *Utilitarianism*:

> Human beings have faculties more elevated than the animal appetites, and when once made conscious of them, do not regard anything as happiness which does not include their gratification. . . . The pleasures of the intellect, of the feelings and imagination, and of the moral sentiments . . . [must be assigned] a much higher value as pleasures than . . . those of mere sensation. . . .

---

[15] John Stuart Mill, *On Liberty*, ed. David Spitz (New York: W. W. Norton and Co., 1975), 18.

[16] Ibid., 54.

[17] Ibid., 11.

[18] Ibid., 71. It is worth quoting Mill directly here: "Human beings owe to each other help to distinguish the better from the worse, and encouragement to choose the former and avoid the latter. They should be forever stimulating each other to increased exercise of their higher faculties, and increased direction of their feelings and aims towards wise instead of foolish, elevating instead of degrading, objects and contemplations."

Now it is an unquestionable fact that those who are equally acquainted with, and equally capable of appreciating and enjoying both, do give a most marked preference to the manner of existence which employs their higher faculties. Few human creatures would consent to be changed into any of the lower animals, for a promise of the fullest allowance of a beast's pleasure.[19]

Mill also observes that the desire to exercise one's higher faculties is "easily killed," especially in children. The desire and capacity can be extinguished by "hostile influences," and young persons might then "addict themselves to inferior pleasures."[20]

When developing their own "life plans," individual men and women must decide for themselves whether various insights gleaned from the study of history can be applied to their own circumstances. Mill encourages us to take advantage of knowledge culled from centuries of human experience. Neither human society nor human history is a tabula rasa, and to conduct our lives as if we were the first humans to walk the earth would be irrational and, in some cases, reprehensible.[21] The sheer folly of some human pursuits will be evident to most adults in a modern society:

A person who shows rashness, obstinacy, self-conceit—who cannot live within moderate means—who cannot restrain himself from hurtful indulgences—who pursues animal pleasures at the expense of those of feeling and intellect—must expect to be lowered in the opinion of others, and to have a less share of their favorable sentiments.[22]

Pace Berlin, it is impossible for a thinker to be both a defender of discriminatory criticism and a proponent of the view that all human ends or endeavors are "equally ultimate." Mill is at once liberal and critically disposed: an advocate of individual freedom, he is ready to criticize others when they squander that freedom or use it badly.

What are the sources of this outlook? What are the purposes of personal freedom? These questions require a more thorough treatment of Mill's

[19] John Stuart Mill, *Utilitarianism,* in John Stuart Mill and Jeremy Bentham, *Utilitarianism and Other Essays,* ed. Alan Ryan (New York: Penguin, 1987), 279–280. In *Two Faces, of Liberalism,* John Gray offers an important comment on this aspect of Mill's thought. Gray believes that Mill is wrong in thinking that the pleasures of the intellect should always be deemed higher than the pleasures associated with "sensation." Gray is correct about this matter—think, for example, of the vocation of a food or wine critic—but notice that Mill uses the phrase "*mere* sensation" in the passage above. Notice also Mill's references (elsewhere) to "hurtful indulgences" and "animal pleasures." Thus, he could easily criticize gluttony or voracious eating. For a fuller discussion, see Gray, *Two Faces of Liberalism* (New York: The New Press, 2000), 57–60.
[20] Mill, *Utilitarianism,* 281–282.
[21] Mill, *On Liberty,* 55.
[22] Ibid., 72–73.

political philosophy than I can offer here. Confining our analysis to *On Liberty*, we could say that individual freedom is valuable to Mill because it fosters human development and accelerates the progress of the species. Defending individuality and promoting an intellectually active society are two goals of Mill's tract, objectives that sometimes overlap and sometimes conflict.

Numerous passages in *On Liberty* reveal Mill's interest in building an intellectually vibrant society, a place of inquiry and expostulation in which criticism, doubt, and misgivings are aired freely. This mental activity is assumed to have no detrimental side effects. Established doctrines will become unsettled, and faith will give way not to angst or nihilism, but to a pervasive and healthy "tentativeness." As men and women question the wisdom of traditions and long-standing conventions—as well as newer and modish patterns of thought—they will have to ask themselves who they are and what they want to become.

This process of individual development and self-refinement should be continual. Mill pays homage to individuality. He also thinks that gentle prodding and sharp criticism from others can benefit us. He regrets that his contemporaries are reluctant to engage in this practice, writing at one point that "it would be well, indeed, if this good office were more freely rendered than the common notions of politeness at present permit."[23]

To say that Mill envisaged a whole society of philosophers would be inaccurate. His aims in *On Liberty* are more realistic. Citizens can profit in many ways from sustained intellectual exchanges among themselves. Before they can do so, however, men and women must overcome their timidity and learn to speak frankly about what they see as the shortcomings of others. Candor is indispensable, but by itself insufficient. Intellectual rectitude is also necessary. At the end of chapter 2, Mill lists a series of "discourse norms" that must be honored. Willfully misrepresenting an opposing viewpoint, deliberately omitting pertinent information, and disparaging a position merely because it is unpopular all violate Mill's ethical code and deserve opprobrium.[24]

The simultaneous commitments to individuality and an active mental life spawn tensions. Communities spare us countless frustrations, while blinkering us all. Repositories of old and useful knowledge, they also

---

[23] Ibid. This sentence, appearing in chapter 4, is difficult to reconcile with several remarks in chapter 1 regarding "the moral coercion of public opinion." As I argue below, Mill's plea for individuality coexists precariously with his awareness of the benefits that communities provide to their members. Mill's aversion to "community," at its apex in chapter 1, weakens thereafter. On the whole, Mill is disturbed by the *unthinking* deference to convention and society's efforts to discourage people from questioning customs. The only antidote to this intellectual lethargy is to encourage as many persons as possible to become gadflies to society.

[24] Ibid., 51–52.

hinder new and valuable discoveries. Mill might chide us either for comporting ourselves as though no one has lived before us or for emulating our upstanding friends and neighbors. Individuality demands engagement with tradition, even though tradition and thoughtless conformity are first cousins.

When he asserts that "there is no reason that all human existence should be constructed on some one or some small number of patterns," Mill repudiates an important piece of the West's Christian heritage. In another attack on the Christian ethical system, he denies the existence of duties to oneself, now a widely held liberal view.[25] What, then, should we make of the "moral duty" to help others in their efforts to distinguish the good from the bad? Is this a sly way of stimulating the mental life of a society?[26]

Even if someone concludes that Mill's first goal in *On Liberty* is to foster individuality, Berlin's summary of modern liberalism would still be misleading. From Mill's standpoint, the conformist and the independent actor are two different persons, even when outwardly their actions are the same. There is an almost unspeakable difference between someone who exercises only the "ape-like faculty of imitation" and someone who relentlessly questions traditions and conventions in an effort to live freely.[27]

The preceding remarks are offered as a corrective to one of Berlin's rare errors. Constant, Tocqueville, and Mill are liberals, but they are liberals who are unafraid to exhort and criticize and admonish. We may even speak of them, especially Mill, as liberals who distinguish between our "higher selves" and our "lower selves."[28]

Berlin's misstep is puzzling. His other essays on thinkers who shaped the modern world—Montesquieu and Machiavelli, for instance—are so nuanced that we should not attribute this error to a superficial reading or hasty generalization. As Berlin's reputation for careful scholarship is secure, what might explain this mistake?

My view is that it must be understood in context. "Two Concepts of Liberty" is not only a historical synthesis, but also a superior polemic. As both Leo Strauss and Marshall Cohen argued, the essay can be read as a

---

[25] Ibid., 73.

[26] Ibid., 71. I suspect that Mill is attacking the notion of "duties to oneself" in its religious sense. His efforts to stimulate independent thinking among his contemporaries—in part, by asking them to exhort one another to exercise their higher faculties—seem compatible with this attack.

[27] Ibid., 56.

[28] In my discussion of Mill, I quote extensively from *On Liberty,* the gospel of late nineteenth-century liberalism. Yet other works in Mill's corpus support the interpretation offered here. I have limited the references to *Utilitarianism* because I want to emphasize the disjunction between nineteenth-century and contemporary liberalism. To that end, relying on *On Liberty,* a canonical liberal text, seems to be a sensible approach.

forceful critique of Soviet communism.[29] The ideological battles of the Cold War help us to make sense of Berlin's rhetorical strategy and the error identified above. In examining two notions of human freedom, Berlin tried to defend one of them as more humane and more likely to further human dignity. In completing this exercise, he was defending a political and moral sensibility, a civilization, a way of life.[30]

In this ideological struggle, Berlin champions the idea of freedom in the "negative" sense. Roughly synonymous with Constant's idea of "modern freedom," it may be defined as the absence of governmental and societal restraint: "the area within which a man can act unobstructed by others," or, more precisely, "the absence of obstacles to possible choices and activities."[31]

The value of negative liberty rests on a particular view of human nature. Leading proponents of this idea of liberty—classical liberal thinkers such as Jefferson, Paine, Constant, Tocqueville, and Mill—argued that every government is obliged to recognize a realm of personal inviolability, a private sphere beyond the reach of the state. Violating that sphere, regardless of the good that might accrue to the state or other citizens, would degrade or deny the victim's humanity.

These theorists sometimes disagree about which liberties deserve legal protection. For Berlin, however, those disagreements are less important than the common value they all attach to individual freedom:

> To threaten a man with persecution unless he submits to a life in which he exercises no choices of his goals; to block before him every door but one, no matter how noble the prospect upon which it opens, or how benevolent the motives of those who arrange this, is to sin against the truth that he is a man, a being with a life of his own to live. This is liberty as it has been conceived by liberals in the modern world from the days of Erasmus (some would say of Occam) to our own. Every plea for civil liberties and individual rights, every protest against exploitation and humiliation, against the encroachment of public authority, or the mass hypnosis of custom or organized propaganda, springs from this individualistic, and much disputed, conception of man.[32]

[29] Leo Strauss, "Relativism," in *The Rebirth of Classical Political Rationalism*, ed. Thomas Pangle (Chicago: University of Chicago Press, 1989), 16; Marshall Cohen, "Berlin and the Liberal Tradition," *Philosophical Quarterly* 10 (1960): 216, 219.

[30] Additional support for the interpretation sketched in this paragraph is found in Michael Ignatieff's *Isaiah Berlin: A Life* (New York: Metropolitan Books, 1998). See chs. 11 and 15, esp. 168–169. See also John Gray, "The Case for Decency," *New York Review of Books*, 13 July 2006.

[31] Berlin, "Two Concepts of Liberty," 122; *Four Essays on Liberty,* xxxix. Berlin uses the words "freedom" and "liberty" interchangeably, and I follow that usage here.

[32] Berlin, "Two Concepts of Liberty," 127–128.

This account of the human person provides resources for thinking about the nature of a free society. Proponents of the negative concept of freedom hold that in such a society, only rights—and no powers—can be regarded as absolute. In an ideal world, state authorities would never cross those frontiers "within which men should be inviolable." In our world, persistent disregard of those sacred frontiers—when, for example, a state regularly tortures citizens or imprisons men and women without a fair trial—denotes horrible oppression.[33]

So closely does the negative concept of freedom correspond to contemporary intuitions that we may forget about an alternative understanding of freedom. The idea (or ideal) of freedom as self-governance or self-direction, which Berlin designates "positive liberty," arises from the longing to be one's own master and to develop and exercise some distinctly human capacities. The notion of positive freedom reflects the perennial human desires to be independent of the wills of others, to be capable of resisting external forces and stimuli, and to govern oneself by reason. To the extent that persons attain this independence, self-control, or self-governance, they are free; to the extent that they remain prey to forces and passions that they cannot control—even if they live in a society that protects many personal liberties—they are, at least to some proponents of "positive" freedom, in a state of servitude.[34]

This admittedly abstract idea can be better understood by reviewing a central question of this study. Someone partial to the idea of freedom in the negative sense would define liberty as having a wide range of choices in the different pursuits that make up our lives. Many persons with children will contest that definition (or at least point out its limited applicability), because some activities give pleasure or amusement to the young, but do not conduce to their long-term moral, emotional, or intellectual growth. If a child or adolescent becomes preoccupied with such an activity and does not abandon it, the parent might say that the child is in a state of psychological thralldom, even if the activity is freely chosen. This is why some might reject the "negative" definition of liberty and embrace the idea of freedom as self-governance, which encompasses the development of different capacities.

Influential political philosophers have explored and defended this idea. Consider the perspective of G.W.F. Hegel. In his *Philosophy of Right*, Hegel wrote that "the final purpose of education . . . is liberation and the struggle for a higher liberation still. . . . In the individual subject, this liberation is the hard struggle against pure subjectivity of demeanour, against the

---

[33] Ibid., 165–166.
[34] Ibid., 131–134.

immediacy of desire, [and] against . . . the caprice of inclination." Such words convey a central theme in Hegel's political philosophy, which has further meaning with respect to educating the young. In developing this theme, Hegel evidently accepted Rousseau's dictum that "to be driven by appetite alone" is a form of slavery.[35]

As this imagery suggests, a person does not become free in the positive sense simply by being born or by becoming an adult. To be free in this sense can be understood as a long-term endeavor, normally requiring the exercise or realization of certain capacities and much self-discipline. For some persons, the ideal might be unattainable, but its antithesis—being "enslaved" to different passions—is real. Sundry dependencies and addictions are among the forms that such unfreedom might take.

How does one become free in the positive sense? Berlin identifies two main ways: by engaging in different kinds of self-abnegation, or by adhering to a theory of "self-realization," whereby a person espouses a principle, doctrine, or creed as a way of transcending impulse and caprice. Of these two methods, Berlin is more favorably disposed toward the second, but he criticizes both.

Self-abnegation, common to several religious and philosophic traditions, entails eliminating desires as a way of ending dependency and thereby becoming "free." This approach is largely a mental or psychological effort, sometimes involving prodigious inner struggles and personal valor amidst political or social turmoil. The state of mind necessary for achieving this type of freedom was limned by the seventeenth-century poet Richard Lovelace:

> Stone walls do not a prison make,
> Nor iron bars a cage;
> Minds innocent and quiet take
> That for an hermitage. . . .[36]

In "Two Concepts of Liberty," Berlin criticizes this strategy of self-abnegation and asks whether freedom could be more fully realized by the *tangible* elimination or conquest of whatever frustrates the attainment of one's goals and desires. His judgment on this matter appears in the section "The Retreat to the Inner Citadel":

> Ascetic self-denial may be a source of integrity or serenity and spiritual strength, but it is difficult to see how it can be called an enlargement of liberty. If I save myself from an adversary by retreating indoors and locking every entrance and

---

[35] See *Hegel's Philosophy of Right*, trans. and ed. T. M. Knox (New York: Oxford University Press, 1967), 125 (sec. 187). See also Rousseau's *On the Social Contract*, bk. 1, ch. 8.

[36] Richard Lovelace, "To Althea from Prison" (c. 1642). Compare with Wordsworth's "Nuns Fret Not" (1807).

exit, I may remain freer than if I had been captured by him, but am I freer than if I had defeated or captured him?[37]

Of the second method cited by Berlin—freedom as self-identification with a creed, doctrine, or institution—religious observance is a well-known example. To take a familiar case: When an observant Jew rests on the Sabbath and declares that the Law spares him from becoming a slave to the desire for material gain, he claims to be liberated from temptations familiar to all of us. He believes that he is self-directed in a way that his neighbor, who labors joylessly to amass more wealth than he could ever need, is not. We can extend this notion of freedom to other pursuits, as one survey of the teachings of Judaism shows:

> So many of the rules and rituals of the Jewish way of life are spiritual calisthenics, designed to teach us to control the most basic instincts of our lives—hunger, sex, acquisitiveness, and so on. We are not directed to deny or stifle them, but to control them, to rule them rather than let them rule us, and to sanctify them by dedicating our living of them to God's purposes. The freedom the Torah offers us is the freedom to say no to appetite. . . .
>
> Think of it this way: There may come a time in your life when your future happiness will depend on your being able to say no to something tempting: a shady business deal, a compromise of your principles, an illicit sexual adventure. If you have had virtually no experience saying no, if the message from parents and salesmen has consistently been, "If you want it, we can work something out," what are the chances of your acting properly at that moment? And what are your chances for happiness? But if all your life you have practiced the control of instinct, saying no to food, to sexual opportunities, to other temptations, how much better will your chances be?[38]

There are other ways for a person to become free in this sense; individual women and men (or groups) can order their lives by living in accordance with the Categorical Imperative or by seeking to promote the Common Good or General Will or some other secular doctrine.[39]

---

[37] Berlin, "Two Concepts of Liberty," 140.

[38] Harold S. Kushner, *To Life: A Celebration of Jewish Thinking and Being* (Boston: Little, Brown and Co., 1993), 51–52. These remarks have a foundation in classical Judaism. See, for example, Babylonian Talmud (Eruvin 54a), commenting on the passage in Exodus 32:16, regarding the word of God being engraved (*harut*) on the tablets. The word "engraved" is "re-vocalized" to read "freedom" (*herut*), thus making the point that only those who keep God's law are truly free. I thank Professor David Novak of the University of Toronto for sharing his knowledge of these texts with me.

[39] Among other works, see Rousseau, *On the Social Contract*; Kant, *Groundwork of the Metaphysics of Morals*; Hegel, *Philosophy of Right*, esp. secs. 257–258 and 260–261. In a similar vein are the following lines from Wordsworth's "Ode to Duty" (1805): "Me this unchartered freedom tires; / I feel the weight of chance-desires: / My hopes no more must change their name, / I long for a repose that ever is the same."

Like its "negative" counterpart, liberty in the positive sense is cognate with a certain understanding of human nature. Traditionally, the idea of freedom as self-governance is linked to an image of a divided person—a "higher" self associated with the faculty of reason, and a "lower" self associated with various passions, impulses, and appetites. Self-governance or self-direction means that the faculty of reason holds sway and that the passions and appetites are in check or have been directed to worthy purposes.

The idea of freedom in the positive sense sometimes serves as the basis of public policies intended to help both adults and children resist self-destructive impulses or potentially dangerous choices. When viewed from the standpoint of "negative" freedom, such policies reduce freedom; but from this alternative standpoint, they can be said to promote it.[40]

Consider two policies. The first criminalizes the sale and use of addictive drugs; the second enacts compulsory schooling until the age of sixteen. If freedom is understood as self-governance, both policies are, over the long run, likely to expand freedom. Those defending the policies would point out that self-governance in any meaningful sense is impossible if a person is addicted to drugs or wholly unschooled. Defenders would also say that since no rational person wants to be addicted or unschooled, the policies are reasonable restrictions on choice.

These and similar policies are still controversial. When they apply to adults, some charge that the policies are "paternalistic." When they apply to children, some object that "outsiders" should not have the power to determine a child's future. Nevertheless, the examples show that we cannot apply the idea of negative freedom when trying to resolve some matters of public policy, because doing so leads to morally intolerable outcomes. Scarcely anyone, for example, would say that parents should be free to deny their children a rudimentary education or that preteens should decide for themselves whether they will be schooled.

Other examples support this point. While some may be more controversial than others, the following policies still enjoy wide support in the United States: restrictions on child labor; a minimum age for military service; compulsory vaccinations for infants and older children; prohibitions on selling oneself into servitude; and "self-protective" measures for adults, such as laws requiring them to wear a seatbelt in a car or a helmet on a motorcycle.

Policies based on the idea of freedom in the positive sense are sometimes said to presuppose a theory of self-realization. If such a theory is presupposed, its content is usually modest. In the examples given, the

---

[40] Here I also draw from Berlin's short essay "Liberty," in Isaiah Berlin, *The Power of Ideas*, ed. Henry Hardy (Princeton: Princeton University Press, 2002).

policies assume that a person prefers life to death, education to ignorance, and decent health to chronic or debilitating illness. The policy projects what a *reasonable* person would choose, rather than a person whose behavior is impulsive or whose patterns of thinking are self-deluding or irrational.

When thinking of policies such as these, readers should keep both the imagery of "self-governance" and its antithesis in mind. It might be a stretch to say that the youth who must attend school every day exercises his freedom as he trudges off to class in the morning; it would be less fanciful to say that being illiterate means being highly or dangerously dependent on others and is therefore a state of unfreedom.

Berlin does not deny the need for policies like those just described, but the associated imagery and theory trouble him. He connects that imagery and the corresponding theories of self-realization to illiberal politics in modern history. Those connections explain why, on balance, he endorses negative freedom as the more humane alternative.

The illiberalism associated with positive freedom can be seen by extrapolating from the examples above. Berlin cites periods in which entire institutions, political parties, and social movements were said to embody or represent "reason." Different political actors demanded allegiance to these entities, with grave penalties for those who resisted their directives. Large numbers of people identified their "higher selves" with the institution or party or movement. Too often, such wholehearted identification affects the moral and intellectual faculties of both individuals and groups and paves the way for gross violations of human rights.

Berlin summarizes the dynamic in this way:

> The real self may be conceived as something wider than the individual (as the term is normally understood), as a social 'whole' of which the individual is an element or aspect: a tribe, a race, a church, a state, the great society of the living and the dead and the yet unborn. This entity is then identified as being the 'true' self which, by imposing its collective, or 'organic', single will upon its recalcitrant 'members', achieves its own, and therefore their, 'higher' freedom. . . . What gives . . . plausibility . . . to this kind of language is that we recognize that it is possible, and at times justifiable, to coerce men in the name of some goal (let us say, justice or public health) which they would, if they were more enlightened, themselves pursue, but do not, because they are blind or ignorant or corrupt. This renders it easy for me to conceive of myself as coercing others for their own sake, in their, not my, interest. I am then claiming that I know what they truly need better than they know it themselves. . . . But I may go on to claim a good deal more than this. I may declare that they are actually aiming at what in their benighted state they consciously resist, because there exists within them an occult entity—their latent rational will, or their 'true' purpose—and that this

entity, although it is belied by all that they overtly feel and do and say, is their 'real' self. . . . Once I take this view, I am in a position to ignore the actual wishes of men or societies, to bully, oppress, torture them in the name, and on behalf of their 'real' selves, in the secure knowledge that whatever is the true goal of man (happiness, performance of duty, wisdom, a just society, self-fulfillment) must be identical with his freedom—the free choice of his 'true', albeit often submerged and inarticulate, self.[41]

This tendency is exacerbated by the willingness of many people to sacrifice themselves on what Berlin (following the Russian writer Alexander Herzen) calls the "altar of abstractions."[42]

In support of these views, Berlin mentions the crimes of the French Revolution, citing Constant's criticisms of unlimited sovereignty, and the history of totalitarian regimes, hinting at the despotic potential of Marx's thought. To follow the subtleties of the argument, it helps to be well versed in modern European history and the political thought of such disparate figures as Kant, Fichte, and Bradley. With its allusions to dark chapters in modern history, "Two Concepts of Liberty" chastens while it instructs. The essay induces a wariness of all philosophic and political theories of self-realization.[43]

Yet we must remember that Berlin in a few places affirms the legitimacy of both the positive and the negative concepts of freedom. It is in connection with education—and, by implication, children—that Berlin recognizes the limits of negative freedom and the importance of the positive concept. At one point, he reminds us that "we compel children to be educated."[44] For these reasons, Berlin wrote that he was "not offering a blank endorsement of the 'negative' concept as opposed to its 'positive' twin brother."[45]

---

[41] Berlin, "Two Concepts of Liberty," 132–133. Responding to critics in the "Introduction" to *Four Essays on Liberty*, Berlin mentioned other collective entities that might be thought to represent one's "true self," such as social classes, political parties, and "the vanguard of the most progressive class" (*Four Esays on Liberty*, xliv).

[42] Isaiah Berlin, in *Russian Thinkers*, ed. Henry Hardy and Aileen Kelly (New York: Penguin Books, 1978), 192–194.

[43] Berlin, "Two Concepts of Liberty," 145–154. The historical references and allusions in "Two Concepts of Liberty" become clearer if one reads Berlin's posthumously published essays collected in *Freedom and Its Betrayal: Six Enemies of Human Liberty*, ed. Henry Hardy (Princeton and Oxford: Princeton University Press, 2001).

[44] Berlin, "Two Concepts of Liberty," 169.

[45] Berlin, *Four Essays on Liberty*, lviii. Note also that Berlin did not favor a policy of strict noninterference (or laissez-faire) in economics. Even though such a policy rested on the idea of negative freedom, he believed that it led to brutal exploitation (including the exploitation of children in the nineteenth century). Most contemporary liberals follow Berlin on this point. I devote little space to this matter, since the focus of this book is noneconomic freedoms and putative rights.

Despite these important qualifications, Berlin's work gives the impression that freedom in the positive sense is less valid than freedom in the negative sense. As noted, he wanted to defend negative freedom as, on balance, more humane. To that end, he developed a stylized contrast in "Two Concepts of Liberty," putting different political thinkers into one of two camps. Constant, Tocqueville, and Mill belonged to one team (gathered under the banner of "negative" freedom); Rousseau, Kant, Hegel, and T. H. Green belonged to the other (under the standard of "positive" freedom). It is a neat contrast—in fact, too neat.

By now, Berlin's error in mischaracterizing modern liberalism should be clearer. In presenting Constant, Tocqueville, and Mill as wholehearted proponents of negative freedom, Berlin neglects to discuss those passages in their writings which contain elements of a theory of self-realization. This neglect is conspicuous in the case of Mill, given the statements quoted above.

Even though the point is seldom recognized, Berlin's defense of negative liberty implicates interests of children. The implications are likely to be even more significant because of the way Berlin mischaracterized modern liberalism.

In retrospect, "Two Concepts of Liberty" marked a turning point in Anglophone political theory in the twentieth century. The essay asserted that our theoretical priorities were misplaced and needed to be reordered. In other papers written between 1949 and 1969—including "Political Ideas in the Twentieth Century," "John Stuart Mill and the Ends of Life," and several passionate tributes to Alexander Herzen—Berlin asked for a renewed appreciation of individuality, human spontaneity, and improvisation, which are all associated with freedom in the negative sense. As other parts of this book will show, these emphases within liberal thought persist to this day.[46]

We should not underestimate the influence of these ideas in the United States. Widely admired as a political theorist, literary critic, and historian of ideas, Berlin had a large academic audience in the country for at least three decades. His reputation grew over the years, and his stature among educated Americans was confirmed by the front-page obituary in *The New York Times* on 7 November 1997. The following year, the New York

[46] Berlin, *Four Essays on Liberty*, xlvi–xlvii. "Political Ideas in the Twentieth Century" and "John Stuart Mill and the Ends of Life" are found in *Four Essays on Liberty*. See also Berlin's writings on Alexander Herzen, two of which are included in Hardy and Kelly, *Russian Thinkers*, and one of which is found in *Against the Current*, ed. Henry Hardy (New York: Penguin Books, 1982).

It is questionable whether Berlin's later writings on nationalism, which appear in the anthologies *Against the Current* and *The Crooked Timber of Humanity* (New York: Vintage, 1992), dilute the strength of his earlier pieces on individuality and personal freedom.

Institute for the Humanities held an important conference to consider Berlin's contributions and legacy.[47]

The next section provides further evidence of Berlin's influence. Yet it is possible that Berlin's admirers might not wish to acknowledge his influence fully.

MORAL RETICENCE AND THE WELFARE OF CHILDREN

We might gauge Berlin's influence in liberal political theory by noticing the special status of "negative" liberty in American liberalism. Leading theorists and legal scholars express their wariness of freedom in the positive sense, often characterizing it as inherently bad, but without acknowledging the limited applicability of negative freedom in some contexts. Freedom in the positive sense has thus been on the defensive for several decades.[48]

Another possible effect of "Two Concepts of Liberty" should be noted. Having essentially denied the affinities between the idea of positive freedom and the political philosophies of Constant, Tocqueville, and Mill, Berlin may have given some scholars an inaccurate picture of nineteenth-century liberalism. As a result, they may have concluded that liberalism entails *both* a commitment to rights *and* an attitude of indifference to the exercise of those rights.[49]

The phenomenon I am describing—the moral reticence of contemporary liberalism—is seen in many places. The phenomenon also appears to be unprecedented. Whereas leading nineteenth-century liberals spoke

[47] The proceedings of the conference were later published. See *The Legacy of Isaiah Berlin,* ed. Ronald Dworkin, Mark Lilla, and Robert B. Silvers (New York: New York Review Books, 2001).

[48] The tendency has been to assume that a cogent political theory can rely solely on freedom in the negative sense. See, for instance, Leon Wieseltier, "When a Sage Dies, All Are His Kin," *The New Republic* (1 December 1997): 29: "It was plain to him [Berlin] that the crimes of this century were the crimes of monism, and he toiled to make this plain to others. In political theory, monism took the form of what he called 'positive liberty.' He was against it; it was a fancy invitation to compulsion, a theory of authority disguised as a theory of freedom." See also the comments of Ronald Dworkin in the "Introduction" to *Freedom's Law* (Cambridge, Mass.: Harvard University Press, 1996), 21–26, and Dworkin's essay on "Two Concepts of Liberty" in *Isaiah Berlin: A Celebration,* ed. Edna and Avishai Margalit (Chicago: The University of Chicago Press, 1991).

[49] My point is that Berlin's philosophic emphases, both intended and unintended, affected perceptions of nineteenth-century liberal thought. In time, those perceptions may have become tenets of some overtly theoretical works, as the rest of this chapter suggests.

Berlin's interpretation of Mill, presented in "John Stuart Mill and the Ends of Life," has little in common with mine. Only in a footnote on the last page of the essay (*Four Essays on Liberty,* 206) does he (fleetingly) touch on the issues discussed here.

frankly about the responsibilities and possible abuses of freedom, contemporary liberals are too often silent about these topics.

If we compare the writings of Mill and Tocqueville with those of, say, Ronald Dworkin and Thomas Nagel, the transformation seems indisputable: a momentous change has occurred. Other prominent liberals who display a willingness to dispense with moral judgment of all "self-regarding" conduct (to use Mill's language) include George Kateb, Stephen Holmes, Amy Gutmann, and Judith Shklar. Again, I refer to actions that enjoy legal protection.

One reason for documenting this change is to show that liberalism is not only a political theory and a political program; it is also a "state of mind." Since Stephen Holmes insists that we view antiliberal thought in this way, we should look at liberalism from the same perspective.[50]

Here some will ask: Why should anyone care about this mindset and this reticence? Isn't the only real issue the criminalization or decriminalization of conduct? These are valid questions. Before I answer them, however, let me provide several examples of moral reticence.

Holmes's and Dworkin's statements on this topic are found in essays that reflect their main scholarly interests. As generalizations about the liberal ethos, they depart significantly from Mill and Tocqueville. In the often-cited "Liberalism," Dworkin writes that "liberals, as such, are indifferent as to whether people choose to speak out on political matters, or to lead eccentric lives, or otherwise to behave as liberals are supposed to prefer."[51] In "The Permanent Structure of Antiliberal Thought," the essay that gave rise to *The Anatomy of Antiliberalism*, Holmes suggests that modern societies must either let individuals be the sole judges of what constitutes their good and their happiness, or allow an oppressive, antiliberal state to take root by allowing the passage of "morals legislation." The implication of this view is that, short of erecting a tyrant state, we cannot criticize anyone's self-regarding conduct. Here are Holmes's thoughts on this topic:

> From the assumption that values are purely subjective, we are told, liberals concluded that all human desires are of equal worth. How accurate is this claim? It is true that liberals wanted to decentralize the authority to define personal happiness, dispersing it into the hands of unsupervised individuals. . . . But liberal skepticism was primarily political, not moral. . . . Liberals assumed that public officials cannot always be trusted to codify and enforce the distinction between the moral and the immoral. From this premise, however, we

[50] See Holmes's comments in *The Anatomy of Antiliberalism*, 5.
[51] Ronald Dworkin, "Liberalism," in *Public and Private Morality*, ed. Stuart Hampshire (Cambridge: Cambridge University Press, 1978), 143.

cannot logically conclude that liberals denied the reality or importance of a substantive moral-immoral distinction.[52]

On the historical matter identified here, Holmes may be correct. But he seems to accept a false dichotomy. He forgets that citizens—including parents, educators, and cultural figures—may *tolerate* some pursuits while discouraging others from engaging in them. That is, decriminalizing certain conduct does not mean that moral judgment is thereafter precluded. Stigmas, disdain, and a "cold shoulder" all convey disapproval without implying that anyone wants to criminalize the objectionable conduct. Since all of these methods are used to promote good manners, we might ask why they cannot be used to promote a more refined culture. Many adults might have as much to gain in this regard as children.[53]

George Kateb's writings are illuminating because he gives a theoretical account of the change being described here. In "Democratic Individuality and the Meaning of Rights" and the papers in *The Inner Ocean*, Kateb observes that a grudging tolerance of practices once frowned upon may be replaced by a greater receptivity toward them. This phenomenon is likened to a "universal absolution." It takes place only in a democratic society that confers dignity on all persons by guaranteeing them rights.[54] Thus, in addition to promoting lives of greater expressiveness and resistance—Emerson's "Self-Reliance" and Thoreau's "Civil Disobedience" are the seminal texts—rights-based individualism also fosters this "almost promiscuous acceptance of one thing after another."[55]

What Kateb describes is attractive in different ways. His account of rights-based individualism helps to explain why so few Americans are now troubled by, say, interracial dating and marriage. Nonetheless, in many instances, "the promiscuous acceptance of one thing after another" should stop long before someone's rights are violated.

At what point? To establish the precise location is difficult, but building on Mill's distinctions between higher and lower faculties and "wise and foolish objects," we have ample resources to criticize some pursuits that liberals such as Nagel seemingly want to celebrate.

---

[52] Stephen Holmes, "The Permanent Structure of Antiliberal Thought," in Rosenblum, ed., *Liberalism and the Moral Life*, 243–244.

[53] Some readers might say that stigmas have no place in a liberal society. I disagree. I cannot imagine a morally decent society without some kinds of *conduct* being stigmatized. Mill, among others, recognized this need (as noted in the next chapter), and Neil Postman was correct in thinking that the welfare of children depends on a social consensus about the wrongness or shamefulness of certain adult behaviors vis-à-vis children. Stigmas often help to preserve that consensus.

[54] Kateb, "Democratic Individuality and the Meaning of Rights," 197.

[55] George Kateb, *The Inner Ocean* (Ithaca, N.Y.: Cornell University Press, 1992), 30.

Nagel's essay "Personal Rights and Public Space" merits scrutiny.[56] After discussing the intrinsic and instrumental value of "personal inviolability," Nagel considers several controversies in civil liberties, including sexual freedom and hate speech. Now it is conceivable that Mill, were he a party to these debates, would agree with Nagel's answers to the relevant *legal* questions. But, as we saw, Mill distinguished the legal dimension from the moral dimension, and his analysis did not end with the former.

By contrast, Nagel seemingly wants to affirm the moral permissibility of any pursuit that does not result in direct, tangible harm to others. This is evident in his views on human sexuality. He accepts the sexual permissiveness of our day *in toto*.[57] He condones adultery.[58] He avoids criticizing the most depraved forms of pornography, even those that depict rape and female mutilation.[59]

Nagel's essay attests to large changes in social and sexual norms in the United States. Notwithstanding our failure to achieve the "worldliness" that he deems desirable, Nagel believes that sexual emancipation is progressing. Yet some might object that Nagel misunderstands what is taking place. Instead of promoting freedom, these changes may jeopardize it. One does not have to be a radical proponent of positive liberty to see this.

The moral reticence of Nagel's liberalism is evident in his strained defense of the vilest pornography. It is difficult for me to believe that at some level Nagel does not recognize such pornography as morally problematic. So his defense suggests that the morally reticent outlook at some point can affect judgment and common sense:

> I don't want to see films depicting torture and mutilation, but I take it as obvious that they do something completely different for those who are sexually gratified by them; it's not that they are delighted by *the same thing* that revolts me; it is something else that I don't understand, because it does not fit into the particular configuration of my sexual imagination—something having to do with the sense of one's body and the bodies of others, release of shame, disinhibition of physical control, transgression, surrender—but I am guessing.[60]

[56] Thomas Nagel, "Personal Rights and Public Space," *Philosophy and Public Affairs* 24 (Spring 1995): 83.

[57] Ibid., 103.

[58] Ibid., 99.

[59] Ibid., 105. At one point (96), Nagel writes that "the expression of what one thinks and feels should be overwhelmingly one's own business, subject to restriction only when clearly necessary to prevent serious harms distinct from the expression itself." Again, whether an action should be criminalized or decriminalized is a separate question from the morality or desirability of that action, but in "Personal Rights and Public Space," Nagel shows no awareness of the importance of that distinction.

[60] Ibid., 105.

To this reader, Nagel's failure to consider *any* secondary effects of the stimuli just described is remarkable, and even more remarkable than his professed concern for the welfare of American women.[61]

As any politically literate citizen knows, these matters have caught the public's attention because the stimuli are so common and because children are widely considered susceptible to their influence. We can therefore see the danger that moral reticence presents to a society like ours.

Based on the statements canvassed above, we can also conclude that liberals such as Nagel, Dworkin, and Kateb have failed to consider how children may be affected by the examples presented to them. A profane torrent of words or grossly outrageous conduct or imagery, when uttered or displayed in the presence of the young, may undermine the efforts of conscientious parents and teachers. And if we agree that home and school should encourage a child to develop his or her innate capacities as far as possible—to exercise the "higher" human faculties and take up substantial rather than crude or insipid pursuits—then it is easy to grasp how outside agents may thwart the attainment of that goal.

John Stuart Mill was aware of these issues. In chapter 4 of *On Liberty*, he asks whether a person can be "injurious by his example." But Mill's treatment of this matter is unsatisfactory, and not only because he failed to explore the connection between this notion of "injurious" and his "harm principle."

In the eighth paragraph of chapter 4, Mill asks (in a roundabout way) whether a man "might be compelled to control himself" for the sake of those who are easily misled. Then, after returning to the topic three paragraphs later, he assumes that the objectionable conduct will be criticized and that the guilty party will change his ways.[62] Despite the curious leap here and the absence of an argument, Mill understood the fragility and corruptibility of children, as noted above. Consider further this statement from *Utilitarianism*:

> Capacity for the nobler feelings is in most natures a very tender plant, easily killed, not only by hostile influences, but by mere want of sustenance; and in the majority of young persons it speedily dies away if the occupations to which their position in life has devoted them, and the society into which it has thrown

---

[61] Despite his failure to criticize such pornography, Nagel says he worries about the social status of American women. But is this a coherent set of views? If a white supremacist made a movie in which actors dressed as Klansmen burned down the churches of African-Americans and then tortured and lynched the members of the congregation, I doubt that Nagel would say that anyone who found the movie piquant (or titillating) simply had a different "configuration of the [racial] imagination." And if he did say as much, many persons would question Nagel's commitment to racial equality.

[62] Mill, *On Liberty*, 75.

them, are not favourable to keeping that higher capacity in exercise. Men lose their high aspirations as they lose their intellectual tastes, because they have not time or opportunity for indulging them; and they addict themselves to inferior pleasures, not because they deliberately prefer them, but because they are either the only ones to which they have access, or the only ones which they are any longer capable of enjoying.[63]

Taking account of the milieu in which so many American children now live, we might ask whether they have an interest in the sustained exercise of their higher faculties. By this, I do not mean an educational regimen like that imposed by James Mill on his son. (Far beyond the ability of most youths, the regimen also stultified the aesthetic and emotional faculties of John Stuart Mill, an outcome he later regretted.) What I have in mind is the creation and maintenance of conditions, both in and outside the home, such that children may exercise these faculties as far as their individual endowments permit.

Critics will say that to create and maintain such conditions gives too much power to the government. That fear is easy to understand, but there is more to consider. In view of the difficulties in securing the child's interest, some persons—including the best-educated members of society—may have a duty to see that society gives the interest its due. Mill recognized this duty and tried to discharge it, whereas the contemporary liberals mentioned above have in an important sense abjured it.

I want to be clear. They have abjured this duty *at the level of theory,* an abjuration that is both regrettable and consequential. To be sure, as academics they may demonstrate to students and the outside world that some human pleasures and pursuits are "higher" or more fulfilling than others. Their lives might also attest to the importance of self-discipline and perseverance in the pursuit of those higher objects. Nevertheless, their statements about the equal value and equal dignity of all "self-regarding" pursuits have had a countervailing effect. The morally reticent outlook of Berlin and others is historically intelligible, and it has both reflected and reinforced certain tendencies within liberal thought and in liberal society. But it would be wrong to suppose that this outlook has had only benign or salubrious effects.

Here we should add that the morally reticent worldview has also been reflected in the liberal postulate that there is no "good life." This notion finds expression in the writings of prominent liberals, including Amy Gutmann, George Kateb, and Judith Shklar. Gutmann submits that we are unable to "specify objectively the good life"; Kateb declares that "there is no good life"; and Shklar contends that "liberalism does not have any

---

[63] Mill, *Utilitarianism*, 281–282.

particular positive doctrines about how people are to conduct their lives or what personal choices they are to make."[64]

As statements about liberal indifference to the exercise of personal freedom in a society that secures basic rights, these are telling. But the statements mislead. To say that there is no *single* good life for citizens in the modern world is different from saying that we have no grounds for distinguishing better lives from worse lives. The former statement is an intelligent response to the defenders of Stalin or Mao; the latter is moral reticence.

As noted at the start of this chapter, we now have some reason to think that the phenomenon of moral reticence is passing away. Some liberal thinkers have reminded us that we have resources to distinguish between the good and bad uses of legally protected freedoms.[65] Other liberals disavowed the moral reticence of their earlier work.[66] Finally, some politicians and political commentators have described the "externalities" of moral reticence, especially as they pertain to children.

All of these developments are welcome. But even today, appeals to various ideals that lie beyond the realm of law ring hollow with many educated persons in the United States. We continue to be told (sometimes in a hectoring tone) that we should not be "judgmental" regarding "lifestyle" choices and the exercise of personal freedom. There is even a tendency—evident in the strange success of Milos Forman's film on Larry Flynt—to valorize those who use their freedom in crude and vicious ways.[67]

To conclude the chapter, and to emphasize the change in liberalism described here, I wish to consider an essay by Aleksandr Solzhenitsyn, a thinker who, in the eyes of Stephen Holmes and others, falls within the "tradition" of antiliberalism.[68] Uttering the names "John Stuart Mill" and "Aleksandr Solzhenitsyn" in the same breath might suggest that we

[64] See Amy Gutmann, *Liberal Equality* (Cambridge: Cambridge University Press, 1981), 12; Kateb, "Democratic Individuality and the Meaning of Rights," 188; Judith N. Shklar, "The Liberalism of Fear," in Rosenblum, *Liberalism and the Moral Life*, 21.

[65] See, for example, William A. Galston, *Goods, Virtues, and Diversity in the Liberal State* (Cambridge: Cambridge University Press, 1991), and Stephen Macedo, *Liberal Virtues* (Oxford: Clarendon, 1991).

[66] See, for example, George Kateb's essay, "The Freedom of Worthless and Harmful Speech," in *Liberalism without Illusions: Essays on Liberal Theory and the Political Vision of Judith N. Shklar,* ed. Bernard Yack (Chicago and London: University of Chicago Press, 1996). Thomas Nagel's essay "Concealment and Exposure," *Philosophy and Public Affairs* 27 (1998): 3, seems to repudiate some of what he wrote just three years earlier in "Personal Rights and Public Space."

[67] See the article by Bernard Weinraub, "'Flynt' Receives Thumbs Up by New Reviewer," *The New York Times,* 21 February 1997, C3.

[68] See, for example, the introduction to Holmes, *The Anatomy of Antiliberalism,* 5–7.

are searching for antipodes. Mill: cosmopolitan, secular, enlightened; Solzhenitsyn: provincial, Orthodox, reactionary. Upon closer inspection, however, the contrast is misleading. If we can divest ourselves of our intellectual prejudices, we might see that in a famous public address, Solzhenitsyn was discharging an important duty spoken of by Mill.

In his commencement speech at Harvard University on 8 June 1978, Solzhenitsyn made a series of statements that seemed alien to the mainstream of contemporary liberalism. For example, he asserted that

> a society with no other scale but the legal one is . . . less than worthy of man. A society based on the letter of the law and never reaching any higher fails to take advantage of the full range of human possibilities.[69]

This may be alien to the mainstream of *contemporary* liberalism—yet it was familiar to John Stuart Mill when he wrote:

> There is a degree of folly, and a degree of what may be called (though the phrase is not unobjectionable) lowness or deprivation of taste, which, though it cannot justify doing harm to the person who manifests it, renders him necessarily and properly a subject of distaste, or, in extreme cases, even of contempt. . . . We are not bound, for example, to seek his society; we have a right to avoid it (though not to parade the avoidance), for we have a right to choose the society most acceptable to us. We have a right, *and it may be our duty*, to caution others against him, if we think his example or his conversations likely to have a pernicious influence on those with whom he associates. . . . In these various modes a person may suffer very severe penalties for faults which directly concern only himself.[70] (Emphasis added.)

What "pernicious influences" did Solzhenitsyn feel obliged to warn us about? Reading his speech more than twenty-five years after it was delivered, we should concede its prescience, because Solzhenitsyn's worries have become our worries:

> Destructive and irresponsible freedom has been granted boundless space. Society has turned out to have scarce defense against the abyss of human decadence, for example against the misuse of liberty for moral violence against young people, such as motion pictures full of pornography, crime, and horror. This is all considered to be part of freedom and to be counterbalanced, in theory, by the young people's right not to look and not to accept. Life organized legalistically has thus shown its inability to defend itself against the corrosion of evil.
>
> Of course, a society cannot remain in an abyss of lawlessness, as is the case in our country. But it is also demeaning for it to stay on such a soulless and

---

[69] Aleksandr I. Solzhenitsyn, *A World Split Apart: Commencement Address Delivered at Harvard University* (New York: Harper and Row, 1978), 17.
[70] Mill, *On Liberty*, 72.

smooth plane of legalism, as is the case in yours. . . . The human soul longs for things higher . . . and purer than those offered by today's mass living habits, introduced as by a calling card by the revolting invasion of commercial advertising, by TV stupor, and by intolerable music.[71]

Many Americans would say that Solzhenitsyn has no connection to the liberal tradition, because we assume that liberal political principles and astringent social criticism are incompatible. This assumption may need to be questioned: in his attacks on Hollywood and Fleet Street, Solzhenitsyn never once called for censorship.[72]

There are rhetorical flourishes in Solzhenitsyn's address, a few of which merit comment. He submits, for instance, that in American society, "if one is right from a legal point of view, nothing more is required. . . . Self-restraint is almost unheard of: everybody strives toward further expansion to the extreme limit of the law."[73] Liberals who focus on the word "everybody" in the last sentence will accuse Solzhenitsyn of exaggerating wildly. But in pointing out that *some* persons exercise self-restraint, these liberals implicitly affirm the need to preserve the distinction between the good and bad uses of protected freedoms, a large theme in Solzhenitsyn's speech.

Since Solzhenitsyn's address, other public figures in the United States have tried to resist some of the least attractive aspects of American popular culture. Some of these initiatives have tried to raise public and parental awareness.[74] Others involve direct appeals to corporate sponsors to withdraw advertising from objectionable programming.[75] Perhaps because the social interests are so weighty, these initiatives have led to some unusual political alliances.[76]

---

[71] Solzhenitsyn, *A World Split Apart,* 21; 35–37.

[72] I do not know whether Solzhenitsyn considers himself a liberal, but he wrote the "Foreword" to the Russian-language edition of Victor Leontovich's *History of Russian Liberalism.* Leontovich was a Russian émigré who settled in Germany after World War II; his *History* was originally written in German. See V. V. Leontovich, *Istoriya Liberalizma v Rossii 1762–1914* (Paris: YMCA Press, 1980).

[73] Solzhenitsyn, *A World Split Apart,* 17.

[74] See, for example, "A Campaign against 'Degrading' Rock Lyrics," *The New York Times,* 31 May 1996, C12; and Seth Schiesel, "On Web, New Threats Seen to the Young," *The New York Times,* 7 March 1997, A1. For "self-policing," see Martha Bayles, "Attacks on Rap Now Come from Within," *Wall Street Journal,* 28 April 2005, D8.

[75] See Lawrie Mifflin, "Talk-Show Critics Urge Boycott of Programs by Advertisers," *The New York Times,* 8 December 1995, A22.

[76] The campaign against highly offensive rock lyrics mentioned above involved William J. Bennett, Secretary of Education in the Reagan Administration; C. Delores Tucker, head of the National Political Congress of Black Women; and Senators Sam Nunn of Georgia and Joseph Lieberman of Connecticut, both Democrats.

Partly out of their concern for young persons, Solzhenitsyn and these other public figures have reminded us of a danger intrinsic to liberalism, a danger seen by Mill and others in the nineteenth century. The threat that moral reticence poses to children in a liberal society should be evident now, even if some contemporary liberals have been slow to recognize it.

CHAPTER TWO

Children and the False Charms
of Liberal Feminism

IF THE ARGUMENT just presented is sound, then some liberal thinkers have oversimplified an important theoretical matter. To judge from the writings cited in the last chapter, these thinkers hold that the archetypal figure in political society is the adult citizen, living in a world where only adults are present. The pervasiveness of this imagery is important. If the imagery appears regularly, then we might conclude that contemporary liberalism has a bias against children.

As a critique, the preceding chapter has something in common with feminism, since it also offers criticism of archetypal figures and images. According to many feminist thinkers, the archetypal or generic figure in Western political life is the male citizen, usually the de jure or de facto head of a family. Feminists argue that, even in the modern age, when all adults have come to be regarded as free and equal persons, the political world presupposed by most theorists is inhabited solely by adult men, with women and children left out of the picture.

Criticisms such as these, which feminists often direct at classical liberalism, have been extended to the recent revival of social contract theory. Having long lain dormant, social contract philosophy came back to life in the 1970s. Since then, leading academic liberals—including Bruce Ackerman, Ronald Dworkin, Stephen Holmes, George Kateb, Robert Nozick, and T. M. Scanlon—have either endorsed the idea of a social contract or presented their own versions of it.[1]

The rudiments of social contract theory are uncomplicated. The parties to the contract make a reciprocal agreement to promote various ends, the foremost being the protection of life and essential liberties. The parties advance these ends by instituting political authority and honoring universally binding laws. Depending on its provisions and the surrounding

---

[1] Among other works, see Bruce Ackerman, *Social Justice and the Liberal State* (New Haven: Yale University Press, 1980); Robert Nozick, *Anarchy, State, and Utopia* (New York: Basic Books, 1974); George Kateb, "The Liberal Contract," in *The Inner Ocean*; Stephen Holmes, "The Permanent Structure of Antiliberal Thought"; Ronald Dworkin, *Sovereign Virtue* (Cambridge, Mass.: Harvard University Press, 2000); T. M. Scanlon, *What We Owe to Each Other* (Cambridge, Mass.: Harvard University Press, 1998).

circumstances, the contract could be regarded as either a hypothetical thought experiment or an actual event in a nation's history.[2]

The best-known contribution to the revival of contractualism is John Rawls's *A Theory of Justice,* published in 1971.[3] Rawls's treatise has elicited both lavish praise and much thoughtful criticism. Among the many responses, one is highly pertinent to my purposes.

In *Justice, Gender, and the Family,* Susan Moller Okin praises Rawls's philosophic method and principles while arguing that his political theory gives insufficient attention to several crucial topics.[4] Okin commends Rawls for discussing women, children, and families, but she criticizes his account of the intellectual and moral development of the contracting parties. In her eyes, Rawls's theory is untenable because of the role he expects the traditional, two-parent family to play. Arguing that the traditional family is the site of substantial injustices—largely because of the "social construction of gender" and the division of labor based on it—Okin concludes that Rawls's vision of a just society will remain unrealized unless those injustices are redressed.

Some of these criticisms have intellectual precedents. Notwithstanding its feminist bearings, Okin's critique in some ways resembles G.W.F. Hegel's critique of social contract theory in his *Philosophy of Right* (1821). The burden of Hegel's critique might be expressed in this way. Because they give so much attention to the terms of the contract and the deliberations that lay behind it, contractarian theorists create the impression that societies are composed exclusively of rational adults and that the intellectual capacities needed to forge the contract develop effortlessly. Okin would deny that she and Hegel are kindred spirits—a point that none of her readers will contest—but each argues that the contract often obscures the importance of education and moral development, especially in young persons.

The surprising affinity between Okin and Hegel shows that one does not have to be a feminist to think about the welfare of children and the political relevance of the family. Okin, however, believes that contemporary feminists have surpassed Hegel's achievement and identified other serious problems in both the liberal and the contractarian traditions.[5]

---

[2] On these matters, see, for example, Thomas Hobbes, *Leviathan,* chs. 17–20 and 26; John Locke, *Second Treatise,* chs. 2 and 7–9, esp. secs. 13–15, 87–89, 99–108, and 112–122; and Jean-Jacques Rousseau, *On the Social Contract,* bk. 1, secs. 5–6, and bk. 2, secs. 6–11.

[3] John Rawls, *A Theory of Justice* (Cambridge, Mass.: The Belknap Press of Harvard University Press, 1971). A revised edition was published in 1999, but in this chapter, all references are to the first edition of the book.

[4] Susan Moller Okin, *Justice, Gender, and the Family* (New York: Basic Books, 1989).

[5] The contractarian and liberal traditions overlap in places, but they are distinct. Many scholars, for example, resist the idea that Hobbes and Rousseau are liberals.

Okin's relationship to liberalism is a bit curious. Besides faulting it for being insufficiently attentive to family life, she maintains that the "public/private" dichotomy in liberal theory hides substantial injustices. At the same time, she accepts key tenets of contemporary liberalism, such as its wariness of the very idea of "public morality." She also takes liberal views on civil-liberties jurisprudence.

Okin refers to herself as both a feminist and a liberal, while arguing that liberalism would be a far more compelling public philosophy if it incorporated elements of feminism. She aspires to develop a liberal theory devoid of any patriarchal bias: a "humanist liberalism," which is the title of one of her essays. Other political and legal theorists whose work is informed by feminism share this aspiration. For this reason, Okin is a representative thinker. She is also an influential thinker, mainly because of her critique of Rawls and her attempt to extend the Rawlsian contract so that it encompasses both gender and family life.[6]

Because of its attention to family life and children, Okin's liberalism might seemingly be able to avoid problems such as those discussed in the last chapter. Okin seeks to provide a fuller account of the foundations of political and social life, working (one might say) from "bottom to top." It is a promising approach for anyone who worries that, with respect to children, most liberal theorists take too much for granted today.

In the end, however, Okin fails to provide sound principles of "humanist" justice. The overriding weakness in her work is an insufficiently critical posture toward a host of rights. Presenting herself as deeply concerned about the welfare of American children, Okin fails to anticipate how certain freedoms, when exercised, may affect them.

This is a peculiar oversight. Okin has sought to add complexity and nuance to accounts of political and social life, and she tries to show that some ostensibly "private" behavior by men has a real impact on women in both the public and the domestic realms. Yet her analysis is less probing when facing issues that affect children, and she too often assumes that the interests of women and children coincide. Moreover, she fails to apply principles uniformly, a tendency that invites the charge of bad faith.

---

[6] On the matters discussed here, see Okin, *Justice, Gender, and the Family,* 127–133; "Gender, the Public, and the Private," in *Political Theory Today,* ed. David Held (Stanford, Calif.: Stanford University Press, 1991); and "Humanist Liberalism," (1989), in Rosenblum, *Liberalism and the Moral Life.*

Soon after Okin's untimely death in March 2004, her colleagues at Stanford University spoke of her influence within academic political theory. Philosophy professor Debra Satz remarked that Okin was "perhaps the best feminist political philosopher in the world," while political scientist John Ferejohn added that Okin "revolutionized the field." These comments were included in Okin's obituary at Stanford University (published at the Political Science Department's website).

In offering these criticisms, I do not wish to suggest that in our liberal democracy, the interests of women and children routinely conflict, or that they conflict more often than do the interests of men and children. (Nor do I wish to say that the interests of children should *always* prevail over the competing interests of adults.) But some conflicts between various interests of adults and children are inevitable, and given Okin's interests, she should be expected to say something about these conflicts.

In this chapter, I first review Okin's main theses about gender, family life, and the welfare of women and children, explaining why Okin believes that other liberal theorists have failed to recognize some important interests of women and children. I then assess Okin's novel theoretical initiative: her attempt to derive new principles of justice from the framework of Rawls's "original position." Those principles are applied to family life to redress the injustices deriving from gender, which Okin defines as "the deeply entrenched institutionalization of sexual differences."[7] In the conclusion, I offer a critique and argue that Okin needs to consider and reconsider various matters, if she truly wants to develop humanist principles of justice and avoid the charge of indifference to children.[8]

GENDER AND INJUSTICE: AMERICAN FAMILIES AND THE WELFARE OF WOMEN AND CHILDREN

Any thorough evaluation of Okin's work should begin by looking at her views about feminism as an academic discipline. This might seem to be a needless digression, but it is warranted because Okin's criticisms of recent political theory are based on its alleged inattention to feminist scholarship. By her estimate, the achievements of feminist scholars elsewhere in the humanities and social sciences can scarcely be overstated.

A few examples will suffice. In *Justice, Gender, and the Family,* Okin credits feminism and its theorists—"Firestone, Friedan, Oakley, Mitchell, Chodorow, Pateman, and all the other great feminist thinkers of the last two decades"—for making gender recognized as "a social factor of major importance." In "Humanist Liberalism," Okin expresses the obverse of that idea, arguing that because of its failure to incorporate feminist insights, contemporary political theory remains mired in the "Dark Ages." And in

---

[7] Okin, *Justice, Gender, and the Family,* 6.

[8] This chapter seeks to provide a comprehensive account of the themes found in *Justice, Gender, and the Family.* To that end, I rely on articles written before and after that book was published in 1989. In the last years of her life, Okin explored the relationship between "multiculturalism" and the welfare of women, asking whether a "multicultural" outlook tends to be too accepting of injustices that women suffer (*qua* women) in disparate social and political circumstances. Those inquiries are of only slight relevance to my concerns here.

"Gender, the Public, and the Private," Okin insists that the marginalization of feminist theory "will continue only at the expense of the . . . coherence, comprehensiveness, and persuasiveness of political theory."[9]

Such praise may seem self-serving, but it should be placed in context. The most relevant context is the long-standing struggle of women to be recognized as fully human and to be treated as such in all spheres of life. Feminist ideas have contributed to this cause, and one can therefore make sense of the encomia above. Greater personal and professional opportunities and the elimination of various forms of sex discrimination are signal changes, having enhanced the lives of many women. Those changes have in turn affected the expectations of millions of girls now growing up in the United States and elsewhere.

A critic might contend that these developments are just as easily explained by the extension of liberal-democratic principles. In this interpretation of modern politics, nearly all forms of ascriptive status have been abandoned. Thus, regardless of the common understanding of the words in 1776, the notion that "all men are created equal" is now read as a synecdoche. "All men" really means "all persons": female and male, black and white, Asian and European.[10] Although Okin faults liberalism for different things and says little about its origins, she concedes feminism's large debt to liberalism. That debt is reflected in what Okin regards as the central thesis of feminism: that "women are human beings in no way inferior to men . . . [and] warrant equal consideration with men in any political or moral theory."[11]

So where does liberalism go wrong? Okin's criticism is both theoretical and historical. She reminds us that even if the central thesis of feminism is now familiar, from a historical standpoint its implications are bold and novel. The boldness and novelty might be seen by briefly reviewing an important chapter in Western intellectual history.

In their reflections on politics and social life, premodern thinkers such as Aristotle and Aquinas assumed that women are in different ways inferior to men and could be excluded from politics and assigned to a subordinate

---

[9] Okin, *Justice, Gender, and the Family,* 61 and 6; "Humanist Liberalism," 39; "Gender, the Public, and the Private," 68.

[10] The outline of such an argument is found in works by historians and contemporary political theorists, including the essays by James M. McPherson in *Abraham Lincoln and the Second American Revolution* (New York: Oxford University Press, 1990), esp. chs. 2, 3, 6, and 7; Harry V. Jaffa, *How to Think about the American Revolution* (Durham, N.C.: Carolina Academic Press, 1978); and George Kateb, "Democratic Individuality and the Meaning of Rights." See also the introduction in Gordon Wood, *The Radicalism of the American Revolution* (New York: Vintage, 1991).

[11] Okin, *Justice, Gender, and the Family,* 61.

status at home. This lower status was said to be grounded in nature, an apparent sign of which was the (alleged) intellectual inferiority of women.[12]

These notions were increasingly questioned in the modern age, when critics (some of them women) detected inconsistencies in new works of political theory. Here is Okin's gloss on this momentous shift:

> When political theories were built on assumptions of natural hierarchy or of a God-given great chain of being, there was no particular difficulty supporting the idea that women were among the inferior categories of human beings. They could therefore legitimately be excluded from political life, denied legal equality, and relegated to a subordinate position within the family. . . . While other whole categories of people—slaves, serfs, and so on—were held to be "naturally" subjected to the rule of their superiors, it was not so difficult to apply this argument to women, too.
>
> By the seventeenth or eighteenth century, however, theories of natural or God-given hierarchy were facing serious challenge, from both scientists and political theorists. . . . The idea of the natural equality and freedom of human beings, as argued by philosophers such as Hobbes and Locke, presented an important intellectual problem to a society still determined to uphold the unequal treatment of men and women.[13]

The "intellectual problem" that Okin speaks of here might be called self-contradiction or disingenuousness or blindness. Having propounded the ideas of natural freedom and government by consent, thinkers such as Hobbes and Locke failed to extend their principles to different matters affecting women. Similar criticisms could be made of Rousseau and Kant.

Why did these thinkers fail to apply their principles categorically? Okin's reference to societies "still determined to uphold the unequal treatment of men and women" suggests a large conspiracy, abetted by influential philosophers. There may be simpler reasons for the inconsistencies, having to do with unreflective adherence to tradition and social conditions very different from those in the West today. Perhaps because she assumes such a conspiracy, Okin overlooks different ideas of theorists such as Locke and Rousseau to explain or justify paternal authority in the family. Those ideas may seem feeble now, but they may be of greater historical significance than Okin realizes.[14]

---

[12] See Aristotle *Politics* bk. 1, esp. 1254b, and Aquinas *Summa Theologiae* I, q. 92 ("Woman is naturally subject to man in this kind of subjection [i.e., of the household, as distinguished from slavery] because by nature man possesses more discernment of the reason").

[13] Okin, "Woman and the Making of the Sentimental Family," *Philosophy and Public Affairs* 11 (1982): 65.

[14] Compare, for instance, Locke's comments on Genesis 3:16 ("Your desire shall be for your husband, and he shall rule over you") in sec. 47 of the *First Treatise* with Okin's words

The foregoing gives us an inkling of what Okin considers a grave deficiency of classical liberalism. Liberal theorists have long argued that certain associations and individual pursuits ought to lie beyond state control. Those associations and pursuits—such as religious observance (or nonobservance), the choice of a spouse, and the management of a household—are said to belong to the realm of private life, which is contrasted with the public realm, comprising politics and much of modern economic life.

Okin criticizes this neat division. Her criticism may be read as both an expression of solicitude and a demand for justice. She writes that men have over time inhabited both the public and the private realm, whereas the law confined women to the private realm, which Okin prefers to call the "domestic realm." That relegation made women vulnerable in different ways. Apart from having to rely on men to identify and promote their interests in politics, they depended on their husbands for sustenance and were obliged to respect certain domestic prerogatives that belonged to him. Women were also mainly responsible for raising the family's children, a division of labor that allowed men to enter political society.[15]

The long-standing dependence of women informs Okin's readings of texts and social practices. It is the basis of her critique of theorists such as Rousseau, Kant, and Hegel for "sentimentalizing" the family and thinking that women belonged at home and would be unhappy everywhere else. Besides leaving many women and children in a precarious economic position, these ideas reinforced common notions about the moral dissimilarity of the sexes and the limited capacity of women to perform certain types of work.[16]

Okin thus faults classical liberalism for the injustice in the public/private dichotomy and for perpetuating harmful superstitions about women. Someone might say that the people of the United States repudiated these elements of classical liberalism with the ratification of the Nineteenth

---

in the last paragraph of p. 71 in "Women and the Making of the Sentimental Family." Regarding Rousseau, Okin writes (ibid., 77) that his justification for patriarchal rule is that the family is an institution based on sentiment and that the father "has only to consult his heart" to govern the family well (*Discourse on Political Economy*, 6th par.). I cannot understand why Okin refers to this passage as a *justification* for patriarchal rule, because the passage identifies one difference between governing a family and governing a polity. In the same essay, Okin fails to mention several of the reasons Rousseau offers in the fourth paragraph of *Political Economy* to justify a father's authority in the home. Even if those reasons will persuade few persons today, they may have had greater force at a time when the personal security of family members from outside threats (both human and nonhuman) could not be taken for granted.

[15] Okin, "Gender, the Public, and the Private," 68–70 and 84–86; *Justice, Gender, and the Family*, 8–9 and 128–131.

[16] See, for example, Hegel, *Philosophy of Right*, sec. 166, and the "Addition" to that section in the Knox edition.

Amendment, but Okin argues that the historical legacy of patriarchy is formidable and is reflected in the relatively small number of women occupying positions of leadership in government and business. For this reason, among others, Okin refuses to refer to the United States as a "post-patriarchal" or "post-feminist" society.[17] In an essay from 1998, she even asserted that American women remain "second-class" citizens.[18]

However it is understood, patriarchy in American society derives from sources besides classical liberalism. To Okin, another prominent source is Christianity, about which she has nary a kind word. Critical of both liberalism and Christianity, Okin is more interested in the former than the latter because liberalism is said to have emancipatory potential that Christianity lacks.[19] Yet contemporary liberalism has some of the same defects as classical liberalism, so it can only modestly counteract the influence of Christianity in American life. Hence the need for feminism, which Okin sees as a new intellectual discipline and a political and social movement working to secure the real—and not merely formal—emancipation of women.[20]

Of the *political* achievement of feminism, little needs to be said. By any honest reckoning, its record is impressive, even if it can only be fully understood by glancing backwards. For in assuming that women are "naturally" inferior to men (or by assigning a host of "fixed" attributes to each sex), philosophers such as Aristotle, Kant, and Hegel unknowingly issued a provocation to posterity. That provocation is now acted on every day in the United States, where cadres of feminist scholars and activists analyze any law or policy that affords different treatment to men and women on the basis of sex.

Though not shared by all citizens, such wariness of sex-based classifications reveals something crucial about feminist theory. To Okin, the most notable accomplishment of feminist thinkers has been conceptualizing "gender," that familiar term which refers to the socially constructed meanings of sexual difference. The emphasis is on "socially constructed": from a feminist perspective, the irreducible biological differences between males and females ought to have little, if any, social significance.

This postulate regarding the social construction of sexual difference raises questions about many conventions. Consider child-rearing. Perhaps because of a woman's capacity to bear and nurse a child, many persons still believe that she should be mainly responsible for raising the young. In

[17] Okin, *Justice, Gender, and the Family,* 3–4 and 65–66; "Gender, the Public, and the Private," 81–83.

[18] Okin, "Feminism and Political Theory," in *Philosophy in a Feminist Voice: Critiques and Reconstructions,* ed. Janet A. Kourany (Princeton: Princeton University Press, 1998), 116.

[19] Okin, *Justice, Gender, and the Family,* 56–57, 61–62, and 101–109.

[20] Ibid., 7–10, 62–68, and chs. 5 and 6.

response, Okin writes that the biological capacities of a woman should not be confused with an innate or a superior talent for spoon-feeding an infant or changing a soiled diaper. Men can also perform these tasks, and the prejudice that women are "naturally" suited for this work has persisted alongside the belief that they cannot acquit themselves with distinction in politics, intellectual endeavors, or economic pursuits.[21]

What Okin calls the social construction of gender is linked to the public/private dichotomy in liberal theory. Gender produces psychological and social expectations in women and men. Those expectations often implicate politics, insofar as politics involves justifying the "differential treatment of persons by social institutions, laws, and customs."[22] Gender is thus concerned with power and relations of power, in both the public and the domestic sphere.

The following example should clarify this point. From the perspective of much liberal theory, a married woman who quits a job to have more time with her family has made a personal decision with little or no political content. Okin, by contrast, would assume that in a "gendered" society such as the United States, this decision has some political dimensions. She would ask: Who is mainly responsible for the child-rearing and domestic labor in this household? If the wife is mainly responsible, why is that so? Does she feel obliged to sacrifice professional advancement for the sake of her family? If so, why must she forego her career while her husband's advances? Finally, will the woman's decision to quit her job make her economically vulnerable in the event of divorce? And will the children be vulnerable?

Such questions suggest that the woman's decision has both a personal and a political component, an interpretation supported by the following excerpt from "Gender, the Public, and the Private":

> What, then, do . . . feminists . . . mean by "the personal is political"? We mean, for one thing, that what happens in personal life, particularly in relations between the sexes, is not immune from the dynamic of *power,* which has typically been seen as a distinguishing feature of the political. And we also mean that neither the realm of domestic, personal life, nor that of non-domestic economic and political life, can be understood or interpreted in isolation from the other. . . . Once the significance of gender is understood, neither the public nor the domestic realm, in terms of its structures and practices, assumptions and expectations, division of labour and distribution of power, can intelligibly be discussed without constant reference to the other. We have demonstrated how the inequalities of men and women in the worlds of work and politics are inextricably related, in a two-way causal cycle, with their inequalities within the family.[23]

[21] Ibid., 33–38.
[22] Ibid., 8.
[23] Okin, "Gender, the Public, and the Private," 77.

The details of this "dynamic of power" are found in chapter 7 of *Justice, Gender, and the Family*, where Okin identifies the key variable as the persistence of the traditional division of labor at home. Even with many more women taking jobs outside the home, wives still do most of the housework and remain primarily responsible for raising a family's children. That fact alone creates disadvantages, but the status of these women is further diminished by the wage and salary differentials between men and women and the common perception that homemaking and child-rearing are less important or less real than "man's work." Another indignity occurs when a husband "pulls rank" on his wife and refuses to share his wages or salary equitably.[24]

Okin bolsters this argument with statistics. She divides married women into two categories: "predominantly houseworking" and "predominantly wage-working." The first group, making up 40 percent of the married women in this country in 1975–76, consists both of women working exclusively at home and of women who work at home as well as less than twenty hours per week outside it. The second group consists of wives and mothers working more than twenty hours per week outside the home. In the "predominantly houseworking" group, women work fewer hours per week than their husbands. Full-time homemakers worked 49.3 hours per week, part-time wage-workers 55.2 hours, and husbands 63.2 hours. Yet Okin still sees injustice here, since more than four-fifths of the husband's work is remunerated and since the wife must contend with an unpredictable schedule (such as attending to a crying baby in the middle of the night) and tasks of greater drudgery (such as washing and ironing clothes and cleaning a house).[25]

In the "predominantly wage-working" group, Okin writes that fully employed husbands do less than half as much domestic work as their fully employed wives. Wives, on average, worked 71.1 hours per week (43 hours of paid labor; 28.1 hours of unpaid labor) and husbands 64.9 hours per week (55.8 paid; 9.2 unpaid). Even unemployed husbands do substantially less work at home than their spouses.[26]

Although the structure of the University of Michigan study appears not to have been replicated in other studies, more recent data suggest that the patterns just described have persisted. With a greater percentage of American women employed outside the home, husbands now do more housework than before, but some tasks previously performed by wives are being

[24] On these matters, see Okin, *Justice, Gender, and the Family*, 144–146 and 156–159.

[25] Ibid., 150–152. The data in this paragraph are from a University of Michigan study, completed in 1975–76. See ibid., 150 n. 44. More recent research is discussed below.

[26] Ibid., 154 n. 60 (citing data in Barbara Bergmann, *The Economic Emergence of Women* [New York: Basic Books, 1986]).

left undone. The result? A "leisure gap" is still found in many American marriages, with husbands usually having more free time each week.[27]

In a study published in 1996, two scholars provided a summary of trends during the previous thirty years:

> As more wives took on paying jobs over the past few decades, their proportional contribution to family earnings increased. In the 1990s, working wives contributed about 30 percent of their family's income; 40 percent when they worked full-time, year round. This development has tended to give wives greater power within their marriages.
>
> Despite their growing economic independence, however, women continue to allocate less time to market work and more time to family than men do. For example, 96 percent of married men ages 35 to 44 were employed in the year preceding the 1990 Census, compared with 77 percent of married women in that age group. . . . But wives put in almost 900 fewer paid work hours than husbands. The full-time year-round employment rate of married women (ages 35 to 44) was 39 percentage points lower than that of married men of the same age.
>
> Most likely, these disparities reflect the continuing differences in the domestic roles of men and women in the American family and economy. To be sure, married mothers have scaled down their hours of housework—from about 30 hours in 1965 to about 20 hours per week in 1985; married fathers, however, picked up only part of the slack, increasing their household work from about five hours to about 10 hours per week. . . . By 1985, married mothers performed about two-thirds of the housework compared with 85 percent in 1965.[28]

---

[27] See Arlie Hochschild, *The Second Shift: Working Parents and the Revolution at Home* (New York: Viking, 1989). For a summary of studies completed during the 1960s and 1970s on housework and the division of labor between spouses, see chapter 1 of Hochschild's book. For more recent studies and a statement on the methodology in Hochschild's own research, see the appendix to *The Second Shift*. Hochschild's work is cited by Okin in her essay "Sexual Orientation and Gender: Dichotomizing Differences," in *Sex, Preference, and Family: Essays on Law and Nature,* ed. David M. Estlund and Martha C. Nussbaum (New York: Oxford University Press, 1997).

According to a Census Bureau report based on data from 1998, families in which both spouses are working outside the home now constitute a majority in the United States, even among married couples with children. Both husband and wife are employed at least part-time outside the home in 51 percent of such families. See Tamar Lewin, "Now a Majority: Families with 2 Parents Who Work," *The New York Times,* 24 October 2000, A14 (national edition).

[28] Suzanne M. Bianchi and Daphne Spain, "Women, Work, and Family in America," *Population Bulletin* 51, no. 3 (Washington, D.C.: Population Reference Bureau, Inc., December 1996), 31–32. As used in this passage, the term "housework" comprises cooking, housecleaning, laundry, yardwork, and family finances; it does not include child care. Regarding the last point, Bianchi and Spain estimate that husbands are now responsible for about 40 percent of the tasks associated with child care. See ibid., 32, citing Frances Gold-

If these disparities are so pervasive, some readers may wonder how Okin accounts for the popularity of marriage and motherhood. (As Okin notes, in the past century nearly 90 percent of American women have been married by the age of thirty, and between 80 and 90 percent have had a child by the age of forty.[29]) Part of the answer allegedly lies in the ideology of patriarchy, which leads a substantial number of women to become mothers and homemakers unreflectively.[30] Other women are said to choose these vocations because they lack the same employment opportunities as men.[31]

While the demands of homemaking and motherhood continue to obstruct women's social and economic advancement, their social position may have worsened with the spread of "no-fault" divorce. Like several other scholars, Okin argues that no-fault divorce has heightened women's economic vulnerability.[32] She traces the problem to family courts treating the divorcing husband and wife as social equals when they are in various respects unequal.

The inequality is easily described. In 90 percent of the cases, a mother takes custody of the children and has more obligations to meet. A woman sometimes has far fewer "career assets" than her husband, especially when she foregoes her education or professional advancement to help her family. She is then at a disadvantage in the job market, particularly if the divorce occurs later in life and she has not worked outside the home for many years.[33]

Different studies support Okin's interpretation. According to scholars such as Lenore Weitzman, Mary Ann Glendon, and Heather Ruth Wishik, the economic prospects of most American women worsen after a divorce, whereas the disposable income of their ex-husbands usually increases. In a widely discussed study cited by Okin, Weitzman reported that in the first year after divorce, the standard of living for divorced men on average improves by 42 percent, whereas that of divorced women falls by 73 percent. She also noted that the legal notion of "fault" previously helped women in their efforts to receive an equitable share of the couple's tangible

---

scheider and Linda Waite, *New Families, No Families?* (Los Angeles: University of California Press, 1991), ch. 7.

The reader should notice that even if the total number of hours devoted to housework has declined since the 1960s, it may not mean that less work is being completed, because of labor-saving devices and declining fertility rates in the United States. (Fewer children in a family would seem to mean that less time is required for both child care and housework.)

[29] Okin, *Justice, Gender, and the Family*, 142.

[30] Ibid., 142–146.

[31] Ibid., 146–148.

[32] Ibid., 161, and Okin, "Economic Equality after Divorce," *Dissent* (Summer 1991): 383.

[33] Okin, *Justice, Gender, and the Family*, 160–167.

assets, but "no-fault" laws removed much of that leverage. (The notion of fault in divorce proceedings typically referred to cruelty, abandonment, or adultery.) Diminishing alimony payments and insufficient child support only add to the mother's vulnerability.[34]

After another scholar scrutinized her findings, Weitzman admitted that she overstated the economic impact of divorce on women.[35] Nevertheless, most scholars agree that divorce in the United States usually puts women (and the children in their custody) at an economic disadvantage. The debate continues, and it involves questions of methodology and of whether divorced women fared better in state courts before the no-fault era. For the sake of argument, however, I will accept Okin's thesis about the economic effects of divorce.[36]

Besides showing this solicitude toward divorced women, Okin expresses some anxiety about single mothers who have never married. She worries about the financial stresses associated with absent fathers and "deadbeat dads," but she does not find single-parent families (i.e., with an unmarried mother) problematic or objectionable. Seemingly in full agreement with Iris Marion Young (whose essay on this subject Okin praises

---

[34] See ibid., ch. 7, esp. 160–167; Lenore J. Weitzman, *The Divorce Revolution: The Unexpected Social and Economic Consequences for Women and Children in the United States* (New York: The Free Press, 1985); Heather Ruth Wishik, "Economics of Divorce: An Exploratory Study," *Family Law Quarterly* 20 (1986): 79; and Mary Ann Glendon, *Abortion and Divorce in Western Law* (Cambridge, Mass.: Harvard University Press, 1987).

A history of the no-fault divorce movement in the United States is presented in Herbert Jacob, *Silent Revolution* (London and Chicago: University of Chicago Press, 1988).

[35] See Richard R. Peterson, "A Re-Evaluation of the Economic Consequences of Divorce," *American Sociological Review* 61 (1996): 528; Lenore J. Weitzman, "The Economic Consequences of Divorce Are Still Unequal: Comment on Peterson," *American Sociological Review* 61 (1996): 537; and Peterson, "Statistical Errors, Faulty Conclusions, Misguided Policy: Reply to Weitzman," *American Sociological Review* 61 (1996): 539.

[36] On the scholarly consensus about the economic consequences of divorce, see Sanford L. Braver, "The Gender Gap in Standard of Living after Divorce: Vanishingly Small?" *Family Law Quarterly* 33 (1999): 111; and Katharine T. Bartlett, "Feminism and Family Law," *Family Law Quarterly* 33 (1999): 475. The general view is that the standard of living of the divorcing wife and her children will decline between 15 and 33 percent, while the standard of living of the divorcing husband will increase by about 10 percent. Braver concedes the existence of a scholarly consensus, but argues that most of the studies behind it (including one of his own) were flawed, and that if the errors were corrected, the standard of living in the two households would be recognized as equal or nearly equal. Bartlett seems to think that Braver's points on methodology need to be considered; see note 22 of her essay cited above.

At least a few scholars believe that the disparities in the standard of living cannot be attributed to the emergence of "no-fault" divorce. See the two contributions by Richard R. Peterson in the previous note. See also Jana B. Singer ("Divorce Reform and Gender Justice," *North Carolina Law Review* 67 [1989]: 1103, 1105), who rejects the notion that divorcing women and their children were better off under the fault-based system.

as "clearheaded" and "persuasive"), Okin believes that no one should second-guess a single woman's decision to have a child, even if the woman does not intend to marry the child's father. As Young baldly asserts:

> A liberal society that claims to respect the autonomy of all its citizens equally should affirm the freedom of all citizens to bear and rear children, whether they are married or not, whether they have high incomes or not.[37]

For several reasons, including the apparent difficulty of reconciling this broad endorsement of personal freedom with her criticisms of the public/private dichotomy in liberal theory, we should consider Okin's thoughts on this topic. Her endorsement is linked to her support for the constitutional "right to privacy" in matters of sexuality and reproduction, but her arguments in defense of that right are unpersuasive.

Consider, first, Okin's position on abortion. Until her essay "Women, Equality, and Citizenship" (1992), there was some doubt about where she stood.[38] In a few places, she seemed dismissive of the pro-life position.[39] Elsewhere she wrote that abortion is a moral and constitutional issue of great complexity, and that both pro-life and pro-choice views deserve respect.[40] Her position was further complicated by her view that disparities in power between men and women prevent us from reaching a satisfactory resolution on this issue.[41]

Keeping these points in mind, we may take note of a later and less equivocal statement. Near the end of "Women, Equality, and Citizenship," Okin asserts that women "have to be able to make their own moral decisions about their reproductive lives . . . [since] no one can be an equal citizen without this fundamental right."[42]

As a moral argument, this line of thinking is underdeveloped, since it nowhere considers the possibility that the fetus or unborn child might also be an "equal citizen." As a constitutional argument, it is even more problematic, since many scholars—including, in a sense, Okin herself—

---

[37] Iris Marion Young, "Mothers, Citizenship, and Independence," *Ethics* 105 (1995): 535, 554. A similar statement is found in Okin's essay "Families and Feminist Theory," in *Feminism and Families*, ed. Hilde Lindemann Nelson (New York and London: Routledge, 1997), 24. See the same essay (pp. 23–24) for Okin's remarks in praise of Young's work.

I have yet to find a statement by Okin that matches Young's in its directness. But Okin gives us no reason to think that she has any reservations about single women becoming mothers. In addition to her comments on Young's essay, see also *Justice, Gender, and the Family*, 83, and "Sexual Orientation and Gender," 44–45.

[38] Okin, "Women, Equality, and Citizenship," *Queen's Quarterly* 99 (1992).

[39] See her remarks in "A Critique of Pregnancy Contracts," *Politics and the Life Sciences* 8 (1990): 205, 209 (n. 9).

[40] See, for example, the footnote on p. 66 of Okin's *Justice, Gender, and the Family*.

[41] See, for instance, Okin, "Gender, the Public, and the Private," 72.

[42] Okin, "Women, Equality, and Citizenship," 56, 70.

recognize that the right to abortion promulgated in *Roe v. Wade* was difficult, if not impossible, to justify on the basis of precedent. The pivotal case here, decided shortly before *Roe* in 1973, was *Eisenstadt v. Baird*. Despite being pleased with the decision, Okin properly (though modestly) describes the ruling in *Eisenstadt* as "something of a leap from precedent."[43]

Okin's failure to probe the weak foundations of the right to "reproductive privacy" makes it hard to accept her ideas about extending that right. In "Sexual Orientation and Gender" (1997), she endorses Jed Rubenfeld's view that the Supreme Court's decision in *Bowers v. Hardwick* "eviscerates . . . privacy's principles."[44] (Though later overruled, *Bowers* upheld Georgia's constitutional authority to criminalize homosexual sodomy.[45]) In the same essay, Okin affirms the freedom of homosexuals to "marry" and adopt children and avail themselves of new reproductive technologies to start their own families.[46]

These affirmations are grounded in both liberalism and feminism. As a liberal, Okin wants to enlarge the scope of individual freedom. As a feminist, she wants to "dismantle" or "confound" gender by attacking conventional sex roles. The latter goal is described in the following passage from *Justice, Gender, and the Family*:

> More and more, as the extent to which gender is a social construction has become understood, feminists have come to recognize how variable are the potential forms and practices of family groups. The family is in no way inevitably tied to its gender structure, but until this notion is successfully challenged, and nontraditional groupings and divisions of labor are *not only recognized but encouraged*, there can be no hope of equality for women in either the domestic or the public sphere.[47]

At this point, one possible criticism is clear. Since Okin champions a host of "lifestyle" freedoms while attacking the public/private division in liberal theory, she seems caught in a great contradiction. She affirms a lesbian's decision to use artificial insemination and raise the child alone or

---

[43] Okin, "Sexual Orientation and Gender," 52. In *Eisenstadt v. Baird*, 405 U.S. 438 (1972), the Supreme Court struck down a Massachusetts law prohibiting the distribution and sale of contraceptives to the unmarried. Previously, in *Griswold v. Connecticut*, 381 U.S. 479 (1965), the Supreme Court had held that a Connecticut statute banning the use of contraceptives violated an unenumerated constitutional right of *associational* privacy belonging to married couples. The boldness of *Eisenstadt* (recognized by Okin) consisted in its declaration that the rights of access to contraceptives must be the same for both married and unmarried persons. *Griswold* and *Eisenstadt* are examined in the next chapter.

[44] Okin, "Sexual Orientation and Gender," 51.

[45] *Bowers v. Hardwick*, 478 U.S. 186 (1986), overruled in *Lawrence v. Texas*, 539 U.S. 558 (2003).

[46] Okin, "Sexual Orientation and Gender," 54.

[47] Okin, *Justice, Gender, and the Family*, 125 (emphasis added). A similar statement is found in "Sexual Orientation and Gender," 44–45.

with a partner, yet is reluctant to accept at face value a married woman's decision to be a homemaker and assume most of the duties in raising her family's children.

Perhaps the contradiction is less significant than it first appears, because with respect to policy, Okin would *tolerate* a "traditional" division of labor if a husband and wife agreed upon it. Okin nonetheless worries about the life prospects of women and children in such families, and that worry lies behind her novel proposal to reduce economic vulnerability in families. The proposal emerges in the course of a wide-ranging discussion on gender and social justice.

BRINGING JUSTICE TO THE FAMILY: OKIN AND THE EXTENSION OF THE SOCIAL CONTRACT

Thus far, I have described the injustices that Okin links to gender in American society. I have presented most of Okin's political and social concerns independent of Rawls's work because such a presentation accords with the design of *Justice, Gender, and the Family*. That is, Okin approaches Rawls's work having already defined some important theoretical issues. She largely accepts Rawls's method and endorses the principles he derives, but she criticizes *A Theory of Justice* for paying insufficient attention to gender.

Okin's attraction to Rawls's work is easy to understand, since Rawls tries to justify a highly egalitarian liberalism. Okin extends Rawls's project and reaches similarly egalitarian, though no less controversial, conclusions.[48] In extending the project, Okin retains its core elements. For that reason, some might even describe her as a "Rawlsian."

So that the reader knows where this section is going, let me provide a map. I first review the premises, method, and conclusions of *A Theory of Justice*. I then discuss Okin's critique and revision of the main ideas, after which I spell out what her critique and revision are supposed to mean for our political and social institutions. Readers who already know Rawls's work should be able to move through this section briskly.

A Theory of Justice is a contribution to the social-contract tradition in Western political thought. In this instance, the contract is purely hypo-

---

[48] Okin refers to *A Theory of Justice* as a "helpful tool" for feminist criticism: *Justice, Gender, and the Family*, 101.

In this section, I follow Okin and use the first edition of *A Theory of Justice*. Some elements of *A Theory of Justice* were superseded by Rawls's *Political Liberalism* (New York: Columbia University Press, 1993) and the second edition of *A Theory of Justice* (1999). For different reasons, however, Okin regretted the changes in Rawls's thinking in *Political Liberalism*. See especially Okin's "*Political Liberalism*, Justice, and Gender," *Ethics* 105 (1994): 23.

thetical; for that reason, Rawls likens it to Kant's contract.[49] The Rawl-sian "contract" results from a thought experiment, a choice situation known as the "original position." Rawls asks his readers to imagine that they are responsible for choosing principles of justice that will apply to major social and economic institutions, which he calls "the basic struc-ture of society." So anyone reading Rawls's book is supposed to imagine that she or he is a party to the original position. The parties are referred to as heads or representatives of families, and within the constraints of the theory, they aim to advance their welfare and the welfare of at least the next two generations.[50]

The thought experiment has a stipulation. Those choosing the prin-ciples of justice lack knowledge of those contingencies which often prej-udice such choices. More specifically, we know nothing about our wealth, social status, interests, or talents. We are even supposed to be ignorant of our race and religious affiliation (if any). This stipulation—called the "veil of ignorance"—excludes principles that would be rational for us to accept if we knew any of those facts said by Rawls to be "irrelevant from the standpoint of justice."[51]

The veil of ignorance allows us to choose principles in a way that re-sembles dispassionate deliberation about justice. In this context, such de-liberation gives rise to a choice of principles, entailing an agreement or "contract" among different persons. What principles would we choose in the original position? Rawls formulates them in this way:

a. Each person has an equal right to a fully adequate scheme of equal basic lib-erties which is compatible with a similar scheme of liberties for all.

b. Social and economic inequalities are to satisfy two conditions. First, they must be attached to offices and positions open to all under conditions of fair equality of opportunity; and second, they must be to the greatest benefit of the least advantaged members of society.[52]

---

[49] Rawls, *A Theory of Justice*, 12 (n. 5).

[50] The subject of justice in Rawls's theory is "the way in which the major social institu-tions distribute fundamental rights and duties and determine the division of advantages from social cooperation." The major institutions that make up the basic structure of society in-clude the political constitution, (competitive) economic markets, and the monogamous family (ibid., 7). The parties are also described as "free and equal" and "mutually disinter-ested" persons who do not suffer from envy (see ibid., 142–149). They have "general facts" about the society in which they reside, including the fact that "the circumstances of justice" obtain (ibid., 137).

[51] Ibid., 18 and 128. It is questionable whether the parties know their sex, but as Okin points out, Rawls later indicated that the parties are ignorant about this matter as well. See Okin, *Justice, Gender, and the Family*, 91.

[52] Rawls, *Political Liberalism*, 291. In *Political Liberalism*, published twenty-two years after *A Theory of Justice*, Rawls slightly revised the first principle of justice. In the first edi-

These two principles apply to the "basic structure" of society; they do not cover the distribution of particular goods to individuals identifiable by their proper names.[53]

How, then, is the social system to be judged? Because the second principle, commonly known as the "difference principle," requires us to identify the least-advantaged representative person, we need concern ourselves only with ordinal judgments.[54] The basis of interpersonal comparison in Rawls's theory is the set of "primary goods," which includes basic rights and liberties; income and wealth; opportunities and powers, including freedom of movement and free choice of occupation; the powers and prerogatives of offices in the basic structure of society; and the social bases of social respect.[55]

A few other elements of the "original position" merit comment. Before putting forth the two principles of justice, Rawls considered philosophic alternatives. He singled out and rejected principles grounded in utilitarianism largely because of its failure to take the "separateness of persons" seriously. Many commentators say that this is the heart of Rawls's political theory. He affirms the inviolability of each person, reflecting his fear that some persons might be regarded merely as a means to promote the total welfare of society.[56]

Along the same lines, Rawls concludes that the two principles would be serially or lexically ordered. By this he means that departures from the equal liberty required by the first principle "cannot be justified by, or

---

tion of *A Theory of Justice* it read: "Each person is to have an equal right to the most extensive total system of equal basic liberties compatible with a similar system of liberty for all" (302). Elsewhere in *Theory* (61), the basic liberties are said to include political liberty (meaning the rights to vote and hold public office), freedom of speech and assembly, freedom of conscience and freedom of thought, freedom of the person, and the right to hold (personal) property.

[53] Rawls, *A Theory of Justice*, 61 and 64.

[54] Ibid., 91.

[55] Ibid., 90–95. To understand how this idea of the set of primary goods is to be applied, consider the following statement by Rawls: "As far as possible . . . justice as fairness [Rawls's own designation for his theory] appraises the social system from the position of equal citizenship and the various levels of income and wealth. Sometimes, however, other positions may need to be taken into account. If, for example, there are unequal basic rights founded on fixed natural characteristics, these inequalities will single out relevant positions" (ibid., 99). Among such inequalities, Rawls mentions distinctions based on sex, race, and culture. So if men are in a better position in the assignment of basic rights, that inequality would be justified by the difference principle only if it is to the advantage of women and acceptable to women.

[56] See, for example, ibid., 27 and 29 ("utilitarianism is not individualistic"). Of course, Rawls believed that persons who engaged in the thought experiment (i.e., his readers, the real parties to the original position) would reach the same conclusion that he did about utilitarianism.

compensated for, by greater social and economic advantages." The first principle has lexical priority.[57]

To strengthen the idea of "personal inviolability," Rawls argues that the parties to the original position would reject all "perfectionist" principles there. This matter is handled in a curious way in *A Theory of Justice*. Rawls raises the issue of perfectionism in the beginning of the book, but he does not present his views until much later. By "perfectionism," Rawls means a standard of excellence in art, science, culture, or morals. In its extreme form, which Rawls (perhaps wrongly) associates with Nietzsche's philosophy, perfectionism means that "we give value to our lives by working for the good of the highest [human] specimens."[58] As a more moderate doctrine, a principle of perfection might be one standard among several in an "intuitionist" theory. (By "intuitionism," Rawls means the view—which he rejects—that we have no way of adjudicating competing claims of political value.[59])

With respect to more moderate versions of perfectionism, Rawls worries that persons apply perfectionist criteria in an ad hoc manner, falling back on "subtle aesthetic preferences and personal feelings of propriety."[60] He comes close to saying that it is impossible to justify any standard of cultural or moral excellence for political purposes:

> When it is said, for example, that certain kinds of sexual relationships are degrading and shameful, and should be prohibited on this basis, if only for the sake of the individuals in question irrespective of their wishes, it is often because a reasonable case cannot be made in terms of the principles of justice. Instead we fall back on notions of excellence. . . . Since these uncertainties plague perfectionist criteria and jeopardize individual liberty, it seems best to rely entirely on the principles of justice which have a more definite structure.[61]

As a corollary, Rawls writes that before restricting any mode of conduct, we should be required to show that it interferes with the basic liberties of others or "violate[s] some obligation or natural duty."[62]

Rawls's strictures on perfectionism are now part of the language of liberal theory. The ideas are controversial, and they might have been even more controversial if Rawls had discussed putative rights and liberties

[57] Ibid., 61.
[58] Ibid., 325.
[59] Ibid.
[60] Ibid., 331.
[61] Ibid. On a related note, Rawls elsewhere (206) writes that the parties must choose principles that secure "the integrity of their moral and religious freedom" because they do not know anything about their moral or religious convictions.
[62] Ibid., 331.

more specifically. For the most part, he avoided such details, and controversy has tended to focus on the second of his two principles of justice.[63]

The most common criticisms of the difference principle, especially as it pertains to income and wealth, are that it is too egalitarian and that it reflects an unnatural aversion to risk on the part of the deliberating parties. Let me comment on each of these criticisms, because they are also relevant to Okin's work.

By requiring that social and economic inequalities be "to the greatest benefit of the least advantaged members of society," Rawls implies that the natural distribution of ability, character, and talent is morally arbitrary. No person really *deserves* the character and talent he or she has, so no one really deserves the income and accolades that such character and talent might bring.[64] Rawls has much compassion for those who are unlucky in the "natural lottery," but some would say that his compassion goes too far, as when he broadly asserts that "even the willingness to make an effort, to try, and so to be deserving in the ordinary sense is itself dependent upon happy family and social circumstances."[65] A more important issue, I think, is that Rawls nowhere seems to admit that a person's talents and abilities may be *squandered* through self-destructive conduct or the corruption of an institution. Because Rawls fails to discuss that common occurrence in any sustained way, his theory appears incomplete.

The compassion or egalitarianism just described might be related to the aversion to risk reflected in the difference principle. Some argue that the parties in the original position have little reason to be preoccupied with the status of the "least advantaged," given the small likelihood that this will be their status when the veil of ignorance is lifted. This is a complex issue, requiring one to take account of the "maximin principle" and

---

[63] One controversy about Rawls's views on civil liberties merits comment. In *Political Liberalism* (243 n. 32), Rawls seemed to argue that the concept of "public reason" (as developed in that book) lent philosophic support to the Supreme Court's decision in *Roe v. Wade*. These remarks provoked wide discussion and some criticism. Then, after the paperback version of *Political Liberalism* appeared, Rawls wrote that his earlier statement should not have been interpreted as an argument in support of a right to abortion in the first trimester. For further remarks, see Robert P. George, "Public Reason and Political Conflict: Abortion and Homosexuality," *Yale Law Journal* 106 (1997): 2475, reprinted in his *In Defense of Natural Law* (Oxford: Clarendon Press, 1999), 206–207.

Besides these matters, it is worth asking whether Rawls's desire to shun "perfectionism" accords with the larger aims of his theory. A settled disposition to act justly and promote just institutions *is* a standard of moral excellence—embraced by Rawls, and notwithstanding his strictures on perfectionist principles. I am grateful to Daniel N. Robinson for discussing this point with me.

[64] Rawls, *A Theory of Justice*, 100–108.

[65] Ibid., 74.

the appropriateness of game-theoretic models to the deliberations in the original position.[66]

Okin expresses few reservations about either of Rawls's two principles, and her criticisms fall outside mainstream commentary on *A Theory of Justice*. She focuses on four issues: the family as part of the "basic structure"; the knowledge about society attributed to the parties in the original position; the assumption that those parties are "heads of families"; and the idea (thus far undiscussed) of the family as the "first school of justice." These issues overlap slightly, but I shall discuss them in the order just listed.

A fundamental question about the basic structure is its status as the "subject of justice." Because Rawls lists the monogamous family as part of that structure, Okin asks whether the two principles of justice apply to it.[67]

She poses this question for another reason. In part 3 of *A Theory of Justice*, Rawls writes that a just and "well-ordered" society can endure only if its citizens acquire and retain a "sense of justice," meaning "a strong and normally effective desire to act as the principles of justice require."[68] Where does this disposition come from? Rawls says that we ordinarily acquire it during childhood and adolescence in the monogamous family.

In a just family, according to Rawls, parents love their young children, and that love is crucial for a child's sense of self-worth. Children soon reciprocate this love, but the more important phase of moral development occurs later. Rawls calls it "the morality of association." In this phase, children are said to develop a capacity to see things from another's perspective. This capacity develops because children learn, largely through family life, that all persons occupy different roles and positions in their lives.

To Okin, Rawls's description of this phase of moral development is flawed because it is expressed in "gendered and hierarchical terms."[69] Yet Okin also likens the morality of association to what ideally takes place in the original position.[70]

---

[66] Ibid., 150–161. For a helpful discussion, see Alan Ryan's essay on Rawls in Quentin Skinner, ed., *The Return of Grand Theory in the Human Sciences* (Cambridge: Cambridge University Press, 1985), esp. 109–111.

[67] In "*Political Liberalism*, Justice, and Gender," Okin asserted (26) that families received less attention in Rawls's second book than in his first book. She objected to Rawls's characterization of the family in *Political Liberalism* as nonpolitical, asking, "How can families be both part of the basic structure and not political?"

[68] Rawls, *A Theory of Justice*, 454.

[69] Okin, *Justice, Gender, and the Family*, 98.

[70] Okin develops this view in "Reason and Feeling in Thinking about Justice," *Ethics* 99 (1989): 229. Here Okin argues against the idea that Rawls's thought experiment should be considered an exercise in rational-choice theory. Relying on part 3 of *A Theory of Justice*, she submits that "feelings such as empathy and benevolence are at the very foundation of his principles of justice" (ibid., 239).

By now, the reader should understand why Okin criticizes Rawls for assuming that the family is just. She enters the original position with the expectation that whatever principles of justice we choose there also apply to the family. She further assumes—reasonably enough, I suppose—that the parties to the original position understand society and family life as she does and that the parties must confront the injustices associated with gender.[71]

Okin believes that Rawls should hold these views, and she points out another ambiguity in *A Theory of Justice*. Rawls sometimes refers to the parties in the original positions as "heads of families" and at other times as "representatives of families." But on Okin's reading, the former designation presents many problems, so she insists on a corrective. She argues that if "all human adults" deliberate behind the veil of ignorance, then Rawls should directly say that the family must be governed in accordance with the principles of justice.

What, concretely, does this mean for Rawls's theory? Even though it contains no references to policies, the following statement is the essence of Okin's critique:

> In innumerable ways, the principles of justice that Rawls arrives at are inconsistent with a gender-structured society and with traditional family roles. The critical impact of a feminist application of Rawls's theory comes chiefly from his second principle, which requires that inequalities be both "to the greatest benefit of the least advantaged" and "attached to offices and positions open to all." This means that if any roles or positions analogous to our current sex roles—including those of husband and wife, mother and father—were to survive the demands of the first requirement, the second requirement would prohibit any linkage between these roles and sex. Gender, with its ascriptive designation of positions and expectations of behavior in accordance with the inborn characteristic of sex, could no longer form a legitimate part of the social structure, whether inside or outside the family.[72]

Although I cannot pursue the theme in detail, Okin's thoughts on the family as the "first school of justice" should by now be intelligible. Much

---

[71] Here I refer to Rawls's assumption that parties to the original position have "basic facts" about the society in which they live. With Okin, I am willing to interpret this phrase broadly, but many persons in our society will dispute Okin's notion that gender is purely a social construct. It would have been helpful if Okin had told her readers that a few societies (e.g., the kibbutzim in Israel, studied by Melford and Audrey Spiro) have made prodigious efforts to extirpate sex-role identification (i.e., "gender"). By reliable accounts, those efforts failed, because some types of behavior commonly believed to rest on the male-female dichotomy reasserted themselves. For an analysis, see James Q. Wilson, *The Moral Sense* (New York: The Free Press, 1993), ch. 8, esp. 182–186.

[72] Okin, *Justice, Gender, and the Family*, 103.

of her thinking on the subject appears in connection with her interpretation of part 3 of *A Theory of Justice*. In the late 1990s, however, she presented her views in other contexts with few references to Rawls's work. The main point, however, is the same: children are influenced by what they see at home, and the injustices associated with gender can be easily perpetuated across generations.[73]

On the basis of the foregoing, what conclusions does Okin derive from Rawls's theory? Here is how she characterizes the original position:

> Let us first try to imagine ourselves, as far as possible, in the original position, knowing neither what our sex nor any other of our personal characteristics will be once the veil of ignorance is lifted. Neither do we know our place in society or our particular conception of the good life. Particularly relevant in this context . . . is our lack of knowledge of our beliefs about the characteristics of men and women and our related convictions about the appropriate division of labor between the sexes. Thus the positions we represent must include a wide variety of beliefs on these matters. We may, once the veil of ignorance is lifted, find ourselves feminist men or feminist women whose conception of the good life includes the minimization of social differentiation between the sexes. Or we may find ourselves traditionalist men or women, whose conception of the good life, for religious or other reasons, is bound up in an adherence to the conventional division of labor between the sexes.[74]

Okin then describes two "models" of social life and public policies. The first would "absolutely minimize gender," whereas the second would allow others "to follow gender-structured modes of life."[75]

Readers may have noticed that Okin departs slightly from Rawls's theory. First, she describes alternative "models" of life, each of which is allegedly consistent with the theory. Second, as we shall now see, she describes public policy in more detail than Rawls did. Someone might say that these departures are unfaithful to Rawls's work, but let us leave that matter aside. The more important point is that Okin believes that only the first of the two models of social life truly accords with principles of justice.[76]

---

[73] As Okin writes: "Unless the first formative example of adult interaction children usually experience—that between their parents—is one of justice and reciprocity, rather than one of domination and manipulation or of one-sided altruism and self-sacrifice . . . their moral development is likely to be extremely stunted." Okin, "The Gendered Family and the Development of a Sense of Justice," in Edward S. Reed et al., eds., *Values and Knowledge* (Mahwah, N.J.: Lawrence Erlbaum Associates, 1996), 67. See also "Reason and Feeling in Thinking about Justice," 237.

[74] Okin, *Justice, Gender, and the Family*, 174.

[75] Ibid., 175.

[76] See ibid., 182–183. See also ibid., 105: "The disappearance of gender is a prerequisite for the *complete* development of a nonsexist, fully human theory of justice" (italics in original).

The traditional model of life is easier to describe. Okin would allow couples to choose a "traditional" division of labor, but to protect economically vulnerable women and children, she proposes that both husband and wife have "equal legal entitlement" to all earnings coming into the household. If the wife is a full-time mother and homemaker, the husband's employer should be required to endorse his paycheck to both him and his wife. If both husband and wife work outside the home, then each paycheck should be endorsed to both spouses.[77]

Okin believes that justice requires this policy of "shared income." It takes account of the wife's unremunerated work at home, and it would amount to public recognition of the importance of domestic labor. Okin makes these points while conceding that some couples already divide the household income freely and equitably.

Because of their vulnerability arising from divorce, a similar remedy must be offered to wives and children in a household with a traditional division of labor. Specifically, both post-divorce households should have the same standard of living. If the wife has not worked outside the home, alimony should continue "at least as long as the traditional division of labor in the marriage did."[78] In the event of a short marriage that produces a child or several children, Okin recommends that alimony continue until the youngest child starts first grade and "the custodial parent has a real chance of making his or her own living."[79] Thereafter, child support should continue at a level such that the child's standard of living is equal to that of the noncustodial parent.[80]

The second model of society put forth by Okin is more detailed than the traditional model. The policies just described would obtain in both models, but the second model could be described as a "best-case scenario" for Okin. It is her vision for the future.

With gender "absolutely minimized," equal parental responsibility would be "both assumed and facilitated." Before reaching that point, however, we will have rethought "the demands of work life":

---

[77] Ibid., 180–182. It is difficult to understand how this policy would operate if the husband were self-employed—say, for example, he painted houses. If the policy became law, he might be regularly writing his wife a check in the amount of 50 percent of his pay. (It seems unlikely that each customer would be required to issue payment to both the man and his wife.)

[78] Ibid., 183.

[79] Ibid.

[80] Okin's policy concerning divorce seems as though it would be far more complicated to administer than the shared-income policy for husbands and wives. Furthermore, because of the many contingencies relating to divorce (including the possibility of remarriage for each spouse), it is doubtful that the standards Okin proposes could ever be adopted as a state's default policy.

Parental leave during the postbirth months should be available to mothers and fathers on the same terms, to facilitate shared parenting. . . . All workers should have the right, without prejudice . . . to work less than full-time during the first year of a child's life, and to work flexible or somewhat reduced hours at least until the child reaches the age of seven. . . . The professions whose greatest demands (such as tenure in academia or the partnership hurdle in law) coincide with the peak period of child rearing must restructure their demands or provide . . . flexibility for those of their workers who are also participating parents. Large-scale employers should also be required to provide high-quality, on-site day care for children from infancy up to school age. And to ensure equal quality of day care for all young children, *direct government subsidies* (not tax credits, which benefit the better-off) should make up the difference between the cost of high-quality day care and what less well paid parents could reasonably be expected to pay.[81]

If equal parental responsibility for children is to be the norm, education must prepare students for it. To that end, both boys and girls should be taught about combining work and parenthood. Public schools might make students aware of that combination by functioning as a day-care center when classes are over (i.e., by offering more after-school programs).[82]

When shared parenting is not feasible because a mother is divorced or has never married, the programs just described, according to Okin, should ease the mother's burden. If affordable day care is available, it will allow the mother to improve the family's economic prospects. Like Rawls, Okin favors a large welfare state, and she argues that the government must accept and discharge many economic duties irrespective of obligations already assigned to individual persons. (The government should therefore provide money to a single mother in the event that the father of her children fails to pay child support.)[83]

As noted, Okin believes that gender will become less important if "nontraditional" households become more common. All of the policy proposals described here allegedly accord with living arrangements that challenge conventional marriage and sex roles.

The bases for that judgment are uncomplicated. Regarding single motherhood "by choice," Okin, like Iris Marion Young, seems to consider it a basic right. Part of the reason for supporting same-sex "marriage" and parenthood is that "the dichotomizing of masculine and feminine attributes, and the privileging of the former, are closely related to the stigma-

---

[81] Okin, *Justice, Gender, and the Family*, 176–177.

[82] Ibid., 177. Okin also suggests (ibid.) that affirmative-action programs may be needed to promote parity in professions that until recently had few women.

[83] Ibid., 178.

tization of homosexuality."[84] Thus, if homosexuality is less stigmatized, the privileging of masculine attributes will be reduced. Or so Okin believes.

As these examples suggest, the project of eradicating gender has many dimensions. For different reasons, it is a project that many liberals have endorsed. But it is also a controversial project, and no one should suppose that it lies beyond criticism. One may ask, for example, whether the project is even faithful to its central premise.

Toward a More Fully Human (and Still Humanist) Liberalism

Before offering a critique of her political theory, I want to express qualified support for one of Okin's boldest initiatives. Her proposal to reduce the economic vulnerability of many mothers and children—the policy of "shared income" between spouses—might serve that end, and I expect that some moral or cultural conservatives would be receptive to the proposal if it were restricted to the traditional family. (By "traditional family" I mean a lawfully married husband and wife and any children they may have, including any children they may have adopted.)

My support for Okin's proposal rests on my understanding of marriage as a social institution and a special type of friendship between a man and a woman. I accept Okin's thesis that marriage in the United States can make women economically vulnerable, but Okin overstates the extent of injustice in American marriages. Confusing the potential for injustice in marriage with its actual incidence, Okin needs to revise or discard some ideas.

Consider, as a theoretical matter, the issue of "unpaid labor." If, on Okin's view, notions of distributive justice should apply to marriage, then certain practices within marriage must be assessed from the same quasi-economic perspective. So rather than describe women's domestic work as "unpaid labor," Okin should admit that this work usually receives "payment in kind"—meaning material support in exchange for the work performed.

Other problems are apparent in Okin's interpretation of the traditional household (a husband with a full-time job outside the home whose wife is a full-time mother and homemaker). Relying on the University of Michigan study discussed above, Okin concludes that even when a husband works more total hours per week than his wife does, the marriage is usually unjust because the woman's schedule is less predictable, her work is less interesting, and her labor is unremunerated. The first point here is probably true for most marriages, the second is highly contestable

---

[84] Okin, "Sexual Orientation and Gender," 44.

(and I shall return to it later), and the third (as I have just argued) is also contestable.[85]

Okin also needs to be mindful of other aspects of human work. For different reasons, a husband's work may be much more stressful than his wife's work. Indeed, from the standpoint of "gender as a social construct," how can we explain the greater life expectancy of American women? Finally, as more and more women balance a career outside the home with motherhood and homemaking, we must be aware of the ambiguity in saying that both a husband and a wife have full-time jobs outside the home. In some families, for example, the wife may work thirty-five hours a week outside the home, the husband fifty to sixty hours. In such circumstances, it would not necessarily be unjust if the wife does more housework than her husband does.

Other issues merit attention. While supporting Okin's "shared income" policy, I have doubts about its success in any American legislature, state or federal. These doubts arise from the rapidly improving economic position of younger American women. Today, many educated women would likely oppose Okin's proposal, for they are unlikely to surrender their financial independence.

Consider these statistics. In 1998—the same year in which Okin announced that American women remain "second-class citizens"—women earned 55.1 percent of the baccalaureate degrees in our colleges and universities. In professional schools, they earned 43.5 percent of the law degrees, 40.9 percent of the medical degrees, and 37.6 percent of the MBAs. These figures may seem unremarkable, but they are striking when compared with those from 1960. In that year, women earned 38.5 percent of the baccalaureate degrees, 2.5 percent of the law degrees, 5.5 percent of the medical degrees, and 3.6 percent of the MBAs.[86]

It is true that the "wage gap" persists—in 1998, women with full-time jobs outside the home earned 26 percent less than men with full-time positions—but women are now well represented in nearly every "white collar" profession in the United States. So it is not uncommon for a university-educated woman to earn considerably more money than her husband. Thus, if Okin's proposal were introduced into an assembly, the female voices most likely to be heard by legislators would belong to women who stand to lose the most from the measure.[87]

---

[85] Moreover, contrary to what Okin often asserts, the economic value of homemaking and child-rearing has been reflected in some public policies; recall that a widow with children has been able to receive government benefits (e.g., under Aid to Families with Dependent Children) even if she has never had a job outside the home.

[86] Bureau of Labor Statistics, cited in Andrew Hacker, "The Unmaking of Men," *New York Review of Books*, 21 October 1999, 26.

[87] The only white-collar profession in which women now seem to be significantly underrepresented is architecture, one of the less lucrative vocations for those with a college or uni-

Regardless of the fate of the "shared income" proposal, it takes account of the needs of both women *and* children. Regrettably, such solicitude toward children is absent elsewhere in Okin's work. I refer specifically to her efforts to normalize single motherhood "by choice" and to expand our notions of marriage and family so that they encompass same-sex couples.

As noted above, these efforts are supposed to hasten the arrival of a genderless world. They also have a corresponding rhetorical strategy. To make freely chosen single parenthood and same-sex "marriage" more palatable, Okin ascribes to the traditional American family the iniquity of forced servitude or impressment. Okin's readers need to be mindful of this rhetoric, because she in many places overstates the historical subordination of women.[88]

Notwithstanding the defects of her historical scholarship, we would still expect Okin, as a political theorist, to ask whether the traditional two-parent family has some normative bases that explain its prevalence and longevity in the West. But instead of exploring this theme, Okin merely observes that other types of families—such as extended families living under one roof and families in which a parent has died—have always existed alongside the traditional family. From this observation, she quickly concludes that each type of family in existence today merits equal respect.[89]

The peculiar reasoning here merits comment. From the fact that a plurality of cultures exists in our world, Okin does not—especially in her later work—conclude that every culture or cultural practice is of equal dignity. So why does she interpret a plurality of family forms in that way? At a minimum, we would expect Okin to ask whether, from the standpoint of basic interests of children, there might be important differences between different family structures.

Okin's unwillingness to face that question leads to many problems. She applies principles inconsistently, and issues that figure prominently in her assessment of traditional marriages and families are absent when she considers same-sex couples. Most important, her desire to eradicate gender exceeds her desire to promote the welfare of children and prevents her from seeing how these new family forms are likely to affect them.

---

versity degree. In 1998, women constituted 42.3 percent of college and university faculty, 46.3 percent of American economists, and 44.4 percent of managers and executives. For these and other data, see Hacker, "The Unmaking of Men," 27.

For a sense of the growing economic power of American women, see Margaret A. Jacobs, "Court Ruling Favors At-Home Dads," *Wall Street Journal*, 17 July 1998, B1, which describes divorce proceedings in Dade County, Florida, between a corporate litigator earning more than $300,000 a year and her stay-at-home husband, a Miami-area architect.

[88] I have documented the many errors in Okin's historical scholarship in "Imagining Patriarchy," *Academic Questions* 17 (2004): 45.

[89] Okin, *Justice, Gender, and the Family*, 18; "Families and Feminist Theory," 18–19.

My critique may therefore be read as an extension of Okin's analysis, since the key premise in her reading of Rawls is that theories of justice must consider issues "from everyone's perspective." To my mind, this is a sensible approach—would that Okin herself had followed it. In the end, Okin's analysis is deficient because she fails to consider important interests of children.

This failing seems related to her uncritical acceptance of certain putative rights for adults. Like many liberals, Okin accepts Rawls's strictures on "perfectionist principles," and she construes Rawls's first principle of justice broadly. Neither Rawls nor Okin seems to realize that we can rationally defend perfectionist principles, especially if we remain mindful of the impressionability of children and their dependence on adults.[90]

Let us first assess the problems with "normalizing" single motherhood (including single motherhood "by choice"). Thereafter, I shall look at the difficulties linked with conferring the status of marriage on same-sex couples. As Okin argues, any serious inquiry into these matters must attend to the soundness of principles. That is, Okin rightly rejects the idea that "all knowledge and value claims are contextual, particular, and local."[91]

One problem emerges when we take note of a recurring presumption in modern political thought. Despite many differences among them, thinkers such as Locke, Hegel, Mill, and T. H. Green all submit that the *parents* of a child—notice the plural—are chiefly responsible for its sustenance and welfare.[92] The consensus is significant, especially in view of the shorter life expectancy in earlier ages. Although no one could predict when a parent might die, these theorists assigned the main duty of caring for the child to the mother and father, rather than to the extended family or the whole society. The reasoning here is cogent. Since neither the society nor the extended family brought the child into being, each should have a subordinate role. In the great majority of cases, the main responsibility for the child's welfare must fall to the parents, for they chose to bring the child into the world.[93]

---

[90] Having explained the basis of this critique, I shall add that it avoids the technicalities of Rawls's thought and the Rawlsian heuristic. That is, I do not ask which principles of justice a six-year-old child would choose in the original position, assuming that he or she could think like an adult. (Such an exercise is simply unreal.)

[91] Okin, "Gender and Relativism in Recent Feminist Historical Scholarship," *New Zealand Journal of History* (1995): 211. This essay warns feminist historians and political theorists about the dangers of affirming different tenets of postmodernism.

[92] See Locke, *Second Treatise,* ch. 6, secs. 52–55; Hegel, *Philosophy of Right,* secs. 174 and 175; Mill, *On Liberty* (Spitz ed.), ch. 5, pp. 97 and 100; Green, *Lectures on the Principles of Political Obligation,* sec. O.

[93] The view being expressed here does not mean that the parents own the child. On this point, see Locke, *First Treatise,* sec. 100, and *Second Treatise,* sec. 65; Hegel, *Philosophy of Right,* sec. 175; and Mill, *On Liberty* (Spitz ed.), p. 97.

We can look at this in another way. If there are basic or categorical precepts of justice, one of them must be that any child who comes into the world has a prima facie claim to some of the resources of his or her biological parents. Those resources, both tangible and intangible, are necessarily limited, but, as a moral matter, the claim to a share of them always deserves a hearing. Depending on circumstances, the child's interests may be better served if we reject the claim—no child, for example, should be expected to live with an abusive mother or father, and there are special circumstances relating to adoption—but the presumption must be recognized. The presumption takes account of a child's helplessness and the basic responsibilities linked to the creation of new human life.

By affirming the single woman's liberty to become a mother, Okin flouts the presumption. The single woman who wants to raise a child alone—and plans to visit a sperm bank or "strike a deal" with a male friend—deprives the child of the opportunity to have close relations with his or her father. This deprivation goes beyond money. Time is also a valuable resource, and few parents, even the very wealthy, have it in abundance. And regardless of whether the child is a girl or a boy, the opportunity to interact regularly with both parents should be recognized as a substantial interest.

Another problem is evident. As scenarios like the one just sketched become more common, some single men will invoke the woman's liberty to free themselves from obligations to their children. This possibility seems acute in an era of abortion "on demand." As Mary Ann Glendon observes, after abortion was declared a right that women *could* exercise, many American men found it easy to say that their pregnant girlfriends *should* exercise it.[94] Similar matters apply here, and if some single women insist on their "right" to raise a child alone, other single women—in all likelihood, less educated, less affluent, and less privileged—may be exercising that right against their will.

Okin would probably contest this point. She might say that if the mother needs help from the child's father, he should be obliged to provide both monetary and nonmonetary support. But this response suggests that everything depends on the mother's inclinations (or preferences) and that *principles* are irrelevant. The response also assumes the unmarried father's full cooperation in supporting the child, an optimistic outlook belied by the evidence.

It is easy to see why Okin would sidestep this issue. As someone who thinks that the "real" emancipation of women depends on a certain kind of sexual freedom—including the sexual freedom of homosexuals—she dismisses the idea that only legally married persons should have children.

[94] See Mary Ann Glendon, *Rights Talk: The Impoverishment of Political Discourse* (New York: The Free Press, 1991), 66.

But if Okin were truly interested in the welfare of children, she would consider the ramifications of the freedom she favors.

Other political and legal theorists also dodge these issues. In *Democracy on Trial,* Jean Bethke Elshtain recorded her growing disquiet at

> comfortable upper-middle-class academics blithely celebrating the "diversity" of lifestyles while inner-city children play out in real life what being unmarried-with-child is more likely to be about than the glamour and glitz of "Murphy Brown."[95]

Elshtain adds that only by "an intellectual sleight of hand" can one equate the life prospects of children growing up in single-parent families with those of children in traditional families.

As Elshtain's words suggest, different scholars adopt different strategies to avoid these issues. Okin's strategy has several elements. First, she maintains that she is "pro-family," while adding that one must understand "family" in a less "exclusionary" sense.[96] Second, she says little about the large body of research documenting the disadvantages of growing up in a single-parent family, while she insinuates that such studies have an ulterior aim—namely, to put women and children "back under the control of men."[97] Finally, she favors a grand array of social programs, all of which are supposed to ensure the well-being of children growing up in difficult familial circumstances.

These responses are inadequate. By submitting that the family be understood "more inclusively" so that single-parent families are "normalized," Okin begs the question at hand. Her silence about the research on the disadvantages of growing up in a single-parent family could be interpreted as an indefensible bias, since she cites dozens of studies about gender and the economic and social position of women. And her enthusiasm for vastly expanding the welfare state shifts most of the responsibility for a couple's children to the larger society—meaning bureaucrats and day-care centers.

In offering these criticisms, I am aware of circumstances in which a (heterosexual) woman wants to become a mother and is wary of raising a child with a husband. One thinks, for example, of a woman who suffered psychological or physical abuse in a previous marriage or relationship. Furthermore, some single mothers do a better job as parents than do many husbands and wives working together. But to acknowledge difficult circumstances and the achievements of exceptional mothers is only part of the story. Thoughtful persons will want to know: Since every child has two biological parents, can a woman's decision to give birth and to exclude the father from the child's life be justified? Both commonsensical

---

[95] Jean Bethke Elshtain, *Democracy on Trial* (New York: Basic Books, 1995), 140.
[96] Okin, "Families and Feminist Theory," 14.
[97] Ibid., 23.

and philosophic thinking converge on this point: children need—and as far as possible deserve—two parents. Marriages may fall apart, a father or mother may die prematurely, but at the level of principle, freely chosen single parenthood is deeply problematic.[98]

Apart from the philosophic issues just considered, any scholar who affirms single motherhood by choice should say something about the social-science research attesting to the diminished life prospects of children in single-parent families. To consider that evidence fully is beyond the scope of this chapter, but Okin is reluctant even to probe it.[99]

Other political and legal theorists may acknowledge the evidence, but they quickly play it down. Looking at essays by Martha Minow and Martha C. Nussbaum, for example, one sees the tendencies described by Elshtain. Because of the prominence of these theorists and their sympathies to both liberalism and feminism, we should pause to document this trend.

In the volume containing Okin's essay "Gender and Sexual Orientation," Minow and Nussbaum also propose that we jettison our "crimped" notions of family. In separate essays, they both argue that the extended family offers vital resources to children whose parents live apart. By this, they mean that the extended family can perform nearly all of the same functions as the traditional family does.[100]

What is wrong with this outlook? With respect to philosophic matters, Minow and Nussbaum err in supposing that children have the same prima

[98] Some readers may suspect that my stance is motivated by a desire to scotch the growing independence of American women. That would be a mistake, and the child's prima facie claim to the resources of both parents also affects various interests of men. Unless I have overlooked something, the claim seems to entail that only lawfully married couples (and neither single women *nor* single men) should be permitted to adopt children. (Whether a state chooses to make that a policy is a different matter.) It also suggests that at a certain point it is irresponsible of older men (with wives of child-bearing age) to become fathers. Space constraints prevent me from pursuing these matters further.

[99] The social-science research on the disadvantages for children growing up in single-parent families vindicates common sense: a two-parent household typically means more resources for a child. That the soundness of such research has been affirmed by scholars such as Elshtain, James Q. Wilson, and William Galston—none of whom can be described as a staunch conservative—should count for something. (Wilson's formidable understanding of what constitutes good social research should count for even more.) Okin, however, says next to nothing about this topic. For summaries of the most important research, see Wilson's *The Moral Sense*, 176–180, and, more recently, *The Marriage Problem: How Our Culture Has Weakened Families* (New York: Harper Collins, 2002). See also Galston's "Causes of Declining Well-Being among U.S. Children," in Estlund and Nussbaum, *Sex, Preference, and Family*.

One further point. Even if someone is unpersuaded by the social-science research, single motherhood by choice can still be resisted on philosophic grounds—as I aim to do here.

[100] Minow, "All in the Family and In All Families: Membership, Loving, and Owing," and Nussbaum, "Preference and Family: Commentary on Parts III and IV," in Estlund and Nussbaum, *Sex, Preference, and Family*.

facie claim to the resources of their grandparents and aunts and uncles as they do to the resources of their own parents. Practical matters should also be noted. Although the support from an extended family is valuable, not all American children can depend on the help of such relatives. Because of tremendous geographic mobility in the United States, some children rarely see their grandparents and aunts and uncles. Moreover, those relatives may have other obligations, including duties to their own children. Finally, because of declining health or advanced age, some grandparents cannot assume the role of mother or father for a second time.

In her commentary to the concluding sections of *Sex, Preference, and Family*, Nussbaum concedes the social problems linked to single-parent families, but suggests that the problems will be less severe when the single parent receives support from other adult relatives.[101] Yet Nussbaum fails to ask whether children have the same claim to the resources of those relatives as they do to those of their own parents. Finally, to circumvent the controversy, Nussbaum speaks vaguely of "American traditions of tolerance and noninterference in matters of intimate personal choice," an apparent allusion to the "right to privacy."[102] But as Nussbaum knows, that "tradition" is a recent invention of the Supreme Court.

In "All in the Family and In All Families: Membership, Loving, and Owing," Minow cites the American Home Economics Association's definition of a family as "two or more persons [living together] who share resources, share responsibility for decisions, share values and goals, and have a commitment to one another over time . . . regardless of blood, legal ties, adoption, or marriage."[103] She says little, however, about what qualifies as a "commitment." Minow later writes that we should be "welcoming toward those who are willing to take on family obligations, but serious in enforcing the expectations that these obligations will in fact be fulfilled."[104] Yet within three paragraphs of this statement, she turns to the subject of "governmental duties," which (predictably) leads to a plea for greater state largesse. And like Nussbaum, Minow invokes the extended family, as if to suggest that all forms of "kinship" are substantively equal.[105]

Nussbaum, Minow, and Okin all favor expanding the welfare state; they all favor a larger catalog of sexual and reproductive freedoms; and they all favor an expanded understanding of "family" as a way of relieving (or obscuring) the primary duties of parents. Missing from their work

---

[101] Nussbaum, "Preference and Family," in Estlund and Nussbaum, *Sex, Preference, and Family*, 334–335.

[102] Ibid., 331.

[103] Minow, "All in the Family and In All Families," 254.

[104] Ibid., 262.

[105] Ibid., 271 and 269.

is a clear statement of the basic obligations associated with human pro-creation, like the one found in Mill's *On Liberty*:

> The fact itself, of causing the existence of a human being, is one of the most re-sponsible actions in the range of human life. To undertake this responsibility— to bestow a life which may be either a curse or a blessing—unless the being on whom it is to be bestowed will have at least the ordinary chances of a desirable existence, is a crime against that being. . . . The laws which, in many countries on the Continent, forbid marriage unless the parties can show that they have the means of supporting a family, do not exceed the legitimate powers of the State: and whether such laws be expedient or not (a question mainly dependent on local circumstances and feelings), they are not objectionable as violations of liberty. Such laws are interferences of the State to prohibit a mischievous act— an act injurious to others, which ought to be a subject of reprobation, and social stigma, even when it is not deemed expedient to superadd legal punishment.[106]

I include this excerpt from Mill not because of the substance of his pro-posal, but because it reminds us of basic moral questions linked to human procreation. We need such reminders because the sense of "entitlement" on the part of Minow, Nussbaum, and Okin is so great. In their eyes, adult citizens are entitled to the broadest possible sexual freedom, and they are further entitled to an inordinately generous welfare state, which (in theory) frees them from many duties as parents.

The point can be amplified with respect to Okin's work. Okin main-tains that a single mother who receives public assistance already has a job. She is thus vexed at those who say that such a woman should be gain-fully employed. As Okin writes: "She *is* working. She is doing some of the society's most valuable work."[107]

Even if we grant the importance of the work, Okin forgets or ignores the real issue, because she assumes that a single woman is simply entitled to have a child and then receive a vast array of social supports. But if parental indifference to the interests of children identified above is blame-worthy—as Mill believed and as many Americans still believe—then we ought to expect only modest public support for this mother and her child.

Contrary to what Okin suggests, there is nothing sinister in assigning the main duty for a child's welfare to his or her parents or in expecting men and women to be lawfully married before they have children or adopt them. Lawful marriage signifies a commitment before the world, a will-ingness to take responsibility for any children issuing from a marriage or being entrusted to a married couple by an adoption agency. Even when a

---

[106] Mill, *On Liberty*, 100.

[107] Okin, "Families and Feminist Theory," 21–22. Iris Marion Young takes the same line in "Mothers, Citizenship, and Independence."

government is unwilling (or unable) to allocate resources to enforce the traditional expectation that marriage should precede the begetting of children, the moral issues remain. And if this amounts to a moral or political "perfectionism," it is a defensible perfectionism.

In the present environment, the moral issues are just as important as—if not more important than—the political and legal issues. This is because single women can inseminate themselves or visit a sperm bank, and they can reach agreements with male friends and acquaintances willing to help them become pregnant.[108] Unsurprisingly, the "agreements" sometimes fall apart, giving rise to bitter legal controversies.[109]

Thus, simply because an unmarried woman is at liberty to become a single mother "by choice" does not mean that she should exercise this freedom. In other contexts, Okin easily distinguishes the moral realm from the politico-legal realm. In her eyes, for example, the (legal) right to buy or produce pornography does not make it morally blameless to do so. So the distinction here is familiar to Okin.[110]

Apparently, Okin believes that with enough government largesse, the composition of a child's family would hold no significance for his or her life prospects. However widespread this view may be in academic circles, it is hard to take seriously. The idea that a benign and omnicompetent welfare state can assume the role of an absent parent in many thousands of households is a fantasy and deserves to be exposed as such.

Okin's faith in the capacity of the welfare state is evident in her views on divorce and child support. Because she believes that marital breakdown usually harms woman and children, we might expect her to welcome the efforts of some reformers to make divorce less whimsical and harder (though not impossible) to obtain. But she dismisses these efforts, characterizing them as dangerously reactionary.[111]

---

[108] On these topics, see Amy Harmon, "First Comes the Baby Carriage," *The New York Times,* 13 October 2005, G1.

[109] See, for example, *C. M. v. C. C.,* 377 A. 2d 821 (1977); *Jhordan C. v. Mary K.,* 179 Cal. App. 3d 386 (1986); and *McIntyre v. Crouch,* 780 P. 2d 239 (Or. App. 1989). For related issues, see John A. Robertson, *Children of Choice: Freedom and the New Reproductive Technologies* (Princeton: Princeton University Press, 1994), 29 and 127–128.

[110] For Okin's views on pornography, see "Sexual Difference, Feminism, and the Law," *Law and Social Inquiry* 16 (1991): 553, 560 (n. 5), and 569–573.

[111] Okin, "Families and Feminist Theory," 22–24. Oddly enough, in *Justice, Gender, and the Family* (180 n. 14), Okin says that she endorses Mary Ann Glendon's idea of a "children-first" approach to divorce, a key element of which is an effort to make divorce less capricious, especially when a couple has children.

In response to the problems linked to "no-fault" divorce, various states have sought to create a new framework for marriage and to reduce the incidence of divorce. In this connection, see the articles on "covenant marriage" in the following publications: *The New York Times,* 24 June 1997, A1; *Chattanooga Free Press,* 3 January 1998, C4; and *Indi-*

Regarding child support, Okin shows little awareness of the difficulties in establishing orders and collecting payments. She has much confidence in the relevant bureaucracies, but she fails to ask whether their day-to-day administration and certain features of American life (such as a highly mobile population and porous borders between states) justify that confidence. Thus, the question for Okin might be: Should we propose harsher measures—such as mandatory work permits or domestic passports—to facilitate child-support payments? Okin the liberal would balk at such remedies, but if Okin the feminist wants to improve the material welfare of women and children, she should admit that collecting child support is different from printing new currency.[112]

In pleading for a more generous welfare state, Okin evidently thinks that she occupies higher moral ground than those who worry about its possible disincentives, as suggested by the enormous rise in single-parent families over the last forty to fifty years. But her pleas are rafts against a current, and by steadily dodging the issues here, Okin steadily risks her credibility as a social critic.

Let us now turn to the question of same-sex "marriage" and parenthood. Okin's proposal to extend marriage to homosexuals is just as controversial as freely chosen single-parenthood—and just as likely to affect children. To see the problems, we must first explicate some ideas relating to Okin's understanding of "traditional" or real marriage. When they are explicated, Okin's enthusiasm for "same-sex marriage" becomes puzzling.

Some readers may be surprised to learn that Okin's understanding of traditional marriage is, well, traditional. She opposes polygamy (more precisely, polygyny).[113] She believes that adultery is wrong and can be grounds for divorce, at least when accompanied by "spousal neglect."[114] Finally,

---

anapolis News, 31 January 1998, A8 (editorial). Covenant marriage is a legal reform, freely chosen by the parties. It binds the couple to a more committed relationship through a "Declaration of Intent" and the relevant state legislation. Typically, covenant marriage entails three elements: mandatory premarital counseling; a legally binding agreement to seek counseling in the event of marital problems; and limited grounds for divorce. Covenant-marriage legislation has been enacted in Louisiana (1997), Arizona (1998), and Arkansas (2001). For a fuller discussion, see Katherine Shaw Spaht, "Revolution and Counter-Revolution: The Future of Marriage in the Law," *Loyola Law Review* 49 (2003): 1.

[112] See esp. Okin, *Justice, Gender, and the Family,* 123. For fiscal year 1993, the rate of collection of child support was only 26.1 percent in non-AFDC cases and 11.7 percent in current (that is, non-arrears) AFDC cases. "AFDC" refers to Aid to Families with Dependent Children, originally established by Congress under the Social Security Act of 1935 (as "Aid to Dependent Children") and renamed in 1962. The statistics here are from Jyl J. Josephson, *Gender, Families, and State: Child Support Policy in the United States* (Lanham, Md.: Rowman and Littlefield, 1997), 134.

[113] Okin, *Justice, Gender, and the Family,* 19; "Gender and Relativism," 212.

[114] Okin, *Justice, Gender, and the Family,* 60.

she gives us no reason to think that she favors "open" marriages, "spouse-swapping," or "polyamorous" groupings.

These ideas suggest the following moral framework for marriage. A marriage between a man and a woman is a union of two persons, characterized by love and fidelity (i.e., sexual exclusivity). In a just marriage, the domestic duties (including child-rearing) will be evenly shared by husband and wife. Spouses must share such work because they owe this to their children and because a just society requires such sharing. Here again I refer to Okin's idea that the family is "the first school of justice."

Taking these points into account, someone might ask why American states deny homosexuals the right to marry. In championing that right, Okin assumes that same-sex couples are in most respects (save the biological difference) indistinguishable from married men and women. She also assumes that most homosexuals *want* the right to marry:

> Many gay men and lesbians are very concerned both to maintain ties with their families of origin and to form new families of various kinds. . . . What prevents them from officially doing the latter is far less often the lack of desire to be part of a family than the fact that the laws in all of our states prohibit homosexual marriage and in most states place many other formidable obstacles in the way of gay and lesbian family formation, especially gay and lesbian parenthood. Thus it seems that most gay men and lesbians are not anti-family, but anti [sic] a legal and social definition of family that excludes and stigmatizes them.[115]

For the sake of argument, I grant that many homosexuals in the United States seek the right to marry and start families. But I submit that most homosexuals do not understand marriage in the same way that most husbands and wives do. Substantial evidence shows that many (if not most) same-sex couples favor a framework for their "marriages" at cross-purposes with the moral framework that Okin favors.

Okin overlooks this possibility. Consequently, she fails to anticipate how the behavior, norms, and living arrangements of same-sex couples might affect other persons in society, especially women in real marriages and children being raised by homosexuals. Recall Okin's minimal expectations of heterosexual marriage. It involves love and sexual exclusivity between two persons. Do most American homosexuals share these expectations? Many sources reveal that they do not.

Consider an essay by Shane Phelan in the *American Political Science Review*.[116] Offered as a contribution to the new academic discipline known

---

[115] Okin, "Sexual Orientation and Gender," 50. As of summer 2006, same-sex marriage is legal in one state, owing to the decision in *Goodridge v. Department of Health* (798 N.E. 2d 941 [Mass. 2003]) by the Supreme Judicial Court of Massachusetts.

[116] Shane Phelan, "Queer Liberalism?" *American Political Science Review* 94 (June 2000): 431.

as "queer theory," Phelan's essay reviews six books: *Gay and Lesbian Politics* by Mark Blasius; *Sexual Justice* by Morris Kaplan; *Queer Family Values* by Valerie Lehr; *Difference Troubles* by Steven Seidman; *Virtually Normal* by Andrew Sullivan; and *Invented Moralities* by Jeffrey Weeks. Strikingly, none of these authors affirms sexual exclusivity as a precondition of marriage between homosexuals, and most reject the idea that sexual exclusivity should be expected of "married" homosexuals.[117]

Other proponents of same-sex marriage take the same line, and even surveys conducted among American homosexuals show faint support for the idea of sexual exclusivity as a condition of marriage. Historical and sociological accounts also suggest the folly of expecting a real commitment to monogamy from the majority of homosexuals who take marriage vows. In a survey of homosexual couples in Massachusetts, for example, Gretchen Stiers found that only 10 percent of the men and 32 percent of the women thought that a "committed" intimate relationship entails sexual exclusivity. These data are even more striking when one takes account of the author's remark that American homosexuals now have a greater incentive to be monogamous because of AIDS.[118]

---

[117] See Mark Blasius, *Gay and Lesbian Politics: Sexuality and the Emergence of a New Ethic* (Philadelphia: Temple University Press, 1994), 108–109, 124, 184, 196–197, and 202; Morris Kaplan, *Sexual Justice: Democratic Citizenship and the Politics of Desire* (New York: Routledge, 1997), 210–211 and 238; Valerie Lehr, *Queer Family Values: Debunking the Myth of the Nuclear Family* (Philadelphia: Temple University Press, 1999), 48–76; Steven Seidman, *Difference Troubles: Queering Social Theory and Sexual Politics* (Cambridge: Cambridge University Press, 1997), 127–128, 180–184, and 226; Andrew Sullivan, *Virtually Normal: An Argument about Homosexuality* (New York: Knopf, 1995), 202–203; and Jeffrey Weeks, *Invented Moralities: Sexual Values in an Age of Uncertainty* (New York: Columbia University Press, 1995), 10, 142–144, and 175–177.

[118] Gretchen A. Stiers, *From This Day Forward: Commitment, Marriage, and Family in Lesbian and Gay Relationships* (New York: St. Martin's, 1999), 49–50. For an account of male homosexual behavior in San Francisco when that "incentive" was absent—in the decade immediately before AIDS—see Randy Shilts, *And the Band Played On: Politics, People, and the AIDS Epidemic* (New York: St. Martin's Press, 1987), chs. 2–5 and pp. 88–90. For a picture of an "open" homosexual partnership, see James Miller, *The Passion of Michel Foucault* (New York: Anchor Books, 1993). Miller's account of the partnership between Foucault and Daniel Defert should be compared with the sketches of the five male homosexual couples in Philip Blumstein and Pepper Schwartz, *American Couples* (New York: Morrow, 1983), a book often cited by Okin. In interviews, all five of those couples admitted that they had "open" relationships. The sources cited here match the conclusions of traveling journalist Michelangelo Signorile, who uses the terms "post-modern monogamy" and "emotional monogamy" (meaning "monogamy with a little breathing room") to describe the living arrangements of many male same-sex couples in the United States. See Signorile's *Life Outside* (New York: HarperCollins, 1997).

Numerous studies, some of them highly sympathetic to the lifestyle of homosexual men and women, provide further evidence. For a summary, see Jeffrey Satinover, *Homosexuality and the Politics of Truth* (Grand Rapids, Mich.: Baker Books, 1996), 49–61. See also the

The implications of the preceding should be clear. If, as Okin argues, the family is the "first school of justice," then indifference to real fidelity in so many homosexual relationships should have an impact on the moral development of children. "Justice" and "moral development" mean different things to different people, but they always entail serious efforts to keep our promises. Thus, in an environment where the vow of sexual exclusivity is evidently made cavalierly, we should expect children and adolescents to develop some curious notions about morality and justice. Okin, however, says nothing about this theme.

The argument being made here is faithful to Okin's writings on the moral development of children. She considers honesty one of the most important virtues for children to develop, while stressing that "what parents *do* is at least as important as what they say." With respect to vices, she has written that "if any of the vices—not only injustice, but also dishonesty . . . [and] hypocrisy . . .—is frequently exhibited in the practice of parents, it seems unlikely that their children will learn the opposite virtues."[119] In making this argument, I assume that men and women in real marriages expect sexual exclusivity, that a decent society requires it (a requirement long reflected in the law, in part to protect children), and that spouses can and do meet this basic duty.[120]

Okin might respond in two ways. First, she might say that the incidence of fidelity in same-sex partnerships will increase as soon as the laws permit homosexual couples to marry (and to adopt children freely). Second, she might argue that even if homosexual couples are far less likely to be faithful to each other than husbands and wives are, fidelity or monogamy is only one aspect of marriage, and that we should take into account many different things when evaluating the relations of homosexual couples.

With respect to the first point, it is illogical to expect that sexual fidelity

---

sources cited in Stanley N. Kurtz, "What Is Wrong with Gay Marriage," *Commentary* 110 (September 2000): 35.

[119] See Susan Moller Okin and Rob Reich, "Families and Schools as Compensating Agents in Moral Development for a Multicultural Society," *Journal of Moral Education* 28 (1999): 283, 284; and Susan Moller Okin, "Feminism, Moral Development, and the Virtues," in *How Should One Live? Essays on the Virtues,* ed. Roger Crisp (Oxford: Clarendon Press, 1996), 223.

[120] On the last point, see the important work by Robert T. Michael, John H. Gagnon, Edward O. Laumann, and Gina Kolata, *Sex in America: A Definitive Survey* (Boston: Little, Brown and Company, 1994), 105, which found that more than 80 percent of women and 65 to 85 percent of men of every age had no sex partners other than their spouse while married. These figures are impressive, in view of the permissive moral standards of the contemporary era. The figures are also based on the most scientifically rigorous survey of sexual behavior conducted in the United States. See Edward O. Laumann et al., *The Social Organization of Sexuality: Sexual Practices in the United States* (Chicago: University of Chicago Press, 1994).

will become a widely accepted norm among homosexuals if the law permits them to marry. As even a cursory reading of Phelan's essay and the other sources shows, the demand for "queer" recognition is premised on a rejection of (if not hostility toward) traditional marriage and monogamy. Hence the illogic: marriage, a social institution that many homosexuals regard with a variety of misgivings or outright contempt, is supposed to help the selfsame persons become more "domesticated" or "civilized."[121]

The line of thinking in the second point seems at odds with Okin's views on heterosexual marriage (already discussed), views that are widely shared in our society. In the moral framework presupposed by Okin for relations between husbands and wives, monogamy is a *sine qua non* of marriage. Although she could have stated the point more forcefully, Okin believes that sexual infidelity reflects a grave lack of respect for one's spouse.

This notion is both sound and uncontroversial. Furthermore, everyone expects unfailing adherence to certain moral norms from members of other social institutions. Ordinary men and women sometimes fail to meet such expectations, but even allowing for human fallibility, some of these expectations are nonnegotiable. Every sane person, for example, expects parents to refrain from abusing their children, and no one says that such abuse can ever be offset by the generosity of parents or their extraordinary attentiveness to their children's intellectual or cultural development.

Along these lines, I reject Okin's view that homosexual couples can serve as some type of moral exemplar for men and women in real marriages. (In one essay, Okin contends that homosexual couples can serve as a model because they allegedly divide the domestic labor more equitably than do heterosexual couples.[122]) To advance such a thesis is to obscure the importance of sexual fidelity in a real marriage. It is akin to saying that, although the parent who abuses a son or daughter is doing something reprehensible, we must consider other behaviors when evaluating him or her as a parent.[123]

That Okin earnestly recommends homosexual couples as some type of

---

[121] See William N. Eskridge, Jr., *The Case for Same-Sex Marriage: From Sexual Liberty to Civilized Commitment* (New York: The Free Press, 1996). Despite the title of his book, Eskridge is less than candid in discussing the absence of sexual exclusivity in so many homosexual partnerships. See, for example, the paltry analysis on p. 120.

[122] See Okin, "Sexual Orientation and Gender," 54–56.

[123] While on the subject of domestic violence, notice that the incidence of abuse in homosexual partnerships is no lower than in heterosexual relationships. See, for example, John Leland, "Silence Ending about Abuse in Gay Relationships," *The New York Times*, 6 November 2000, A18; and the *San Francisco Chronicle*, 6 October 1998, A13. I mention this fact because of Okin's penchant for "romanticizing" same-sex romance, e.g., suggesting that homosexuals who use new reproductive technologies are more likely than are most husbands and wives to have "really" wanted children. See "Sexual Orientation and Gender," 54.

moral exemplar for our society reveals a certain naiveté in her political and social worldview. It also reveals the extent to which her thinking is shaped by "gender."

Regarding her naiveté, consider the following. At least a few "gay" writers admit that allowing same-sex couples to marry will "liven up" the institution of marriage. By such a remark, they mean that the norm of sexual exclusivity between husbands and wives will grow weaker because of certain realities of the homosexual lifestyle (including the intrinsic sterility of all homosexual "unions") and the greater visibility of homosexuals in America today. Michael Bronski, an unabashed proponent of gay "liberation," provides a valuable perspective on this matter:

> One of the persistent myths of the gay rights movement, and of liberal thinking, is that the dominant culture's fear of homosexuality . . . is "irrational." This is untrue: It is a completely rational fear. Homosexuality strikes at the heart of the organization of Western culture and societies. Because homosexuality, by its nature, is nonreproductive, it posits a sexuality that is justified by pleasure alone.[124]

Such candor is welcome, and one wonders what Okin would make of it. That is, if we recall that the great majority of American women will be married by the age of thirty and will have a child by the age of forty, and if we further recall that virtually all of these women expect sexual fidelity within marriage, the development in question scarcely bodes well for most American women. Thus, given Okin's views on the economic effects of divorce on women and children, her enthusiasm for same-sex "marriage" is hard to fathom. Women in real marriages would seem to have few if any reasons to want the institution "livened up" in the way that Bronski and others predict.[125]

In all likelihood, Okin cannot see this point because she is so committed to eradicating gender. That commitment is a basic tenet of feminism—which still elicits support from liberals and liberal jurists—but the reader should notice the irony. Despite her grudging toleration of the traditional family, Okin is more of a traditionalist than she realizes. That such "traditionalism" conflicts with the project of creating a genderless world is something Okin misses. The conflict is nonetheless an important theoretical problem in her work, a problem with other real-life implications.

[124] Michael Bronski, *The Pleasure Principle* (New York: St. Martin's Press, 1998), 8.

[125] For other statements, see Miller, *The Passion of Michel Foucault*, 8; Blasius, *Gay and Lesbian Politics*, 124; and Lehr, *Queer Family Values*, 49. Because so many American women have children within marriage while expecting fidelity from their husbands, William Eskridge Jr. is mistaken in writing that "in today's society the importance of marriage is relational and not procreational" (Eskridge, *The Case for Same-Sex Marriage*, 11). For more on these matters, see Robert P. George and David L. Tubbs, "Redefining Marriage Away," *City Journal* 14 (Summer 2004): 26.

Because Okin assumes that gender is a social construct, we can see why she is so beamish about a genderless future. If gender is at the root of so many social evils, the welfare of women should surely improve in a genderless world. For other reasons—including, significantly, her faith in the omnicompetent welfare state—Okin also believes that the well-being of children will necessarily improve in a genderless society. But, as the example of homosexual "marriage" suggests, Okin too quickly posits "the best of all possible worlds."

In putting forth ideas for social reform, Okin makes projections about a genderless future and sometimes assumes that persons will behave just as they do today. But if social institutions and norms change as much as Okin wants them to change, men and women may have new incentives and disincentives for different types of conduct. Their behavior in response to these incentives and disincentives might be hard to predict, and their actions (or inaction) might present problems that Okin nowhere considers.

Here is another example, not unrelated to the topic just discussed. In *Justice, Gender, and the Family*, Okin rebukes Allan Bloom for suggesting that, in the wake of the sexual revolution, most men will ignore the feminist demand for a more equitable division of domestic labor. Bloom reasons as follows. Despite their strong sexual drive, most men have no natural desire or need for children. This indifference to parenthood distinguishes the sexes, because most women naturally want to be mothers. By contrast, most men prefer to advance their careers or engage in other activities that test their "male-spiritedness."[126]

In the face of male indifference toward children, women usually won long-term commitments from men by withholding sex until marriage. Today, however, nonmarital sex is common, and men have no incentive to marry, save long-term companionship (whose importance Bloom plays down). Bloom therefore ridicules those who suppose that men not only will remain committed to marriage but also will take on more domestic work than before, thereby allowing their wives to pursue a career outside the home.

Okin is indignant at this line of thought:

The things that make traditional families unjust are not matters of natural necessity, as reactionaries like Bloom would like to have us believe. There is surely nothing in our natures that requires men not to be equal participants in the rearing of their children. Bloom says they won't do it because they are naturally selfish. Even if he were right, which I very strongly doubt, since when did we shape public policy around people's faults? Our laws do not allow kleptoma-

---

[126] Bloom, *The Closing of the American Mind*, 97–118; Okin, *Justice, Gender, and the Family*, 33–40.

niacs to shoplift, or those with a predilection for rape to rape. Why, then, should we allow fathers who refuse to share in the care of their children to abdicate their responsibilities?[127]

This response is to the point, provided that the men in question are married. If that condition obtains, then the redistributive policy Okin favors could reduce the economic vulnerability of wives. If enacted, the policy might also lead husbands to value more highly the domestic work done by their wives.

Notice, however, that Okin says nothing about Bloom's other point: the greater reluctance of "sexually liberated" men to settle down with a wife. Okin may find it unpleasant to admit this possibility, but a long-standing incentive for men to marry may have vanished, and their behavior may have changed accordingly. (Despite my endorsement of the measure, Okin's policy of shared income between spouses may create a disincentive for some men to marry.) Furthermore, in a more permissive sexual environment, fewer husbands are likely to regard their wives as a permanent and exclusive partner, making family life still more fragile, with consequences for both women and children.

Other scholars and writers, very different in style and temperament from Bloom (and from one another), also notice that so much casual intimacy can create a disincentive for men to marry. In this environment, these scholars worry about the prospects of young women finding emotionally mature men and committed husbands.[128]

As the preceding suggests, Okin is disposed to give sunny forecasts and does not anticipate some undesirable changes that may ensue if her ideas win acceptance. The sexual freedom she favors is supposed to ease the emergence of a genderless world, without any adverse consequences. As another example of this tendency in Okin's thinking, consider her idea that justice should be regarded as the primary virtue of marriage and family life.

---

[127] Okin, *Justice, Gender, and the Family*, 39.

[128] See, for example, Wilson, *The Moral Sense*, 165–170; Wendy Shalit, *A Return to Modesty: Rediscovering the Lost Virtue* (New York: The Free Press, 1999); and Patricia Dalton, "Daughters of the Revolution," *Washington Post*, 21 May 2000, B1.

Because Okin so often refers to the "social construction" of gender, Dalton's views on some of the "natural" differences between men and women deserve attention. Dalton reminds her readers of some basic facts about biology and human societies: that a woman's child-bearing years are finite; that men around the world tend to "seek mates the same age or younger"; and that women everywhere tend to mate with men "close to their age or older." Dalton then issues a warning to young women who might suppose that sexual freedom comes without any unpleasant consequences. As a professional therapist, Dalton has counseled many women who "embraced both word and deed of the sexual revolution," only to discover that the years of fertility can "pass pretty quickly."

By this, Okin does not mean that spouses in a good marriage will relate to each other in the same manner as citizens in a good polity. She hopes that love and altruism will coexist with a concern for justice between spouses. That goal is not unreasonable, but Okin should concede that a concern for justice sometimes *cannot* be the chief characteristic of a marriage, including some very good marriages.

Here is what I have in mind. In some circumstances, we cannot expect to find anything like "parity" or "reciprocity" in marriage. If, for example, one spouse becomes disabled from an accident or a prolonged illness, the other spouse may constantly have to "give" and rarely, if ever, "receive." Such self-sacrifice may be required for many years—*if* the healthy spouse stays in the marriage. But if he or she chooses to stay, then a concern for justice is no longer the defining characteristic of the marriage.

Another implication should be noted. If men and women begin to believe that a concern for justice is the groundwork of marriage, they might be disinclined to stay in a marriage where the likelihood of parity or reciprocity (i.e., "justice") is remote or nonexistent. ("Parity" and "reciprocity" should be understood broadly, encompassing a range of goods and types of support, some of them intangible.) The law of averages should ensure that wives and husbands are equally affected by grave accidents and illnesses, but a change in the spouses' perception of marriage, in accordance with Okin's wishes, might make divorce even more common. In such an environment, the women and children in a family are apt to suffer the most.

A little candor by Okin would have gone a long way here. It might have also reduced the amount of scorn she heaps on Christianity. For as almost everyone knows, Christian wedding vows ("For better and for worse . . . in sickness and in health") acknowledge that self-sacrifice of a high order may be required of either spouse at any time (and for any length of time) in marriage. Thus, unless she is indifferent to spousal and familial abandonment in circumstances like those described above, Okin should admit that something valuable may be lost if a concern for justice comes to be regarded as the most important trait of a good marriage.[129]

Even if Okin would concede the point just made, no one should expect

---

[129] The traditional Christian account of marriage seems to hold that marital love is more an act of will than an emotional response to one's spouse (however deeply felt the emotions may be at any time before or during marriage). As an act of will, marital love affirms the importance of steadfastness in the face of life's misfortunes: the onset of old age, various illnesses, the inevitable decrepitude of the body. For supporting evidence, see Aldous Huxley, *The Perennial Philosophy* (New York: Harper, 1944), ch. 5, esp. 85 and 90.

Of course, spouses who profess Christianity do not always live up to the marital ideal of that religion. Furthermore, some husbands and wives who accept Okin's account of marriage

her to rethink her views on the traditional family. Those views are of much relevance to policy debates about day care, the last subject to be considered here.

Though less controversial than her ideas about marriage and family life, Okin's views on day care should be considered in conjunction with her vision of a genderless society. Here we should recall that Okin has both short-term and long-term goals. In the short run, and from the standpoint of Rawls's "original position," she will tolerate traditional families and a traditional division of labor between husbands and wives. In the long run, however, justice demands the elimination of gender. Again, this means parity in domestic labor between husbands and wives and roughly the same number of women as men in all jobs. It also means a vast increase in day-care centers and the number of children in them.[130]

This distinction between short-term and long-term goals is revealing. If Okin believes that "demolishing" gender is the only sensible policy in the long run, then the traditional family is somehow "unreasonable." That is in fact her view, and Okin often tells her readers that traditional gender roles draw sustenance from traditional religion. Assigning much of the resistance to feminism in the United States to Christianity, Okin characterizes the religion as "sexist," "misogynist," and "elitist," and concludes that a thinking woman would never espouse it.[131]

This conclusion attests to Okin's inability to understand the mindset of many Americans, especially with regard to children and day care. Because of her antipathy to Christianity, Okin has no real appreciation of why some American parents might be wary of leaving their children for long stretches of time with persons who do not share the family's faith. Praising democracy and inveighing against "elitism," Okin wants her readers to believe that she has the interests of ordinary women and men at heart. But from several standpoints, her views on Christianity bespeak condescension and an aggressively secular elitism.

Apart from the religious convictions that might influence their decisions about day care, American women may have other reasons for choosing homemaking and motherhood as a full-time job. At least a few polls suggest that the women who make this choice are primarily motivated by the

---

might stay with their spouses in circumstances like those described here. Still, my point remains: the way a society characterizes marriage is likely to affect the behavior of husbands and wives within it, and Okin is wrong in thinking that only happy consequences will result if her ideas take hold. In this context, see her remarks in *Justice, Gender, and the Family*, 26–33, and "*Political Liberalism*, Justice, and Gender," 27 n. 12.

[130] See, generally, *Justice, Gender, and the Family*, ch. 8.

[131] See the hypothetical "thought experiment" in *Justice, Gender, and the Family*, 58–60, which is supposed to demonstrate the "unreasonableness" of Christianity. See also "*Political Liberalism*, Justice, and Gender," 31.

welfare of their children.[132] If that hypothesis is correct, could anyone question the woman's choice? Well, Okin questions it, and she believes that others should also question it. To suggest that the choice is problematic or indefensible, Okin and like-minded theorists must seemingly hold views such as the following:

> That motherhood and homemaking are less fulfilling, less challenging, or less important than a career outside the home; that day-care centers and the persons who work in them will be as solicitous of a child's needs as the child's mother is; that even if the policy of "shared income" between spouses were enacted, a traditional division of labor (i.e., husband as sole or principal breadwinner, wife as primary homemaker and caretaker of the children) is still unfair or unjust to women.[133]

Okin either explicitly or implicitly endorses each view here. But a reasonable person could hold the contrary positions.

Consider the first view above. In several places, Okin says that being a mother and homemaker is hard work. She also worries that American society undervalues the work of mothers and homemakers.[134] By this remark, she means that men often take it for granted. As my support for the "shared income" policy suggests, I agree with Okin that men too often take the work for granted and that it lacks the prestige of other vocations in our society.

Nevertheless, what our society esteems and disesteems may not affect the thinking of a wife and her husband regarding the welfare of their own children. As the sons and daughters of most immigrants know, parents often endure great hardship and even humiliation to better the lives of their progeny. Thus, that parenthood as a full-time vocation lacks social prestige does not mean that a mother who chooses it is being unreasonable. Her husband and children, moreover, may love her deeply for all that she does.

What about fulfillment? Are motherhood and homemaking less fulfilling or less challenging to a woman than most careers available to her outside the home? Perhaps we should distinguish between "challenging" and "fulfilling," because Okin routinely says that motherhood and homemaking are challenging (meaning hard or demanding), while she sometimes says (and more often intimates) that they are less fulfilling than a career outside the home.

---

[132] See Tamar Lewin, "Americans Attached to Traditional Roles for Sexes, Poll Finds," *The New York Times*, 27 March 1996, A15, and the research summarized in *The American Enterprise* (Sept./Oct. 1992): 85–86.

[133] See, generally, *Justice, Gender, and the Family.*

[134] See, for example, Okin, "Are Our Theories of Justice Gender-Neutral?" in *The Moral Foundation of Civil Rights*, ed. Robert K. Fullwinder and Claudia Mills (Totowa, N.J.: Rowman and Littlefield, 1986), 137.

On the latter point, I suspect that Okin generalizes from her experience. If so, she errs in assuming that most jobs, even most "white-collar" jobs, are as stimulating as that of a university professor.[135]

Another explanation for Okin's view is possible. As readers may have noticed, Okin has a fondness for sharp dualisms. Just as she posits an implacable opposition between the interests of women and the claims of traditional religion (such as Christianity), she overdraws the contrast between a man's work outside the home (scintillating and life-enhancing) and a woman's work in the home (pure toil and moil). Yet no one should think that women in this country ever had a monopoly on undesirable work. Immigrant life speaks volumes on this subject as well.[136]

It is true that in the last century, most white-collar jobs were the preserve of men. It is also true that most academics would find white-collar work to be more stimulating than blue-collar work. But not all women are suited for white-collar jobs, and even when they are, they might find those jobs less satisfying than full-time motherhood, particularly in our present milieu. Being a full-time parent could be more demanding (yet more fulfilling) than it was a generation or two ago. Some of the greater demands may have arisen from affluence and ennui, but parents of all social classes may now have to contend with them.

Many parents, even nonreligious parents, might still try to discourage their children from becoming sexually active during adolescence. These parents might deplore the libertine attitudes so common in popular culture, including the relentless prodding to "experiment" with one's sexuality. Okin dismisses some of these concerns as outdated—she evidently

---

[135] In a note in *Justice, Gender, and the Family* (116), Okin writes that "in favorable circumstances"—a telling qualifier, it seems—child-rearing "can be immensely pleasurable and rewarding." She adds that child-rearing is also immensely time-consuming, making it difficult for women to achieve other "social goods," such as education, earnings, and political office.

Like so many persons affiliated with feminism, Okin believes that women should want those other social goods as much as (if not more than) they might want motherhood and homemaking as a full-time career. See, for example, "Families and Feminist Theory," 15–16, and *Justice, Gender, and the Family,* 150–151. See also the petitions, scattered throughout her work, for *subsidized* day care. The repeated calls for subsidized day care and Okin's indifference to whether most Americans want it reveal much about her political worldview.

[136] This contrast is accentuated by the (historically false) image of women laboring endlessly at home while their husbands, one and all, debated politics in the assembly. See, for instance, Okin, "Families and Feminist Theory," 14. In the modern West, the percentage of white men who could vote was quite small until the nineteenth century, and in most European countries, women were enfranchised within one to two generations after universal male suffrage was attained. See the summary in Norman Davies, *Europe: A History* (New York: Harper Perennial, 1998), 1295. Recall, too, that some jobs, either highly undesirable (e.g., trash-collecting) or highly dangerous (e.g., fire-fighting), have almost always been held by men.

thinks it is pointless to discourage teenage sexuality—but she knows that the *consequences* of teenage sexuality can severely affect a young person's future.[137] Furthermore, Okin would have to acknowledge a new fear shared by nearly all American parents: the threat of explosive and unprovoked violence, as evidenced in schoolyard shootings across the country in the 1990s and beyond.

These considerations alone might lead some husbands and wives to opt for a traditional division of labor. Even if it involves sacrificing income and professional opportunities, couples may be willing to do so. As parents, they may feel that their foremost duty is to be attentive to all of the things—ideas, people, stimuli, media—that can affect the moral development of their child.

Perhaps it will sound extreme, but this outlook might even extend to day care. By this I mean that parental regard for a child's moral environment might entail using day care as little as possible. This concern is in some ways similar to (though in other ways different from) the reservations religiously devout parents might have about day care. In either case, parents may want to exert greater control over the child's environment to reinforce the religious or moral convictions of the family. These remarks do not imply that persons who work in day-care centers are morally lax or indifferent to the children in their presence. The point is narrower: conscientious parents are more likely than anyone else to know the needs and susceptibilities of their child.

We can hope that Okin would recognize the reasonableness of such concerns, but that might be expecting too much. Her commitment to a genderless future is strong, and something so starkly at odds with it—such as full-time motherhood and homemaking—is hard for her to accept. Moreover, Okin is less than candid in discussing day care. She always uses the same adjectives to describe it—"low-cost" (or "affordable"), "subsidized," and "high-quality"—but these refer to day care as she envisions it, not (even by her own admission) as we find it today.[138] More important, Okin fails to ask whether we can expect day care to be generously subsidized by the state (and its taxpayers) if a substantial percentage of American parents hold views such as those just described.

These criticisms might be misunderstood. I am not saying that every woman should want to be a full-time mother and homemaker. Nor am I saying that having a full-time mother and homemaker ought to be the norm for every American family. Day care is an important matter for many parents, and it may be a necessity for those who plan to send their children to college. Contrary to Okin, however, I think that gener-

---

[137] Okin, *Justice, Gender, and the Family,* 178; "Families and Feminist Theory," 22–23.
[138] Okin, *Justice, Gender, and the Family,* 17, 116n, and 175–177.

alizing about these matters on the basis of personal preference is presumptuous.

Let me put this differently. Despite the greater overall need for day care, people have different attitudes toward it. Some couples want it for the same reasons that Okin wants it, and, like her, they may want the government to play a large role in providing it. Other couples regard it as a regrettable necessity. Still others sacrifice a great deal to go without it. The *reasons* for such sacrifice should be noted. Just as they might forego several vacations or a new car to further their children's education, parents might deny themselves income and career advancement to promote their children's moral or intellectual development.

Where Okin goes wrong is in supposing that all couples should adopt her priorities. In the main, her priorities strike me as legitimate. A career outside the home is hugely important to many women, and, if my opinion were sought, I would urge any woman to think carefully before quitting a job outside the home to become a full-time mother. That choice may entail different costs and risks (some noted by Okin), and if the opportunity is present, these women should perhaps continue working outside the home, if only for a few hours each week. Those few hours might allow women to maintain vital professional skills.

Having affirmed the validity of Okin's priorities, I will add that it would be good of her to do the same for other women, including full-time mothers. Her unwillingness to do so seems related to her sense that even if the policy of shared incomes were enacted, a traditional division of labor would still be unfair to women.

This task involves some speculation—because Okin is less than clear on some matters—but I shall try to sketch her position. Despite being dismissive of certain moral concerns of traditional parents, Okin could still challenge the traditional division of labor as the preferred means of promoting them. She might ask: If these moral matters are so weighty that a full-time parent and homemaker are needed, why can't the man take on those roles?

The short answer is that a man *can* take them on, and he is more likely to take them on in the new century. (Because of demographics and the career choices of professional couples, a more frequent occurrence will be the father as the *primary* caretaker of the children.) But Okin probably has another question in mind: Will the full-time, stay-at-home father be as common as the full-time, stay-at-home mother? That seems to be a crucial question for Okin, and until such fathers are as common as such mothers, she will maintain that the disparity is an injustice, rooted in gender.

Is she right? For different reasons, I believe that she is mistaken, and badly so. To understand her error, we need to consider the economic basis of the traditional division of labor. Rather than regard the disparity just mentioned as an injustice, we should regard it as the persistence of a tradition. And to those who will reply that it is an *unjust* tradition, we must respond that the notions of "just" and "unjust" are in significant respects inapplicable here.

Here is why. As noted above, Okin leads her readers astray in suggesting that women have had something like a monopoly on undesirable work in this country. Even if we ignore the immigrant experience, other economic realities, grounded in history, complicate the picture that Okin presents.

Consider rural life, mocked by Karl Marx and others, yet the basis of American economic life for much of our history. In the late eighteenth century, roughly 75 to 80 percent of the nation's population made its living from agriculture or independent artisanship. In such circumstances, husbands and wives and whole families functioned as an economic team, often as a matter of survival and usually with little margin for error. For many Americans, this way of life persisted well into the twentieth century.[139]

The point here is clear. Under conditions such as these, particularly in the more distant past, it makes little sense to talk about the justice or injustice of a division of labor between husband and wife. When even minimal levels of human welfare could not be taken for granted, the division of labor belonged more to the realm of necessity than to that of "free choice." Being on average stronger, men usually had to perform the more physically demanding labor, while women did most of the child care and housework. (This does not imply that child care and housework have ever been easy.)

The basis of this sexual division of labor is less apparent than before, and time and technological change have obscured its importance. Because she so often repeats that gender is a "social construct," Okin might be slow to concede that the traditional division of labor had a real biological basis. But upon reflection, who could deny it? Anyone with lingering doubts would do well to spend some time in rural America and observe the lives of many families there. Failing that, they could read a few novels by John Steinbeck.[140]

The preceding helps us to understand why the traditional division of labor has persisted and why the current disparity between full-time mothers and full-time fathers should not be deemed an injustice. Today, relatively few persons in the United States make their living directly from

---

[139] See, for instance, Robert Heilbroner, "Reflections: Boom and Crash," *The New Yorker* (28 August 1978): 68.

[140] One scholar reminds us: "In the seventeenth century our modern phrases 'domestic economy' or 'household economy' would have been redundant. Retaining the spelling of the Greek word for household, 'oeconomie' on its own still referred to the small scale, defined as 'the knowledge of well ordering matters to the household'" (Amy Louise Erickson, *Women and Property in Early Modern England* [London and New York: Routledge, 1993], 18).

the earth. The arrangements described above, however, lasted for centuries, promoting patterns of behavior and cultural norms that are likely to be with us indefinitely.

Until very recently, another type of work was without exception assigned on the basis of sex, and this division of labor has also promoted scores of cultural norms and ideals. I refer to armed combat, and the long history of sex-based conscription provides further evidence (if further evidence were needed) that the traditional division of labor is not the manifest injustice that Okin takes it to be.

To forestall an objection, let me say that the analysis here is not exhaustive. As noted, the still-widespread belief that a mother is the "natural" caretaker of a family's children seems related to her capacity to bear and nurse a child. Too often, however, Okin writes as though that belief by itself explains the origins and persistence of the traditional division of labor.[141]

Consider one further point. Anyone truly interested in how individual women establish priorities in their lives must take account of the joy—or, to use the economists' word, "utility"—they derive from giving life to another human being. (A similar question must be asked about a married woman's choice to be a full-time mother and homemaker.) But Okin fails to do this, and she seems unwilling to face the relevant matters squarely.[142]

Greater awareness of the issues raised here might lead Okin beyond her grudging toleration of the traditional division of labor, particularly when couples choose it for the sake of their children. But once again, this may be wishful thinking. To judge from many passages, Okin is strongly, almost reflexively, disposed to equate the "traditional" with the "irrational." She does this while making only cursory efforts to understand the choices and behavior of persons whose priorities differ from hers.

To conclude this chapter, we should review the achievements and shortcomings of Okin's political theory. I said that Okin deserves credit for urging liberal theorists to give more attention to the family and for stressing the political relevance of family life. She also merits praise for having presented various interests of women and children within the framework of Rawls's influential theory. Thus, in important respects, Okin has added complexity to contemporary debates about social justice and the life prospects of women and children.

---

[141] See, for example, "Families and Feminist Theory," 14; "Are Our Theories of Justice Gender-Neutral?" 140–142; "*Political Liberalism*, Justice, and Gender," 29; and "Gender, the Public, and the Private," 76–77.

[142] In addition to the de rigueur feminist musings on "compulsory" heterosexuality for women (provoked by an essay by Adrienne Rich), see the peculiar analysis in Okin's "Politics and the Complex Inequalities of Gender," in *Pluralism, Justice, and Equality*, ed. David Miller and Michael Walzer (New York: Oxford University Press, 1995), 132–133.

In other respects, however, Okin oversimplifies or obscures fundamental questions. She does this in several different ways: by sometimes insisting that what is perceived by others as a problem is just an irrational or sexist prejudice; by routinely supposing that every problem she associates with gender has a straightforward solution; and by nearly always assuming that all of those solutions (and her political values more generally) harmonize.

We see these tendencies throughout Okin's work. Consider two topics already examined: family life and sexual freedom. While finding nothing per se objectionable about single-parent families or single motherhood by choice, Okin is sure that the economic difficulties of single-parent families (which almost everyone acknowledges) can be easily overcome. Only by iterating her strong faith in a large welfare state is she able to evade the truth: that the greater sexual freedom of the day has indeed contributed to the economic vulnerability of women and children.

This lack of forthrightness is distressing. As another example, consider Okin's views on pornography and the First Amendment, a topic only touched on above, though plainly relevant to this study. Because of Okin's loyalty to both liberalism and feminism, one might expect that this subject would yield an interesting tension in her thinking, owing to liberalism's concern for freedom of expression and feminism's concern for the public perception of women and girls and the social status of women and children.

Why, then, are Okin's judgments about pornography so facile? Why is she so confident that the next generation of Americans will be able to "find a means of regulating pornography that . . . [does] not seriously compromise freedom of speech"?[143] And why does she nowhere explore the connection between the sexual freedom *she* favors and the sexual freedom that producers and consumers of pornography favor? Is there *no* intersection or overlap?

To use a distinction associated with Isaiah Berlin's thought, Okin is a monist, not a pluralist. In view of Okin's twin loyalties to liberalism and feminism, the appellation might sound strange, but it is correct. Okin is a monist because she assumes an easy harmonization of the political values dearest to her. Moments of candor in Okin's work about the conflict of values are rare, and those infrequent instances almost always involve a disagreement between political activists on the left.[144] *Philosophic* candor, like that found in the writings of distinguished theorists such as Berlin,[145]

---

[143] Okin, *Justice, Gender, and the Family,* 105.
[144] See, for example, "Sexual Difference, Feminism, and the Law," 565–567.
[145] See, for instance, the essays in Berlin's *The Crooked Timber of Humanity.*

Elshtain,[146] and Kateb,[147] is virtually nonexistent in Okin's work from the late 1970s through the 1990s.

From the standpoint of this study, what is most maddening about Okin's work is her recurring assumption that the interests of women and children coincide. Most reflective readers are likely to be curious about the source of this assumption, so I would like to suggest two possible reasons for it.

First, because of her strong desire to make theory directly relevant to practice, Okin seems to cut corners, just as politicians cut corners. In some places—notably the essay "Feminism and Political Theory"—Okin seems more concerned with the vocation of politics than with the vocation of theory. That choice is her own prerogative as a scholar and a politically engaged citizen, but we ought to be frank about what the choice entails. Few politicians are philosophers, and an unwillingness to explore where the interests of women and children diverge might be ascribed to the temperament of the political activist.

Okin's reluctance to assess the interests of children independent from the interests of women could also be attributed to her preoccupation with the concept of gender. Okin knows that a concern with gender is sometimes considered tantamount to interest-group politics and theorizing, but she insists that this criticism is invalid.[148] Okin's work, however, lends validity to the criticism. The themes are familiar: gender as artifact, gender as curse, gender as destiny. The themes are also persistent, consuming nearly all of Okin's mental energy.

Conscientious readers and critics may disagree as to why Okin so casually assumes that the interests of women (as she defines them) coincide with the interests of children. But if the arguments in this chapter have merit, then the assumption must be rejected, regardless of its provenance. To cling to it, in the face of so much evidence to the contrary, might make one's work as a theorist easier, but at a cost that no serious thinker should be willing to pay.

[146] See, e.g., Elshtain's *Democracy on Trial.*
[147] See, for example, Kateb, *The Inner Ocean,* 27–35.
[148] Okin, "Feminism and Political Theory," 135.

CHAPTER THREE

The "Right to Privacy" and Some Forgotten Interests of Children

IN THE LAST TWO CHAPTERS, I explored some theoretical problems in liberal thought as they relate to the lives of American children. In this chapter and the next one, I add concreteness to the discussion by reviewing some cases decided by the Supreme Court of the United States.

Several justices of the Supreme Court uncritically champion "negative" freedom while disregarding important interests of children. Without expressly endorsing the idea of negative freedom, some of the judicial opinions by these justices display a moral reticence akin to that of the liberal political theorists described in Chapter One. Given the critical role of the judiciary in American politics, these developments deserve close attention.

In this chapter, I identify various interests of children that the Supreme Court ignored when it formulated the controversial "right to privacy" and invalidated various laws relating to the use, sale, and distribution of contraceptives. To identify these interests is a valid scholarly exercise because of a long-standing perception that some of the laws were "purposeless restraints." Besides identifying these interests, I offer a critique of the decisions.

The holdings in the relevant cases can be summarized as follows. In *Griswold v. Connecticut, Eisenstadt v. Baird,* and *Carey v. Population Services International,* the Supreme Court declared that various state laws regulating the use and distribution of contraceptives were unconstitutional.[1] In *Griswold,* the Court held that a Connecticut statute prohibiting the use of contraceptives violated an unenumerated constitutional right to marital privacy. In *Eisenstadt,* the Court struck down a Massachusetts law forbidding the sale and distribution of contraceptives to unmarried persons; in the majority opinion, Justice William J. Brennan Jr. cited *Griswold* and asserted that "whatever the rights of the individual to access to contraceptives may be, the rights must be the same for the unmarried and the married alike."[2] In *Carey,* the Court extended the right to purchase contraceptives to unmarried minors and invalidated various regulations on the sale of contraceptives.

---

[1] *Griswold v. Connecticut,* 381 U.S. 479 (1965); *Eisenstadt v. Baird,* 405 U.S. 438 (1972); *Carey v. Population Services International,* 431 U.S. 678 (1977).

[2] *Eisenstadt v. Baird,* 453.

When many Americans hear the phrase "right to privacy," they think of abortion rights and cases such as *Roe v. Wade* (1973) and *Planned Parenthood v. Casey* (1992).[3] I do not discuss the constitutionality of abortion here, but my critique of *Griswold* and *Eisenstadt* can be extended to *Roe* and *Casey*.

I have two main goals in this chapter. First, I argue that the Supreme Court wrongly decided the three contraception cases. Second, I argue that the public policy in each of the three states was morally defensible. I hasten to add that "morally defensible" does not necessarily mean that each state's policy was the best or only way to achieve the goals it set for itself.

In making these arguments, I will show that the relevant laws had legitimate public purposes. Specifically, they promoted the monogamous, two-parent family as a social norm and as the family structure most conducive to the welfare of children. The Supreme Court's failure to acknowledge these purposes is regrettable, and the majority opinions in *Griswold, Eisenstadt,* and *Carey* miseducated scholars, jurists, and others about various duties of parents and certain interests of children. As the last chapter suggests, signs of such miseducation are apparent in contemporary scholarship.[4]

Some readers might say that the "right to privacy" still deserves respect because it describes a fundamental value of our polity. This response suggests that a decisive rhetorical battle has been won and the real meanings of these cases have been obscured.

I say this because if the justices in the majority in *Eisenstadt* and *Carey* had been candid, they would have characterized the right in question as the freedom to have consenting, nonmarital intercourse, regardless of the social consequences. The Court failed to explore the link between one's freely consenting sexual relations and basic parental duties—duties that would seem to transcend any cultural or political divisions in our society. Furthermore, the Court said nothing about the diminished life prospects of children issuing from nonmarital relations—a matter well understood by many state legislators before the *Griswold* era.

Other problems must be noted. A close reading of the opinions in *Griswold, Eisenstadt,* and *Carey* reveals lapses of logic, ignorance of or indifference to the traditional bases of morality, and disdain for the judgments of state legislatures. Taken together, these judicial writings provide

---

[3] *Roe v. Wade*, 410 U.S. 113 (1973); *Planned Parenthood of Southeastern Pennsylvania v. Casey*, 505 U.S. 833 (1992).

[4] Besides Okin's work, see Kenneth Karst, "The Freedom of Intimate Association," *Yale Law Journal* 89 (1980): 624; and John Robertson, *Children of Choice*, both of which are discussed below.

evidence of indifference to children's welfare at the highest levels of American jurisprudence.[5]

My analysis begins with an assessment of basic constitutional matters, an overview intended mainly for nonspecialists. Thereafter, I review the purposes of the relevant laws and offer a defense of the policies.

Constitutional Preliminaries

The most direct way to criticize the Supreme Court's decisions in *Griswold, Eisenstadt,* and *Carey* is to point out that each state involved (Connecticut, Massachusetts, and New York) was validly exercising its authority to promote public health, safety, and morals. Before the Court's decision in *Griswold v. Connecticut,* state and federal courts rejected a variety of constitutional challenges to state regulations on contraceptives. Just thirty-four years before *Eisenstadt v. Baird,* for example, the Supreme Court dismissed a similar appeal originating in Massachusetts, holding that the suit did not present a substantial federal question.[6] So we ought to ask what accounts for this tremendous change.

Before turning to that question, we should discuss the state's constitutional authority to promote public health, safety, and morals. That authority, sometimes called the "police power," is an attribute of each state. A clear account of the police power was offered by the first Justice John Marshall Harlan (1833–1911) in the majority opinion in *House v. Mayes*:

> There are certain fundamental principles which . . . are not open to dispute. . . . Briefly stated, those principles are: That the Government created by the Federal Constitution is one of enumerated powers, and cannot, by any of its agencies, exercise an authority not granted by that instrument, either in express words or by necessary implication; that a power may be implied to give effect to a power expressly granted; that while the Constitution of the United States and the laws enacted in pursuance thereof, together with any treaties made under the authority of the United States, constitute the Supreme Law of the Land, a State of the Union may exercise all such governmental authority as is consistent with its own constitution, and not in conflict with the Federal Constitution; that such a power in the State, generally referred to as its police power . . . is the power to

[5] Throughout this chapter, the term "nonmarital relations" refers to any sexual relations that occur outside marriage. The term encompasses both premarital and extramarital (i.e., adulterous) relations. For many years, "fornication" was a widely used term for premarital sexual relations, as evidenced by some cases discussed here.

[6] *Gardner v. Massachusetts,* 305 U.S. 559 (1938). The Massachusetts statute made it a crime to sell, lend, or give away "any drug, medicine, instrument or article whatever for the prevention of conception": 15 N.E. 2d 222 (1938).

so regulate the relative rights and duties of all within its jurisdiction so as to guard the public health, as well as to promote the public convenience and the common good; and that it is with the State to devise the means to be employed to such ends, taking care always that the means devised do not go beyond the necessities of the case, have some real or substantial relation to the objects to be accomplished, and are not inconsistent with its own constitution or the Constitution of the United States.[7]

A famous nineteenth-century reference work in constitutional law defines the police power in similar terms. According to Thomas Cooley's *General Principles of Constitutional Law in the United States,* the police power is "a most comprehensive branch of sovereignty," extending to "everything in the nature of property, every relation in the State, in society, and in private life." By virtue of this power, a state has the authority to pass laws governing marriage and divorce and requiring the education of children. A state can also regulate prices and industries and establish licensing requirements and occupational safety standards.[8]

In numerous cases decided between 1865 and 1940, the Supreme Court defined the police power as the authority of the individual states to promote public health, safety, and morals. This shorthand definition is still sometimes used in the contemporary era.[9]

A survey of cases from the nineteenth and early twentieth century shows the range of legislation passed under the rubric of the police power. As the country's highest appellate court, the Supreme Court affirmed the authority of individual states to pass laws proscribing usury;[10] establishing professional criteria to practice dentistry;[11] regulating the storage fees in grain warehouses;[12] restricting the hours of operation of public laundries;[13] banning the sale and consumption of alcoholic bev-

---

[7] *House v. Mayes, Marshall of Jackson County, Missouri,* 219 U.S. 270, 281–282 (1910).

[8] Thomas M. Cooley, *The General Principles of Constitutional Law in the United States,* 3d ed. (Boston: Little, Brown, and Company, 1898), 250. It is crucial to take note of Cooley's remark that "the Fourteenth Amendment is held not to have taken from the States the police power reserved to them at the time of the adoption of the Constitution" (251). This view had been corroborated in the Supreme Court's decision in *Barbier v. Connolly,* 113 U.S. 27 (1885). Section One of the Fourteenth Amendment reads in part: "No state shall make or enforce any law which shall abridge the privileges or immunities of citizens of the United States; nor shall any State deprive any person of life, liberty, or property without due process of law."

[9] See, for instance, *Barbier v. Connolly,* 31, and the dissenting opinion of Justice William J. Brennan, Jr., in *Paris Adult Theatre v. Slaton,* 413 U.S. 49 (1973).

[10] *Missouri, Kansas, & Texas Trust Company v. Krumseig,* 172 U.S. 351 (1899).

[11] *Graves v. Minnesota,* 272 U.S. 425 (1926).

[12] *Munn v. Illinois,* 94 U.S. 113 (1887).

[13] *Barbier v. Connolly* (note 8, supra).

erages;[14] and permitting the recovery of punitive damages from railroads in tort claims.[15] From 1917 to 1953, state courts in Massachusetts, New York, Connecticut, Wisconsin, and New Jersey sustained the power of their respective legislatures to restrict or forbid the sale or use of contraceptives.[16]

Although used much less than before, the term "police power" (and sometimes "police powers") still appears in Supreme Court opinions. Justice Stephen Breyer, for example, used the term in a high-profile case in 1997.[17]

One concession is in order. To some persons, "police power" sounds foreboding, and the term may have fallen into relative disuse because of its connotations. Since most Americans do not want to live in a "police state," they might be wary of a government—even a representative democracy—exercising the "police power." The unpleasant connotations can be avoided by speaking of the state's reserved powers, which comprise its authority to promote public health, safety, and morals. (Despite having this alternative, I shall use the term "police power" because of its historical importance in the cases under review.)

Regardless of terminology, the police power was long recognized as fundamental to our system of government. To quote the first Justice Harlan again:

> Such a power in the State . . . is not granted by or derived from the Federal Constitution but exists independently of it, by reason of its never having been surrendered by the State to the General Government.[18]

This view would have been familiar to the Framers of the Constitution; the same idea, for example, is expressed by James Madison in *Federalist* No. 45.[19] Because of the federal judiciary's long history of deferring to state legislatures when they exercised the police power, proponents of the "right to privacy" should explain what justifies the departure from the

---

[14] *Bartemeyer v. Iowa*, 18 Wall. 129 (1873).

[15] *Minneapolis and St. Louis Railway Company v. Beckwith*, 129 U.S. 26 (1889).

[16] Among other cases, see *Commonwealth v. Allison*, 227 Mass. 57, 116 N.E. 265 (1917); *People v. Byrne*, 163 N.Y. Supp. 682 (1917); *People v. Sanger*, 222 N.Y. 192, 118 N.E. 637 (1918); *State v. Arnold*, 217 Wis. 340, 258 N.W. 843 (1935); *State v. Nelson*, 126 Conn. 412, 11 A. 2d 856 (1940); and *State v. Tracy*, 29 N.J. Super. 145, 102 A. 2d 52 (Super. Ct. 1953).

[17] *Washington v. Glucksberg*, 521 U.S. 702, 792 (1997).

[18] *House v. Mayes*, 219 U.S. 270, 282 (1910). See also Justice Harlan's opinion in *Jacobson v. Massachusetts*, 197 U.S. 11, 25 (1904), and the opinion of Justice Story in *Martin v. Hunter's Lessee*, 1 Wheat. 304, 326 (1816), both of which reiterate the ideas above.

[19] As Madison wrote: "The powers delegated by the proposed Constitution to the federal government are few and defined. . . . The powers reserved to the several states will extend to all the objects which, in the ordinary course of affairs, concern the lives, liberties, and properties of the people, and the internal order, improvement, and prosperity of the State."

status quo ante. Their response is easy to predict. Defenders of "privacy" will say that judicial acceptance of regulations on contraceptives was constitutional obscurantism, on a par with the Supreme Court's earlier decision in *Plessy v. Ferguson,* which upheld laws mandating segregated railway cars in Louisiana.[20]

Here we must concede the blemishes and scars. The police power has been abused. On occasion, it has been egregiously abused. Furthermore, the federal courts have more than once been derelict in their constitutional duties, especially in matters pertaining to race-based discrimination. Besides *Plessy v. Ferguson,* scholars could cite cases such as *Pace v. Alabama* and *State v. Tutty* as shameful examples of legislative transgression receiving judicial approbation.[21]

Few persons now question the important role played by the federal judiciary in dismantling the institutions of Jim Crow. Yet for reasons given below, we should reject the view that the regulations on contraceptives were morally indefensible and, in this regard, no different from the laws that established and perpetuated racial segregation. Many liberals, however, are likely to disagree. Prominent liberal political theorists support the holding in *Roe v. Wade,* and such support implies an acceptance of the rights previously announced in *Griswold* and *Eisenstadt.*[22]

In the next two sections, I review *Griswold, Eisenstadt,* and *Carey.* I first explain the purposes of the laws, then evaluate the arguments offered to justify these new rights. I conclude that all of those arguments have serious weaknesses.

REGULATING CONTRACEPTIVES: PROMOTING CHILDREN'S WELFARE BY PROMOTING MARITAL FIDELITY

In the last chapter, I argued that every child has a prima facie claim to the resources of the parents who have begotten him or her. This argument en-

[20] *Plessy v. Ferguson,* 136 U.S. 537 (1896).

[21] *Pace v. Alabama,* 106 U.S. 583 (1882) (holding that an Alabama statute proscribing fornication and adultery between whites and blacks did not violate the Equal Protection Clause, even though the penalties the law imposed were more severe than those to which the parties would have been subjected "were they of the same race and color"); *State v. Tutty,* 41 Fed. Rep. 753 (1890) (sustaining, as a valid exercise of the police power, a Georgia law "forever" prohibiting in that state marriages between whites and blacks).

[22] Among works already cited, see George Kateb, "The Liberal Contract," 191, in *The Inner Ocean;* Stephen Macedo, *Liberal Virtues,* 72; Thomas Nagel, "Personal Rights and Public Space," 103; Susan Moller Okin, "Women, Equality, and Citizenship," 70. See also Macedo's "In Defense of Liberal Public Reason," *American Journal of Jurisprudence* 42 (1997): 1, 15–24. This list could be extended. In 1987, many liberal scholars and activists opposed Judge Robert Bork's nomination to the Supreme Court of the United States because of his misgivings about the "right to privacy."

tails that biological parents ordinarily have substantial duties to their children. There are exceptions (e.g., because of the circumstances surrounding adoption), but they are comparatively rare.

When reviewing *Griswold, Eisenstadt,* and *Carey,* readers should keep this prima facie claim in mind, because it takes us to the heart of the relevant legislation. The restrictions on the sale and use of contraceptives were meant to promote favorable domestic circumstances for children. The laws aimed to discourage sexual relations outside marriage and to promote the traditional two-parent family as a social norm and as the family structure most conducive to the welfare of children.

Today, despite abundant evidence about the disadvantages of growing up in a single-parent family, many persons will criticize or deride the goals of this legislation. Others will protest that even if the goals were legitimate, the means were not. Such persons will probably say that the Supreme Court performed a great public service by invalidating state restrictions on contraceptives.

I reject this view. The laws—including those in Connecticut—advanced important public purposes. Today, this point is rarely acknowledged, partly because the majority opinions in both *Griswold* and *Eisenstadt* failed to identify any legislative purpose. So a logical way to begin a defense of the laws is by describing their purposes.

In Connecticut, the principal law in question, section 53-32 of the General Statutes (1958 revision), made it a crime to "use any drug, medicinal article or instrument for the purpose of preventing conception." A related provision, section 54-196 of the General Statutes, provided that a person who "assists, abets, counsels, causes, hires or commands" another to commit an offense could be prosecuted and subjected to the same penalties as the main offender. A person who broke either law was to be "fined not less than fifty dollars or imprisoned not less than sixty days nor more than one year or be both fined and imprisoned."[23]

Reading the statutes in isolation, one might suppose that they were meant to realize the vision of a particular faith—namely, the vision that William Blake found so offensive:

> And priests in black gowns were walking their rounds
> And binding with briars my joys & desires.[24]

What were Connecticut's goals in banning the use of contraceptives? Since the majority opinion in *Griswold* says nothing about the state's interests, one must search elsewhere for the answer. The concurring and dissenting

[23] *Griswold v. Connecticut,* 480.
[24] William Blake, "The Garden of Love," in *Songs of Innocence and Experience* (New York: Penguin Books, 1995).

opinions in *Griswold* furnish useful, albeit fragmentary, information. A more important source is the judicial corpus of the highest appellate court in Connecticut. From 1940 to 1964, litigants challenged the constitutionality of the law and on five occasions appeared before the state's highest appellate tribunal, the Supreme Court of Errors.[25]

The logic of the statutory scheme is more fully explained in the following excerpt from the majority opinion in *State v. Nelson*, decided in 1940 by the Supreme Court of Errors of Connecticut:

> The civil liberty and the natural rights of the individual under the federal and state constitutions are subject to the limitation that he may not use them so as to injure his fellow citizens or endanger the vital interest of society. . . . Whatever may be our own opinion regarding the general subject, it is not for us to say that the Legislature might not reasonably hold that the artificial limitation of even legitimate child-bearing would be inimical to the public welfare and, as well, that use of contraceptives, and assistance therein or tending thereto, would be injurious to public morals, indeed, it is not precluded from considering that not all married people are immune from temptation or inclination to extra-marital indulgence, as to which risk of illegitimate pregnancy is a recognized deterrent deemed desirable in the interests of morality.[26]

Recalling that the *Nelson* case was heard roughly twenty years before oral contraceptives were developed, we must fill in some gaps here. When the *Nelson* court writes that illegitimate pregnancy is a "recognized deterrent" to extramarital relations, it presupposes the existence of a moral community that conveys its disapproval to members who fail to observe one of its basic norms. As the excerpt shows, this particular community believed that children should be begotten only by lawfully married men and women.

Of what relevance are the moral judgments of a community? For many persons in the United States today, the judgments of a particular community (e.g., a state or county or town) might have little significance, if they are even recognizable. Implicit in the *Nelson* court's reasoning, however, is the view that most citizens will acknowledge such judgments and try to avoid a community's disapproval.

By limiting access to contraceptives and penalizing their use, the Connecticut legislature discouraged attempts to eliminate the risks of adultery and premarital sex. Apart from the legal duties assigned to parents, the father and mother of a child issuing from nonmarital relations might suf-

---

[25] The five cases were *State v. Nelson; Tileston v. Ullman*, 26 A. 2d 582 (1942); *Buxton v. Ullman*, 156 A. 2d 508 (1959); *Trubek v. Ullman*, 165 A. 2d 158 (1960); and *State v. Griswold*, 200 A. 2d 479 (1964).

[26] *State v. Nelson*, 861.

fer a loss in social status. In the excerpt above, the phrase "illegitimate pregnancy" is telling: it signifies that there is and should be some stigma attached to begetting a child outside of marriage.

The idea of a moral community is reflected in another passage in the *Nelson* case. Here the *Nelson* court quoted the Supreme Judicial Court of Massachusetts, which had resolved a similar controversy twenty-three years earlier:

> Manifestly they [i.e., the laws] are designed to promote the public morals and in a broad sense the public health and safety. Their plain purpose is to protect purity, to preserve chastity, to encourage continence and self-restraint, to defend the sanctity of the home, and thus to engender . . . a virile and virtuous race of men and women.[27]

Some readers will smirk at these words. The dated language notwithstanding, we can identify several goals of the Connecticut laws, including the moral improvement of citizens (by discouraging adultery), the protection of marriages and families, and the advancement of children's welfare. These goals are interrelated, and it might be hard to ascertain which of the purposes (if any) was primary.

The basic strategy of the legislation is still clear: by limiting access to contraceptives, it sought to prevent people from trying to eliminate the potential costs (or risks) of nonmarital sexual relations. With respect to premarital sexual relations, the matter in *Nelson* is at one point stated bluntly: "While there are other reasons that keep unmarried people from indulging their passions, the fear that pregnancy will result is one of the potent ones."[28]

The controversy in *Nelson* involved the putative right of a physician to prescribe contraceptives to married women when, in the doctor's judgment, the "general health" of a woman required them. The defendants, a registered nurse and two medical doctors, asked the court to interpret the two statutes to include the exception just noted. In rejecting this request, the court stated that it was obliged to follow the legislature's construction of the statute:

> Any intention on the part of the Legislature to allow such an exception as would advantage the present defendants is negatived not only by the absolute language used originally and preserved ever since but also, signally, by its repeated and

---

[27] Ibid., 862 (quoting *Commonwealth v. Allison*, 266, decided in 1917). In *Allison*, the Supreme Judicial Court dismissed a constitutional challenge to a Massachusetts law prohibiting the advertisement of drugs or instruments to prevent conception, stating that "the subject matter is well within one of the most obvious and necessary branches of the police power of the state."

[28] *State v. Nelson*, 861, quoting *People v. Byrne*, 686.

recent refusal to inject an exception. . . . Rejection by the Legislature of a specific provision is most persuasive that the act should not be construed to include it.[29]

To clarify the matter, the majority opinion in *Nelson* referred to the decision in *Lambert v. Yellowley,* where the Supreme Court of the United States ruled that the practice of medicine is everywhere subordinate to the exercise of the police power.[30]

Elsewhere, the *Nelson* court faced the appellant's contention that the anti-use statute was unconstitutional because it interfered with the "free exercise of conscience and the pursuit of happiness."[31] The court rejected this view, too, pointing out that a similar and equally unpersuasive argument might be made about laws against adultery. The court then noted that the easy availability of contraceptives and greater sexual permissiveness might lead to grave social consequences.[32]

Today, some might be tempted to describe the Connecticut policy as "patriarchal." But such a description would be misleading in at least two respects: first, as recent scholarship shows, a significant number of women legislators and activists in the state backed the policy;[33] and second, some British feminists in the late nineteenth century (when the Connecticut legislation was passed) also feared the social harms that might arise from the easy availability of contraceptives.[34]

The Supreme Court of Errors made its position known in *State v. Nelson* and adhered to it thereafter. Focusing on the unambiguous language of the laws, the interpretation of similar legislation by the Supreme Judicial Court of Massachusetts in 1938, and the unwillingness of the Connecticut legislature to make any exceptions to the law, the *Nelson* court advised opponents of the policy to direct their requests to the law-making body. "Courts may not by construction supply omissions in a statute, or add exceptions merely because it appears to them that good reasons exist for adding them," wrote Judge Hinman for the majority.[35] The court maintained that the judiciary must not interfere with the exercise of the police power if a piece of legislation has a "real and substantial relation" to the furtherance of public health, safety, and morals.

---

[29] *State v. Nelson,* 858–859.

[30] Ibid., 861, citing *Lambert v. Yellowley,* 272 U.S. 581, 596 (1926).

[31] *State v. Nelson,* 861.

[32] Ibid., 861–862; see the reference to *State v. Hollinshead,* 77 Or. 473, 477; 151 P. 710, 711 (1915).

[33] See generally David J. Garrow, *Liberty and Sexuality: The Right to Privacy and the Making of* Roe v. Wade (New York: Macmillan, 1994).

[34] See Susan Kingsley Kent, *Sex and Suffrage in Britain, 1860–1914* (Princeton: Princeton University Press, 1987), 104–105. On a related note, scholars sometimes suggest that the Connecticut laws were meant to enforce a tenet of Catholic moral theology, but all five of the judges on the *Nelson* court were Protestants. See Garrow, *Liberty and Sexuality,* 75–76.

[35] *State v. Nelson,* 858.

By now, a few things should be apparent. Without feeling obliged to describe all of its features, the judges in the majority in *Nelson* took the two-parent family as normative for society. And like most legislation, the Connecticut statutes presupposed that the law has the capacity to affect human behavior.

Critics might say that the anticontraceptive laws were a needlessly punitive measure for sexual peccadilloes. The laws were nonetheless meant to advance the well-being of children in the state. In ways tangible—the attachment of penalties on the use of contraceptives, for example—and intangible—such as allowing one's standing in the community to be diminished because of irresponsible conduct—the legislature sought to promote favorable domestic conditions for children in the state.[36]

Other states regulated contraceptives for essentially the same reasons. In the 1930s, a majority of the states restricted the distribution of contraceptives, with seven states banning any distribution. Roughly ten regulated advertisements and publications. At least five permitted information to be published only in standard medical works and forbade anyone but licensed doctors and pharmacists to dispense materials.[37]

The legislative strategy in Connecticut was admittedly conservative, and Connecticut was unique among the states in banning the *use* of contraceptives. But these facts do not justify the Supreme Court's decision in *Griswold*. On one reading, part of the attractiveness of our federal system consists in what former Supreme Court Justice Louis Brandeis called "laboratories of democracy," whereby different states experiment with different regulatory schemes to achieve policy goals.

Our federal system at one time allowed the states much leeway in setting their own priorities as they promoted various goods such as personal freedom, stable families, and the welfare of children. In establishing such priorities, legislators might have become aware of some difficult choices and of the public dimensions of much ostensibly private conduct.[38]

---

[36] Many of the nineteenth-century laws on contraception were part of a larger legislative project to protect children by eradicating vices such as indiscriminate sexual relations and the dissemination of lewd materials. See, for example, Carol Flora Brooks, "The Early History of the Anti-Contraceptive Laws in Massachusetts and Connecticut," *American Quarterly* 18 (1966): 3. This initiative was publicly supported in the 1870s by the presidents of Yale and Brown Universities and Amherst and Dartmouth Colleges, all of whom belonged to an organization known as the New England Society for the Suppression of Vice.

[37] Among other works, see Note, "Some Legislative Aspects of the Birth-Control Problem," *Harvard Law Review* 45 (1932): 723; "Recent Case," *Harvard Law Review* 50 (1937): 1312; and "Note: Contraceptives and the Law," *University of Chicago Law Review* 6 (1939): 260.

[38] In suggesting that states should have been allowed to establish their own priorities with respect to personal freedom and other competing interests, I refer to freedoms that lacked the express protection of the U.S. Constitution and the constitution of the particular state. My account of the federal system as an ensemble of laboratories of democracy is indebted

These comments about experiments in legislation are offered so that another aspect of this controversy may be understood. Some states were unwilling to change old laws, and such unwillingness was long considered a prerogative of the police power. This point deserves stressing, because by the 1960s, the two Connecticut statutes seemed fantastically outdated to some critics. Still, based on many years of judicial precedent, the state's legislators had ample reason to believe that the statutory scheme was consistent with the U.S. Constitution.

Why, then, did the Supreme Court in *Griswold* declare the two Connecticut laws unconstitutional? To answer that question, let us first review the facts of the case.

In November 1961, authorities invoked the two laws in the prosecution of Estelle Griswold, the executive director of the Planned Parenthood League in Connecticut, and C. Lee Buxton, a physician and medical director for the League at its office in New Haven. Griswold and Buxton advised married persons on how to prevent conception, and, following a medical exam, they prescribed contraceptive devices or materials for the wife's use. They were found guilty as accessories under statute 54-196 and fined $100 each.[39]

In his majority opinion in *Griswold,* Justice William O. Douglas listed a series of cases as evidence for his thesis that "specific guarantees in the Bill of Rights have penumbras, formed by emanations from those guarantees that help give them life and substance."[40] This was a roundabout way of saying that the Constitution includes more personal liberties than those expressly listed, including an unenumerated "freedom of association" and an unenumerated right of "privacy and repose."[41] To Douglas, the marital relationship must be understood as lying within these "zones of privacy," and the ban on using contraceptives was unconstitutional because it sought to "achieve its goal by means having a maximum destructive impact upon that relationship."[42]

Because Douglas never identified any goal of the statute, it is impossible to evaluate the last statement. Even if the law had the incidental effect of increasing the size of many families, someone could argue that having more children in a family tends to strengthen, rather than weaken, a marriage. Douglas's view seems to be that the marital bond will be strongest when couples are free to copulate without having to worry about preg-

---

to Justice Brandeis's dissenting opinion in *New State Ice Co. v. Liebmann,* 285 U.S. 262, 311 (1932).

[39] *Griswold v. Connecticut,* 480.

[40] Ibid., 484.

[41] Ibid., 483, 485.

[42] Ibid., 485.

nancy. The much greater availability of contraception and the parallel rise in the divorce rate in the last fifty years might be cited as evidence against Douglas's position.[43]

In holding that the two statutes were unconstitutional, Douglas denied that the Supreme Court was acting as a "super-legislature."[44] His disclaimer will seem disingenuous unless one keeps in mind his remark about the "destructive impact" of the law; by submitting that marriage falls within one of the constitutionally protected "zones of privacy and repose," Douglas made it appear as though he was not second-guessing the Connecticut legislature, but merely respecting a constitutional constraint on legislative authority.

This approach suffered from an overarching flaw, namely, that such a constraint was the Court's invention. Douglas's invocation of the constitutionally sacrosanct "zones of privacy" was thus the first of several ruses in *Griswold, Eisenstadt,* and *Carey.* In citing many disparate cases to lend credence to this idea and to invalidate the laws, Douglas may have been trying to convince himself that the Connecticut legislature had violated the Constitution. But his indifference to the state's interests and the settled jurisprudence of the police power set an intellectually shoddy precedent for subsequent cases in this realm.

The concurring opinions in *Griswold* provide more information than does the majority opinion about the goals of the Connecticut laws. From the concurrences, we can infer that Douglas was at least apprised of the purposes of the laws when the justices met in conference. Yet to my mind, none of the concurring opinions vindicates the putative right.

Justice Arthur Goldberg's opinion, which was signed by Justice William J. Brennan Jr. and Chief Justice Earl Warren, is a novelty in civil-liberties jurisprudence, relying on the Ninth Amendment as no previous Supreme Court opinion had. Goldberg and the majority agreed that the Connecticut law intruded upon the right of marital privacy, while

---

[43] My comment is offered as an observation, not an argument. It is nonetheless curious that Justice Douglas, married four times in his long life, presented himself as an authority on such matters. It is especially curious in view of Douglas's marital affairs, including an affair that took place around the time of *Griswold.* See Bruce Allen Murphy, *Wild Bill: The Legend and Life of William O. Douglas* (New York: Random House, 2003), and Richard A. Posner's review in *The New Republic* (24 February 2003).

Douglas's defenders might say that his opinion in *Griswold* must be read in conjunction with his dissent in *Poe v. Ullman,* 367 U.S. 497 (1961). This is an unsatisfactory response, since in both cases Douglas failed to consider the purposes of the Connecticut statutes. In *Poe,* the Court dismissed an appeal from three plaintiffs who argued that the Connecticut statutes violated the Fourteenth Amendment by depriving them of life and property without due process of law. The Court dismissed the appeal, arguing that there was not a justiciable legal controversy, since no prosecution had taken place.

[44] *Griswold v. Connecticut,* 482.

disagreeing about the right's provenance. Without rejecting Douglas's penumbral theory, Goldberg tried to ground the right in the broad language of the Ninth Amendment, which reads: "The enumeration in the Constitution, of certain rights, shall not be construed to deny or disparage others retained by the people."

Much of Goldberg's opinion examines the history and original meaning of the Ninth Amendment. His disquisition failed to win over Justices Hugo Black and Potter Stewart, each of whom rejected Goldberg's historical thesis and found its implications disturbing. Seeming to recognize the potentially vast scope of the Ninth Amendment and its possible abuse by the judiciary, Justice Goldberg tried to delimit its application. He denied that judges have a license to invalidate laws on the basis of personal predilection. Rather, he wrote, they are obliged to assay the "traditions and [collective] conscience of our people" to establish whether a principle or putative right should be deemed "fundamental."[45]

This method allowed Goldberg, or so he thought, to invalidate the Connecticut laws. He quoted passages from cases such as *Meyer v. Nebraska*, *Pierce v. Society of Sisters*, and *Prince v. Massachusetts* to defend his action. Since those cases involved the domain of family life—a realm, according to *Prince*, "which the state cannot enter"—Goldberg's strategy was superficially attractive, though ultimately misguided.[46]

In the end, Justice Goldberg seemed unaware of the problem with the test he proposed. Connecticut may have been unique among states in banning the use of contraceptives, but if Goldberg had focused on the com-

---

[45] Ibid., 493, quoting *Snyder v. Massachusetts*, 291 U.S. 97, 105 (1934).

[46] *Griswold v. Connecticut*, 495, quoting *Prince v. Massachusetts*, 321 U.S. 158, 166 (1944).

In *Meyer v. Nebraska*, 262 U.S. 390 (1923), the Court ruled that a state law forbidding the teaching of any modern language except English to a child who has not passed the eighth grade "invades the liberty guaranteed by the Fourteenth Amendment." In *Pierce v. Society of Sisters*, 268 U.S. 510 (1924), the Court denied that the State of Oregon enjoyed the authority to "standardize" children living there by requiring them to be educated in public schools. In *Prince v. Massachusetts*, the Court *upheld* the application of a state statute that prohibited any boy under the age of twelve or girl under the age of eighteen from selling newspapers and periodicals in public. The aunt and custodian of Betty M. Simmons, a nine-year-old girl, challenged the statute as violative of the girl's right to distribute religious literature under the Free Exercise Clause of the First Amendment.

Of what relevance are these rulings for *Griswold*? The problem in citing *Prince* as a warrant to strike down the Connecticut statutes is obvious, and we must note that Justice Goldberg quoted nothing more than obiter dicta from the case. *Meyer* and *Pierce* could be considered the controlling precedents, but there are difficulties. In my judgment, *Meyer* and its companion case *Bartels v. Iowa*, 262 U.S. 404 (1922), were wrongly decided for the reasons given in Justice Oliver Wendell Holmes Jr.'s dissent in *Bartels*. Finally, I reject *Pierce* as a relevant precedent for *Griswold* because the subject matter of the two cases differs so much.

mon aims of those states which regulated contraceptives, he might have dissented in *Griswold*.

I already noted some of the regulations in place when *State v. Nelson* was decided in 1940. About twenty years later, sixteen states regulated either the advertising of contraceptives or their sale through vending machines. Eight states prohibited all persons except physicians and pharmacists from distributing contraceptives. By reliable estimates, thirty to thirty-five states and the federal government had some type of birth-control legislation in force in 1960.[47] The judicial records in different states provide strong grounds for concluding that these laws had essentially the same objectives. Justice Goldberg was therefore mistaken in singling out the Connecticut laws.

The two other concurring opinions in *Griswold* contended that the Connecticut laws violated the Due Process Clause of the Fourteenth Amendment. Referring to the lengthy dissent he had composed in *Poe v. Ullman*, Justice John Marshall Harlan (i.e., the second Justice Harlan) argued in *Griswold* that the laws compromised fundamental values "implicit in the concept of ordered liberty."[48] To Harlan, the Due Process Clause of the Fourteenth Amendment "stands . . . on its own bottom," and it was therefore unnecessary to find an enumerated liberty or one of its penumbras in the Bill of Rights as a justification for striking down the laws. But like Justice Goldberg, Harlan furnished no satisfactory criteria that would circumscribe this doctrine.[49]

Of those justices who voted to invalidate the Connecticut statutes, Justice Byron White was the most solicitous of the state's interests. He assumed that the laws were linked to the policy against extramarital relationships, a "permissible and legitimate legislative goal."[50] His concurrence referred

[47] See "Connecticut's Birth Control Law: Reviewing a State Statute under the Fourteenth Amendment," *Yale Law Journal* 70 (1960): 322; Jack H. Hudson, "Birth Control Legislation," *Cleveland-Marshall Law Review* 9 (1960): 245; and Peter Smith, Comment, "The History and Future of the Legal Battle over Birth Control," *Cornell Law Quarterly* 49 (1964): 275.

[48] *Griswold v. Connecticut*, 500, quoting *Palko v. Connecticut*, 302 U.S. 319, 325 (1937).

[49] *Griswold v. Connecticut*, 500. Justice Harlan's dissent in *Poe* was divided into two parts. Regarding the constitutionality of the Connecticut statutes, the topic explored in the second part, Harlan wrote that they amounted to "an intolerable and unjustifiable invasion of privacy in the conduct of the most intimate concerns of an individual's personal life" (*Poe v. Ullman*, 539). Such laws therefore violated the Due Process Clause of the Fourteenth Amendment. Harlan owned that the state, out of concern for the moral welfare of the citizenry, could forbid certain sexual intimacies, including fornication, adultery, and sodomy. The Connecticut statute, however, went too far by its intrusion into the intimacy of husband and wife, which he referred to as an "unreasonable intrusion" (ibid., 552–553, 550). But Harlan's notion of an "unreasonable intrusion" was underspecified, mainly because he failed to ask whether the Connecticut laws had a rational basis and advanced public purposes.

[50] *Griswold v. Connecticut*, 505.

to the relevant decisions in the Connecticut courts, and he tried hard to understand the logic of the two laws.

Like Justice Goldberg, White cited cases such as *Meyer v. Nebraska, Pierce v. Society of Sisters,* and *Prince v. Massachusetts* to support his view that Connecticut had violated an unenumerated constitutional right. He characterized that right as being free from "regulation of the intimacies of the marriage relationship."[51] Because the Connecticut statutes regulated "sensitive areas of liberty," they required strict judicial scrutiny and could be justified only by a compelling state interest.[52]

Without saying whether Connecticut's interests were compelling, White argued that the ban on using contraceptives failed to reinforce the state's laws against extramarital relations. The sale of contraceptives in some Connecticut drugstores and the infrequent prosecutions led him to reason along these lines:

> Perhaps the theory is that the flat ban on use prevents married people from possessing contraceptives and without the ready availability of such devices for use in the marital relationship, there will be no or less temptation to use them in extramarital ones. The reasoning rests on the premise that married people will comply with the ban in regard to their marital relationship, notwithstanding total nonenforcement in this context and apparent nonenforceability, but will not comply with criminal statutes prohibiting extramarital affairs and the anti-use statute in respect to illicit sexual relationships, a premise whose validity has not been demonstrated and whose intrinsic validity is not very evident.[53]

Because the ban on the use of contraceptives was broad and had a "telling effect" on married persons, White concluded that it deprived persons of liberty without due process of law.[54]

White's opinion raises difficult questions. By most accounts, contraceptives were available in some Connecticut drugstores during the 1960s. Depending on one's viewpoint, this availability could have undermined the purpose of the two laws. Before *Griswold,* however, one commentator noticed that "since adultery and fornication statutes are largely ineffective because of the difficulty of detection and enforcement, prohibition of the use and sale of contraceptives may well be the most effective method of control."[55] Having accepted this as a theoretically valid justification for the anti-use statute, Justice White rejected it because of the "total nonenforcement" of that law and its counterpart.[56]

---

[51] Ibid., 502–503.
[52] Ibid., 503–504.
[53] Ibid., 505–507.
[54] Ibid., 507.
[55] "Connecticut's Birth Control Law," 322 and 331.
[56] For different medical reasons, doctors in the 1960s sometimes prescribed oral contraceptives to *pregnant* women, and such prescriptions were lawful in Connecticut. This practice

Looked at from this perspective, the controversy in *Griswold* might pivot on an empirical question. Did White accurately describe the situation in Connecticut? Recent scholarship reveals that enforcement was selective and that the state wanted its citizens to be aware of a standing threat of prosecution. That approach is hardly unique to this area of the law (think of speed limits), and White, who cited the decisions of the Connecticut courts in his concurring opinion, should have seen that the policy was successful in at least one regard: the ruling in the *Nelson* case in 1940 had kept every birth-control clinic in Connecticut closed for twenty years.[57]

Justice White's opinion suffers from another weakness, also evident in the opinions of Justices Goldberg and Harlan. In describing the Connecticut laws against extramarital relations as "a permissible and legitimate legislative goal," White said nothing about the enforcement of those laws. Upon reflection, they would seem as difficult to enforce as the law forbidding the use of contraceptives. Other members of the Court apparently forgot that enforcement of the anti-use statute was subject to the Fourth and Fifth Amendments. These oversights suggest that some of the justices in *Griswold* were influenced more by contemporary prejudices about individual freedom and human sexuality than by fidelity to the Constitution.

Some light on those prejudices is furnished by the American Law Institute's Model Penal Code on Morals Offenses from the early 1960s. In the drafts of this document, which was offered as a legislative template for states, scholars considered various secular goals that might be served by laws like the Connecticut statutes. Such goals included "promoting the stability of marriage [and] preventing illegitimacy and disease." Without offering any evidence, the authors concluded that "there is no reliable basis for believing that penal laws substantially contribute to those goals."[58] Another commentator, however, argued that some data showed that the laws were helping the state to achieve its goals.[59]

---

explains (at least in part) why some contraceptives were available in drugstores there. I thank Norman Fost, M.D., for discussing these matters with me.

[57] See, for instance, Garrow, *Liberty and Sexuality*, 78. See also the concurring opinion of Justice Brennan in *Poe v. Ullman*, 509: "The true controversy in this case is over the opening of birth-control clinics of a large scale; it is that which the State has prevented in the past, not the use of contraceptives by isolated and individual married couples."

In *State v. Nelson*, none of the three defendants was convicted. The case ended as a *nolle prosequi*, and the prosecutor warned that anyone who violated the law in the future should expect to be tried "in accordance with the literal provisions of the law" (Garrow, *Liberty and Sexuality*, 82). One prosecution and conviction in Connecticut took place in 1961, after North Haven police arrested Thomas Coccomo for distributing condoms to gasoline-station owners for retail sale. See Garrow, *Liberty and Sexuality*, 188 and 201.

[58] See Louis B. Schwartz, "Morals Offenses and the Model Penal Code," *Columbia Law Review* 63 (1963): 669, 674.

[59] See "Connecticut's Birth Control Law," 322 and 331.

Judging from their dissenting opinions, neither Justice Potter Stewart nor Justice Hugo Black was free from the prejudices of the day, but both men put them aside when analyzing the constitutional issues. The candor in the two dissents in *Griswold* is attractive, even if Black and Stewart were too quick to mock the Connecticut laws. Stewart called the anti-use statute "uncommonly silly," and Black wrote that it was as "offensive" to him as it was to his "Brethren of the majority."[60]

Black worried that in the majority and concurring opinions, policy preferences were masquerading as recondite knowledge. He came close to saying that those opinions abound in sophistry, since all of the language about "due process" and "unenumerated rights" was

> merely using different words to claim for this Court and the federal judiciary power to invalidate any legislative act that the judges find irrational, unreasonable, or offensive.[61]

Black aimed to instruct his brethren about the proper role of the judiciary through a history lesson. During the period from 1897 to 1937, the Supreme Court, relying on the theory of laissez-faire economics, struck down many regulatory laws said to infringe an unenumerated right known as "liberty of contract." By 1965, however, very few jurists defended the judiciary's role in supporting that controversial economic theory and the Court's decisions in cases such as *Lochner v. New York*.[62] Black worried that the Court was embarking on another journey that would prove to be as embarrassing as the "Lochner era" and would similarly call the Court's legitimacy into question.[63] To avoid that scenario, he urged the other justices to let the Connecticut legislature resolve the matters at hand, a call repeated in the conclusion of Justice Stewart's dissent.[64]

In sum, Black and Stewart believed that opponents of the Connecticut laws had two political options: repeal the laws through the legislative process or, less plausibly, amend the U.S. Constitution. To think that Black and Stewart stood alone would be a mistake. In the face of growing national criticism of the two laws, Connecticut's Supreme Court of Errors refused to yield, maintaining that judges lacked the authority to strike down these laws. That steadfastness might now seem to be an unforgivable

---

[60] *Griswold v. Connecticut*, 507 and 527.

[61] Ibid., 511.

[62] *Lochner v. New York*, 198 U.S. 45 (1905).

[63] *Griswold v. Connecticut*, 522–524.

[64] Ibid., 521 and 531. In *Lochner v. New York*, the Court invalidated a New York law that prohibited bakeries in the state from having their employees work more than sixty hours a week. Most scholars agree that the *Lochner* era ended with the Supreme Court's decision in *West Coast Hotel v. Parish*, 300 U.S. 379 (1937). Here the Court upheld a minimum-wage law passed in Washington.

obstinacy, but readers should try to understand how these jurists perceived their function.

Today, many persons are likely to say that the state's concern for the integrity of families and the welfare of children was several steps removed from the ban on contraceptives and lacked the immediacy of the claim to privacy within marriage. Critics will say that the reasoning of the *Nelson* court (and the Connecticut legislature) was too speculative, too hypothetical. Husbands and wives were asked to sacrifice part of the happiness of married life—for what?

These charges may have some merit, but they are often presented in a manner that fails to appreciate aspects of the legislation. People often forget, for example, that the legislators themselves were bound by the laws they passed. Precisely because duly enacted statutes in a modern republic bind everyone, legislators are presumed to consider the effects of proposed laws on themselves and those closest to them.[65]

The legislators might have known that contraceptives were available in some pharmacies, while still believing that the statutes served valuable public purposes. They may have feared that the easy availability of contraceptives would gradually weaken the family as a social institution and put children at risk. They may have told themselves that it was necessary to remain vigilant, lest one compromise lead to another. This viewpoint can hardly be scoffed at after *Eisenstadt* and *Carey* and the social changes since those cases were decided.

However remote the concerns of the Connecticut legislature may seem to a contemporary reader, I am convinced that the state's highest court read the Constitution correctly. Even critics of the two statutes, such as Justice Black and Justice Stewart, saw that the state's concerns were legitimate, that it was vested with the power to enact the laws, and that the laws violated no provision of the federal Constitution (or Connecticut's own constitution). Citizens who opposed the law could work to repeal it or, failing that, move to another state.

To some persons, the last suggestion might seem outrageous. But the notion is more consistent with the traditional (i.e., pre-*Griswold*) understanding of American federalism than the view espoused by seven of the justices in that case. Furthermore, the notion is still intelligible.

Consider the following. Today, anyone with moral reservations about prostitution is unlikely to settle in or retire to Nye County, Nevada. We may also assume that *some* persons—even in this permissive age—chose

[65] In my reading, I have seen no intimation or accusation that any Connecticut legislator during the years 1940 to 1964 flouted or circumvented the laws under discussion. The situation in Connecticut was thus morally distinguishable from that in the South, where the sham of "separate but equal" persisted for more than fifty years.

to move their family away from that county for the selfsame reason. On occasion, that decision must have been a large financial burden for such families, but the county's policy of decriminalizing prostitution must be recognized as an attribute of the police power (devolved to the county by the state as a constitutional prerogative of the latter). If that point is granted, then Connecticut's constitutional authority to prohibit the use of contraceptives should also be recognized, even if it led some citizens to move elsewhere.

Those persons who concede the legitimacy of the state's interests but who suppose that the two statutes did little to promote those interests must realize that the opportunity to establish the effectiveness of the laws was lost as a result of *Griswold*. Something similar happened in *Eisenstadt* and *Carey*. These two cases further reduced the likelihood that states in our federal system would function like the "laboratories of democracy" envisaged by Justice Brandeis. That is regrettable, because these decisions also disregard important interests of children.

REGULATING CONTRACEPTIVES: PROMOTING CHILDREN'S WELFARE BY DISCOURAGING SEXUAL PROMISCUITY

In view of the long history of the jurisprudence of the police power, the Supreme Court's decision in *Eisenstadt v. Baird* should have been easy to predict. That is, even if *Griswold* were correctly decided, the decision should still have been considered an anomaly. But *Griswold* soon came to mark a new era in constitutional law. Thus, when analyzed today, *Eisenstadt* and *Carey* could be read as stanzas in a judicial elegy to the police power and those "rude Forefathers" in our republic who once accorded it so much respect.

In the majority opinions in *Eisenstadt* and *Carey*, both of which were written by Justice William J. Brennan, Jr., the Court rejected the rationales for the statutes. The rationales should have been clear to Brennan, who was on the Court when both *Poe* and *Griswold* were decided. Brennan essentially said that the law is powerless to affect human behavior in this area and that unmarried men, women, and teenagers would have sexual relations regardless of the availability of contraceptives.

More than thirty years later, the surprising decision in *Eisenstadt v. Baird* still provokes speculation. The Court's failure to accept the Massachusetts law as a valid exercise of the police power might easily lead one to think that several of the justices simply acceded to the demands of feminists and civil libertarians. In a curious way, the Court affirmed "sexual freedom"—but without saying anything about sexual responsibilities.

The controversy in *Eisenstadt* involved that Massachusetts law penalizing "whoever sells, lends, gives away, [or] exhibits . . . any drug, medicine, instrument, or article whatever for the prevention of conception."[66] Passed in 1879 and attacked as unconstitutional in four cases in the state, the law was revised in 1966 to conform to *Griswold*. After the revision, registered physicians were permitted to administer or prescribe contraceptives to married persons, and licensed pharmacists were allowed to fill such prescriptions.

Even after the revision, the main purpose of the law—to discourage unmarried persons from having sexual relations—was still discernible. The law obviously did not succeed in discouraging all unmarried persons from having sex, but its defensibility as public policy did not depend on that.

In 1967, William Baird, a tireless and peripatetic advocate of birth control and abortion, challenged the constitutionality of the law. He sought to have it invalidated by displaying contraceptives during a lecture at Boston University and giving a young woman a package of Emko vaginal foam. Baird's suit took five years to resolve. Two years after his arrest, the Supreme Judicial Court of Massachusetts set aside the conviction for exhibiting contraceptives, holding that it violated Baird's First Amendment rights.[67] The same court sustained the conviction for giving away the foam, shortly after which the Supreme Court of the United States denied Baird's request for a writ of certiorari.[68] Sentenced to three months in the county jail, Baird then filed a petition for a writ of habeas corpus with the United States District Court in Massachusetts. That court rejected the writ,[69] but was overruled by the United States Court of Appeals for the First Circuit.[70] Thomas Eisenstadt, the sheriff in Suffolk County, Massachusetts, then appealed to the Supreme Court, whose decision was announced on 22 March 1972.[71]

The central holding of *Eisenstadt v. Baird* is that by treating married and unmarried persons dissimilarly, the Massachusetts law violated the Equal Protection Clause of the Fourteenth Amendment. In the majority

[66] *Eisenstadt v. Baird*, 440–441.

[67] *Commonwealth v. Baird*, 247 N.E. 2d 574 (1969).

[68] *Baird v. Massachusetts*, 396 U.S. 1029 (1970).

[69] *Baird v. Eisenstadt*, 310 F. Supp. 951 (1970).

[70] *Baird v. Eisenstadt*, 429 F. 2d 1398 (1970).

[71] The Court's volte-face on the merits of Baird's petition is strange and has provoked little commentary. In denying certiorari on 12 January 1970, only one member of the Court (Justice Douglas) thought that Baird's conviction raised a substantial question of constitutional law. Thus, when Baird's habeas corpus petition was heard by the Court in 1972—after the Court had noted probable jurisdiction on 1 March 1971—there was ample reason to expect a decision in favor of Sheriff Eisenstadt. Changes in the Court's composition cannot explain the turnaround, since Justice Harry Blackmun was the only justice who joined the Court between 12 January 1970 and oral argument in *Eisenstadt*.

opinion, Justice Brennan began his analysis by restating several relevant principles of law. The Fourteenth Amendment permits states to treat different classes of persons in different ways, provided that the classification "rest[s] upon some ground of difference having a fair and substantial relation to the object of the legislation." Classifications based on criteria "wholly unrelated" to the purpose of a statute are, however, forbidden by the Equal Protection Clause.[72]

As part of his argument that the distinction between married and unmarried persons served no legislative purpose, Justice Brennan tried to show that the purpose of the law was neither to deter premarital sex nor to promote public health. Having demonstrated this to his own satisfaction, he then asked whether the statute could be upheld "simply as a prohibition on contraception."[73] He said that it was unnecessary to answer this question because "whatever the rights of the individual to access to contraceptives may be, the rights must be the same for the unmarried and the married unlike."[74] Brennan then crafted an extremely broad reinterpretation of *Griswold*:

> If under *Griswold* the distribution of contraceptives to married persons cannot be prohibited, a ban on distribution to unmarried persons would be equally impermissible. It is true that in *Griswold* the right of privacy in question inhered in the marital relationship. Yet the marital couple is not an independent entity with a mind and heart of its own, but an association of two individuals each with a separate intellectual and emotional endowment. If the right of privacy means anything, it is the right of the *individual*, married or single, to be free from unwarranted governmental intrusion into matters so fundamentally affecting a person as the decision whether to bear or beget a child.[75]

The extraordinary sweep of this language is only one of several problems in the majority opinion. Equally troubling is Brennan's reading of the judicial record in Massachusetts, a selective, tendentious, and sometimes erroneous reading. Of the six noteworthy contraception cases heard by the Supreme Judicial Court of Massachusetts before *Eisenstadt*, Brennan mentioned five. His omission of one case deserves reproach,

---

[72] *Eisenstadt v. Baird*, 446–447.

[73] Ibid., 452.

[74] Ibid., 453.

[75] Ibid.; emphasis in original. Contrary to Brennan's assertions, the Massachusetts statute *was* meant to deter premarital sex and to promote public health. The judicial record in Massachusetts bears this out.

One scholar argues that the language here—in particular, the phrase "to bear or beget a child"—was deliberately chosen to "build a bridge between contraception and abortion." See Rosalind Rosenberg, "The Abortion Case," in *Quarrels That Have Shaped the Constitution*, ed. John A. Garraty, rev. ed. (New York: Harper Torchbooks, 1987), 370.

inasmuch as it qualified the holding in a case that Brennan treated as authoritative.[76]

The constitutional challenges to the law from 1917 to 1970 produced some ambiguity in the state's judicial record, and the Supreme Judicial Court of Massachusetts was less consistent than Connecticut's Supreme Court of Errors in its responses. Had Brennan attempted to explain this ambiguity, the errors in his opinion would be easier to forgive.

The first two contraception cases heard by the Supreme Judicial Court in the twentieth century were clear affirmations of legislative authority in this area. In *Commonwealth v. Allison*, the court upheld the conviction of Van Kech Allison, who was arrested for distributing birth-control pamphlets and advertisements to factory workers.[77] In *Commonwealth v. Gardner*, the Supreme Judicial Court rejected the argument of three physicians and a registered nurse that the law forbidding the distribution of contraceptives was not intended to apply to medical practitioners when prescribing them to promote the general health of women. The defendants then appealed to the Supreme Court of the United States, which ruled that the appeal did not present a substantial federal question.[78]

The ambiguity referred to above took shape in *Commonwealth v. Corbett* and *Commonwealth v. Goldberg*, two cases decided within a decade of *Gardner*.[79] *Corbett* and *Goldberg* are legal conundrums in light of the holding and language of *Gardner*. Let me first discuss *Corbett*.

Lewis Corbett was a pharmacist who sold condoms to a policeman. The condoms were in a package marked "sold for the prevention of *disease*" (emphasis added). After making the purchase, the policeman held the condoms as evidence for the prosecution in Suffolk County Superior Court. Corbett was convicted by a judge of that court (sitting without a jury) for violating the state law that proscribed the sale and distribution of articles "for the prevention of conception."[80]

In the Supreme Judicial Court of Massachusetts, the dispute in *Corbett* involved the meaning of the statute. The defense argued that the condoms

[76] The six cases were *Commonwealth v. Allison; Commonwealth v. Gardner; Commonwealth v. Corbett; Commonwealth v. Goldberg; Commonwealth v. Baird;* and *Sturgis v. Attorney General;* all are discussed below. A seventh case is of little importance since it merely applied the holding in *Commonwealth v. Corbett* to a similar controversy. See *Commonwealth v. Werlinsky,* 29 N.E. 2d 150 (1940).

[77] *Commonwealth v. Allison.* For a discussion of Allison's activities and prosecution, see Garrow, *Liberty and Sexuality,* 12. There are some inconsistencies in the different secondary sources that discuss this case.

[78] *Commonwealth v. Gardner,* 300 Mass. 372, 15 N.E. 2d 222 (1938), and 305 U.S. 559 (1938).

[79] *Commonwealth v. Corbett,* 307 Mass. 7, 29 N.E. 2d 151 (1940); *Commonwealth v. Goldberg,* 316 Mass. 563, 55 N.E. 2d 951 (1944).

[80] *Commonwealth v. Corbett,* 152.

were intended to prevent the transmission of venereal disease and that Corbett should be acquitted. Both the majority and the dissenting opinion expressed some uncertainty about the legislature's intention when it declared guilty of a felony anyone who

> sells, lends, gives away, exhibits, or offers to sell, lend or give away an instrument or other article intended to be used for self-abuse, or any drug, medicine, instrument or article whatever for the prevention of conception or for causing unlawful abortion.[81]

In his majority opinion, Justice Lummus interpreted the phrase "intended to be used" to apply to all three clauses above. Since Corbett did not know the purpose for which the condoms were being bought, Lummus vacated the decision of the county court.[82]

In *Eisenstadt*, Justice Brennan took *Corbett* to mean that "married or single persons [in Massachusetts] may obtain contraceptives from *anyone* to prevent . . . the spread of disease."[83] In fact, this characterization is too broad. The majority opinion in *Corbett* said nothing about who was permitted to distribute contraceptives to arrest the spread of disease; it only directed the lower court to acquit the pharmacist because that court had misconstrued the statute.[84]

More significant than Brennan's mischaracterization of the holding in *Corbett* was his failure to discuss the effect of the ruling in *Commonwealth v. Goldberg* on the scope of *Corbett*. In *Goldberg*, decided four years after *Corbett*, the Supreme Judicial Court of Massachusetts sustained the conviction of the proprietor of a "novelty store" that sold condoms, ostensibly

---

[81] Ibid.

[82] "There is reason for believing . . . that the words 'intended to be used' were in effect to be understood before the word 'for' in the two instances in which they are omitted in the text. They may have been omitted either because to repeat them would have made the wording cumbrous, or because the word 'for' by itself conveys the same idea of intent or purpose" (ibid., 153).

The sole dissenter in the case, Justice Donohue, wrote that the law proscribed the sale of certain articles based on their "character" and that the buyer's intention was immaterial to the legality or illegality of any sale. He added that "as a practical matter, under the construction of the language of the statute adopted by the [majority] opinion, it would be almost impossible ever to obtain a conviction under this statute" (ibid., 156).

[83] *Eisenstadt v. Baird*, 442 (emphasis added). Brennan repeated this assertion at 449 (writing that the Massachusetts law does not "regulate the distribution of contraceptives when they are used to prevent . . . the spread of disease") and at 451 n. 8 ("the same devices the distribution of which the State purports to regulate when their asserted purpose is to forestall pregnancy are available without any controls whatsoever so long as their asserted purpose is to prevent the spread of disease").

[84] Based on sources cited above, the Supreme Judicial Court seems to have acquitted Corbett because it believed that his judgment as a pharmacist was owed more respect than that of ordinary persons.

to prevent disease. The court stated that John Goldberg's wares had a purpose different from the one offered in his defense:

> The evidence in the present case warranted the inference that these instruments or articles were advertised by the defendant with an intention on his part that they be used for the purposes of preventing conception. Of the three cards and the pamphlets—all herein referred to as "cards"—two have the statement "Play safe—Use Jack's high grade disease preventative Rubber Goods." The other two bore similar statements. All of the cards bore stories or anecdotes of a vulgar nature, three of which referred to sexual intercourse, and of the three one referred to the birth of the child as a result of such intercourse. We think that it could be inferred that the instruments or articles were advertised by the defendant for use by purchasers to insure safety in sexual intercourse, not only from disease but also from . . . conception.[85]

The opinion for the unanimous *Goldberg* court finished by citing the Wisconsin case *State v. Arnold* in support of its decision—the same case cited at the end of *Commonwealth v. Corbett* to lend support to *that* decision.[86]

To reconcile *Corbett* and *Goldberg* is difficult. To interpret the latter so that it has no relevance to the former is more difficult. Justice Brennan made the more difficult task easy by ignoring *Goldberg*. It is nowhere mentioned in *Eisenstadt,* though it should have figured prominently there.

In the ruling by the Supreme Judicial Court of Massachusetts in 1969 on William Baird's prosecution, the majority opinion stressed the similarities between the evidence used to convict both Goldberg and Baird. The messages on Goldberg's cards were sufficient to conclude that the condoms were being sold to prevent conception. Likewise, by handing out the vaginal foam, admitting that it was a contraceptive, and inviting the police to arrest him, Baird gave the authorities enough evidence for a conviction.[87]

[85] *Commonwealth v. Goldberg, 953.*

[86] In *State v. Arnold,* the Supreme Court of Wisconsin upheld the conviction of a lessee of a gas station in Milwaukee. The defendant, Ewart Arnold, allowed a vending machine with condoms to be placed in the men's washroom, for which he received a commission on sales. A sign on the machine read "Sold only for the prevention of disease" and "Minors are prohibited to operate this machine."

Arnold was prosecuted for violating section 351.235 of Wisconsin's statutory code. That section forbade the advertising and display of any indecent article, defined as "any drug, medicine, mixture . . . article or device . . . used or intended or represented to be used to procure a miscarriage or prevent pregnancy" (*State v. Arnold,* 844). The court rejected Arnold's argument that the statute denied him liberty without due process of law. Regarding the articles in question, the court held that their sale in a public toilet by a mechanical vending machine gave sufficient grounds for inferring that they were meant to prevent conception, not merely the transmission of disease (ibid., 845, 846).

[87] *Commonwealth v. Baird, 579.*

Brennan's failure in *Eisenstadt* to discuss the *Goldberg* case and the reasoning of the Supreme Judicial Court in upholding Baird's conviction smacks of intellectual dishonesty. If all the relevant precedents are considered, the decision of the Supreme Judicial Court appears "eminently correct," to quote Chief Justice Warren Burger in dissent.[88] We can see that Brennan evaded the relevant issue by directing attention to the purposes of the statute, the subject I now wish to consider.[89]

Brennan's interest in the legislative purpose is understandable when we recall the jurisprudence of the police power. One possible way to invalidate the Massachusetts law—perhaps the only way—would be to show that it had nothing to do with public health, safety, or morals. If that could be shown, someone might then ask—as Brennan asked—whether the statute could be upheld "simply as a prohibition on contraception."[90] Here some persons might (wrongly) suspect that the law was based on theology.

On the question of public morality, Brennan rejected the idea that the law was meant to deter sex between unmarried persons. He reasoned in this way. Because fornication had been classified a misdemeanor in Massachusetts, the legislature must have had another goal in mind when it made distributing contraceptives a felony for all persons except doctors and pharmacists.[91] The different penalties for these two violations provided the evidence: whereas fornication was punishable by a thirty-dollar fine or three months in jail, the unlawful distribution of contraceptives could result in a five-year prison sentence. This disparity made it "hard to believe" that a regulation on distributing contraceptives was meant to deter sex between unmarried men and women.[92]

In Brennan's eyes, to assume that Massachusetts sanctioned pregnancy and the birth of an unwanted child as deterrents to nonmarital sex would mean attributing a wretched "scheme of values" to the state.[93] In striking

---

[88] *Eisenstadt v. Baird*, 465.

[89] On p. 449 of *Eisenstadt v. Baird*, Brennan wrote that the Massachusetts law does not regulate the distribution of contraceptives when they are used to prevent disease. He mentioned the decision in *Corbett* and wrote that it had been "cited with approval" in *Commonwealth v. Baird* (the decision of the Supreme Judicial Court of Massachusetts). But Brennan was guilty either of a large error or a deliberate misrepresentation, because the Supreme Judicial Court did not cite *Corbett* approvingly; it simply paraphrased one of the arguments made by Baird's attorneys. That paraphrase was immediately followed by a discussion of the *Goldberg* decision and its relevance to Baird's case. This is why Brennan's opinion appears intellectually dishonest. Even if Brennan (mis)took the paraphrasing of an argument made by the defendant's counsel for an argument made by the court, he should be criticized for failing to discuss the *Goldberg* case.

[90] *Eisenstadt v. Baird*, 452.

[91] Ibid., 449–450.

[92] Ibid., 449, quoting *Baird v. Eisenstadt*, 429 F. 2d 1398, 1401.

[93] Ibid., 448.

down the statute, Brennan imputed discreditable motives to the Massachusetts legislature. Again, the crucial premise in his argument was that unmarried persons will "persist in having intercourse," regardless of the law.[94]

Regarding public health, Brennan's view was more complicated. He agreed with Chief Judge Aldrich of the Court of Appeals that the law was not meant to be a public-health measure since it was originally characterized as a "morals law." The statute's placement in a chapter dealing with "Crimes against Chastity, Morality, Decency, and Good Order" and the *Gardner* court's refusal to exempt doctors from its operation were, for Aldrich and Brennan, dispositive.[95] Neither of these men took account of the words of Massachusetts Chief Justice Rugg, who in *Commonwealth v. Allison* wrote that the law was meant "in a broad sense" to promote the public health and safety.[96]

Curiously, however, Brennan proceeded to analyze the statute as if it were a health measure. On that supposition, he concluded that the law was unconstitutional because it was both discriminatory and overbroad: discriminatory in denying single persons access to prescriptions for contraceptives, overbroad in restricting to doctors and pharmacists the distribution of all contraceptives, even "harmless" contraceptives.[97]

Brennan chose not to elaborate on these two issues, and his only references were to lower-court decisions dealing with the Massachusetts law. In dissent, Chief Justice Burger noted that the statutory classifications pertaining to public health were ordinarily considered valid even when some harmless articles were found within the proscribed class.[98]

The analysis here reflects Brennan's narrow understanding of public health. Anyone who doubts the narrowness of this understanding should consider some of the likely consequences when a parent refuses to accept responsibility for a child. This is an ever-present possibility in our mobile society, as evidenced by the familiar story of the "deadbeat dad," moving from state to state to elude public authorities and avoid paying child support.

[94] Ibid., 452. Here, as in several places in his opinion, Brennan followed the reasoning of Chief Judge Aldrich, writing for the Court of Appeals for the First Circuit. In this instance, he quoted from Aldrich's opinion.

[95] Ibid., 450–451.

[96] *Commonwealth v. Allison*, 266. Since Brennan quoted from the *Allison* decision when considering the question of public morality, one wonders why he left unexplored the meaning of Rugg's words on the subject of public health and safety.

[97] *Eisenstadt v. Baird*, 450–451.

[98] Ibid., 469. Many cases could be cited in support of Burger's position. See, for example, *Purity Extract and Tonic Company v. Lynch*, 226 U.S. 193 (1912). Additional cases are cited there at 201.

As I argued in the last chapter, the suggested links between single-parent families and the diminished life prospects of children growing up in them are well known to politically literate citizens. The cycle of poverty, underachievement in school, a greater propensity to drug abuse and violence: all of these have been credibly hypothesized to be related to the breakdown of American families. Admittedly, some of these links are unlikely ever to be demonstrated in a way that admits of no uncertainty. Their plausibility, however, is a different matter, and in the traditional exercise of the police power, states were never required to show that the laws achieved a certain level of success in attaining the posited ends. So there were many good reasons for the Supreme Court to regard the Massachusetts law as a measure to advance the public health and safety (as well as public morality), as Rugg observed in 1917.[99]

Believing that he had shown that the law was not meant to further any purpose under the rubric of the police power, Brennan might have tried to explain what it was supposed to accomplish. He declined the opportunity that presented itself,[100] and instead of providing a statement on legislative purpose, he gave an audacious reading of *Griswold*.

By "audacious," I mean that he mocked the intelligence of his readers. He expected them to disregard the repeated references to the right to privacy in *Griswold* as an *associational* freedom. The right was said to be shared by wife and husband as a marital unit, not as individuals.

Brennan's revision of the right to privacy is what distinguishes *Eisenstadt* from *Griswold*. It also makes *Eisenstadt* indefensible as a statement of political principle. Although other scholars may have interpreted the case less expansively, the Court in *Eisenstadt* was telling the nation that all adult citizens had a constitutional right to consenting, nonmarital sexual relations, irrespective of the social consequences.

Since this is a somewhat controversial interpretation, I need to substantiate it. That task first requires us to take notice of Brennan's evasiveness when facing an important argument made by Sheriff Eisenstadt's attorneys:

> Appellant insists that the unmarried have no right to engage in sexual intercourse and hence no health interest in contraception that needs to be served. The short answer to this contention is that the same devices the distribution of which the State purports to regulate when their asserted purpose is to forestall pregnancy are available without any controls whatsoever as long as their asserted purpose is to prevent the spread of disease. It is inconceivable that the

---

[99] This point was developed by Joseph R. Nolan, the attorney for Sheriff Eisenstadt, in oral argument before the Supreme Court.

[100] *Eisenstadt v. Baird*, 452–453.

need for health controls varies with the purpose for which the contraceptive is to be used when the physical act in all cases is one and the same.[101]

As I have shown, the second sentence of this excerpt is an error, if not a misrepresentation. The holding in *Commonwealth v. Goldberg* belies the notion that contraceptives were freely available to adults in Massachusetts "so long as their asserted purpose is to prevent the spread of disease."

Notwithstanding this error (or misrepresentation), let us interpret the passage as Brennan wanted it to be interpreted. In the second sentence, Brennan is saying that unmarried persons have a "health interest" in contraception, an interest that is met if the "asserted purpose" of the contraception is to check the spread of venereal disease. The third sentence says that it is irrational ("inconceivable") for any state regulations ("health controls") on contraceptives to depend on the purpose of the contraceptive (that is, avoiding pregnancy or checking the spread of disease). Because coitus may lead both to conception and to the transmission of disease, it would be wrong for a state to place regulations on contraceptives (e.g., restricting them to married persons) when the contraceptives are used to avoid conception. That is, if an unmarried person's "health interest" in contraception is to avoid disease, and if that interest can be met (legally, according to Brennan) by asserting that the contraceptives are being used to stop the spread of disease, then the same considerations should apply to unmarried persons whose "health interest" in contraception is to avoid conception.[102]

Brennan's language is dense, his argument is convoluted, but in a roundabout way, he has argued (*contra* Sheriff Eisenstadt's attorneys) that the unmarried *do* have a right—presumably, a *constitutional* right—to engage in sexual intercourse. Why should anyone be troubled by that idea? The answer has to do with the facts in the majority opinion in *Eisenstadt*.

As we saw, Brennan argued that the Massachusetts law could not be defended as a valid health measure, since it violated the stricture against overbreadth—that is, it prohibited the sale of some products, such as Emko vaginal foam, which were deemed "harmless." Since Brennan placed so much emphasis on the characteristics of this particular contraceptive,

[101] Ibid., 451.

[102] Again, Brennan tried to demonstrate—unsuccessfully, in my view—that the Massachusetts law was *not* meant to deter premarital sex. Recall also Brennan's indifference toward the central legislative classification (i.e., married vs. unmarried persons) of the Massachusetts law. See, for example, *Eisenstadt v. Baird*, 450. Furthermore, Brennan avoided responding to the claim of the Supreme Judicial Court of Massachusetts in *Sturgis v. Attorney General*, where it submitted that the Massachusetts statute could be upheld as a regulation on "the private sexual lives of single persons," consistent with the state's authority to promote public morals (and for all the reasons adduced in the cases discussed here). *Eisenstadt v. Baird*, 442; *Sturgis v. Attorney General*, 260 N.E. 2d 687, 690 (1970).

we should do the same. In his dissent, Chief Justice Burger pointed out that Emko vaginal foam prevented pregnancy 70 to 80 percent of the time. What does this mean for Brennan's argument? Well, having assumed that unmarried persons will have sexual relations regardless of the law, and having further assumed that the need for access to contraceptives is the same for the married and the unmarried, Brennan was, by any coherent standard of moral argument, obliged to say something about a development that would seem to follow ineluctably from his premises.[103]

Owing to the predictable failure of Emko vaginal foam—20 percent of the time would be a conservative estimate—Brennan should have been expected to say something about the welfare of those children born of nonmarital relations. Would their life prospects in any way be affected by this condition? Could they expect to have lasting and stable relations with their parents? If their parents were only casually acquainted with each other and did not intend to marry—two possibilities mentioned in academic commentary on the "right to privacy"—would these children have the same opportunities in their lives as children with both parents at home?[104]

In fact, the opinion lacks any discussion of these matters. Its absence is as regrettable as Brennan's seemingly crafty elisions. Brennan derided the efforts of the Massachusetts legislature to fashion its own solutions to a set of real problems. His opinion exudes confidence in the Court's "enlightened" revision of the state law, yet it fails to mention that the key premise in its argument could have been tested in our federal system. In assuming that unmarried adults would have sexual relations irrespective of the law, and by interpreting the right to privacy so broadly, Brennan was assigning to chance the domestic circumstances of many American children. And by never broaching the crucial questions—What if contraception fails? What if the partners are strangers to each other? What if a parent is a stranger to his or her child?—Brennan made light of what morally serious persons would regard as significant interests of children. Therein lies the opinion's greatest harm.

Some persons might say that the issue is now moot with the refinement of oral contraceptives and the ruling in *Roe v. Wade*. Because of these changes, they might add that there is no reason for a woman to have a child unless she wants to, and that state governments should not try to influence the decisions made by unmarried adults about their sex lives. Along similar lines, these persons might insist that "even a fool knows how to use a condom."

---

[103] For a discussion of medical research on the effectiveness of vaginal foam, see *Eisenstadt v. Baird*, 470–471, and the sources cited therein.

[104] An argument for expanding the right to privacy to include "casual" sexual relations is found in Kenneth Karst's "The Freedom of Intimate Association," discussed below.

Let me concede there is some truth here. Many unmarried women and men have been and will be responsible in their sex lives and will never have to deal with a sexually transmitted disease, an unplanned pregnancy, or an unwanted child. (Abortion, of course, raises other questions.) As a statement of social life in the post-*Eisenstadt* world, this account of responsible sexuality seems true for a substantial sector of the American populace. But can *Eisenstadt* be justified on this ground and the bases put forth in Justice Brennan's opinion?

I think not. The problem is one of extrapolation. Apart from the other errors in *Eisenstadt*, Brennan was wrong to think that everyone in America would behave in the same manner as university students attending a lecture by William Baird.

One might admit that in a city such as Brookline or Boston, a law forbidding the sale of contraceptives to the unmarried may have seemed irrational because an illegal abortion was a common response to an unplanned pregnancy. (Recall that *Eisenstadt* was decided before *Roe*.) In such circumstances, Brennan may have been correct in thinking that *some* unmarried persons will persist in having sex regardless of the law. But Brennan really had no grounds for thinking that *all* unmarried persons—even in Brookline and Boston—would behave in this way. He therefore had no grounds for thinking that the most sensible course of action was to make contraceptives freely available to anyone wanting them.

We should nonetheless try to imagine some of the consequences of this policy. The ready availability of contraceptives could easily have been taken to mean that nonmarital relations had been "legitimized." Some men and women might have reached this conclusion without fully understanding how different contraceptives are to be used or without the resolve to use them unfailingly. These persons might have had grave reservations about abortion, and some women might have never sought one, even after it was declared a constitutional right. With little foresight, these persons may have accepted some of the social changes taking place, not realizing the full ramifications until they faced a fait accompli, such as a child without a father at home or diminished educational or professional opportunities for the new parent(s).

Because of these potential complexities, the Supreme Court would have done well to stay out of the matter. State legislators would have in all likelihood done a better job of making policy in view of local circumstances.

Let us now consider *Carey v. Population Services International*. Less significant than either *Griswold* or *Eisenstadt*, *Carey* deserves a brief review since it elaborates on the dimensions of the newly minted right.

The decision was predictable. With the rulings in cases such as *Roe v. Wade* and *Planned Parenthood of Central Missouri v. Danforth*, few persons could have expected the Court to uphold the New York restrictions on the sale of contraceptives to minors.[105] Those restrictions criminalized the sale or distribution of contraceptives to any person under the age of sixteen. They also forbade advertisements and displays of contraceptives, and barred any persons except licensed pharmacists and physicians from distributing contraceptives to persons over the age of sixteen. The suit was initiated by Population Planning Associates, a North Carolina corporation selling "nonmedical" contraceptives through the mail. After the federal district court declared the law unconstitutional under the First Amendment and the Fourteenth Amendment as it applied to nonprescription contraceptives, the State of New York appealed to the Supreme Court.[106]

In the majority opinion, Justice Brennan reaffirmed the idea of "constitutionally protected choices," including the choice of "whether to bear or beget a child."[107] This unenumerated right, also known as the "right to privacy," extends to choices regarding contraception, though the right does not preclude regulation. Brennan then introduced a new criterion: a state's regulations are permissible only when its interests are "compelling" and when the regulations are narrowly drawn to express only those interests.[108]

Using this standard, Brennan argued that restricting the distribution of nonprescription contraceptives to licensed pharmacists imposed a "significant burden" on the right of privacy. This restriction made contraceptives less accessible to the public, reduced the opportunities for "privacy of selection and purchase," and lessened the likelihood of competitive pricing that would benefit consumers.[109] Brennan next explained why none of the state's purposes in restricting the distribution could be considered "compelling." Borrowing some of the arguments found in *Eisenstadt*, he made three distinct claims. First, since the statute applied to "nonhazardous" contraceptives, it was irrelevant to any state interest in protecting health. Second, because pharmacists lacked expertise in nonmedical contraceptives, the restriction on distribution could not be considered a "quality control device." Third, even if the restriction facilitated the enforcement of other statutory provisions, the prospect of administrative inconvenience was an insufficient reason to justify an invasion of "fundamental" constitutional rights.[110]

---

[105] *Planned Parenthood of Central Missouri v. Danforth*, 428 U.S. 552 (1976).

[106] *Carey v. Population Services International*, 678–682. The district court case was *Population Services International v. Wilson*, 398 F. Supp. 321 (1975).

[107] *Carey v. Population Services International*, 684–685.

[108] Ibid., 686. This criterion was new in that it cannot be found in the majority opinions in either *Griswold* or *Eisenstadt*. But see Justice Goldberg's concurring opinion in *Griswold*, which Brennan signed.

[109] Ibid., 689.

[110] Ibid., 690–691.

On the prohibition against distributing contraceptives to minors, Brennan drew an analogy with abortion laws: if a state may not prevent a minor from terminating her pregnancy or require her to obtain parental consent before doing so—the holding in *Planned Parenthood of Central Missouri v. Danforth*—then New York could not categorically forbid the distribution of contraceptives to minors. Quoting from his opinion in *Eisenstadt*, Brennan rejected the idea that the sexual activity of minors might be reduced if contraceptives were unavailable to them, again expressing his reluctance "to attribute any such 'scheme of values' to the State."[111]

The majority opinion in *Carey* concluded with a discussion of the provision forbidding the advertisement or display of contraceptives. Brennan held that this provision, too, was unconstitutional. Even if advertisements for contraceptives would legitimize the sexual activity of unmarried minors, none were "directed to inciting or promoting imminent and lawless action and [were] likely to produce such action."[112] The advertisements therefore enjoyed the protection of the First Amendment's Free Speech Clause.

The decision in *Carey* was the Court's final blow in its thirteen-year attack on the sizable body of law relating to contraception. All of the substantive criticisms I directed against *Eisenstadt* apply with equal or greater force to *Carey*. In the latter, Justice Brennan may have sincerely believed that all minors would persist in having sexual relations irrespective of the law, but his view still represents judicial hubris. It is hubris because it disregards both the constitutional prerogative of state legislators and their judgment about particular conditions (including social norms) in a state. Today, the many problems associated with "children having children" are well known, but our policy options are restricted because of the *Carey* decision.

This point was recognized by dissenting Justice William Rehnquist in *Carey*. For Rehnquist, the Court had called its credibility into question by repeatedly second-guessing state legislators and revising policy:

> There comes a point when endless and ill-considered extension of principles originally formulated in quite different cases produces such an indefensible result that no logic chopping can possibly make the fallacy of the result more

---

[111] Ibid., 695. The majority opinion in *Carey* contained references to several studies by social researchers that cast doubt on the view that limiting access to contraceptives discourages adolescent sexual behavior. These studies might have had some merit, but almost all of them were completed in the mid-1970s, by which time the transformation in American (and Western) sexual mores was well under way (thanks in part to the Supreme Court). The results of the studies should therefore be accepted with a measure of skepticism. It is noteworthy that no such studies were cited in either *Griswold* or *Eisenstadt*.

[112] Ibid., 701, quoting *Brandenburg v. Ohio*, 395 U.S. 444, 447 (1969).

obvious. The Court here in effect holds that the First and Fourteenth Amendments not only guarantee full and free debate *before* a legislative judgment as to the moral dangers to which minors within the jurisdiction of the State should not be subjected, but goes further and absolutely prevents the representatives of the majority from carrying out such a policy, *after* the issues have been fully aired. . . .

That legislature has not chosen to deny a pregnant woman, after the *fait accompli* of pregnancy, the one remedy which would enable her to terminate an unwanted pregnancy. It has instead sought to deter the conduct which will produce such *faits accomplis*. The majority of New York's citizens are in effect told that however deeply they may be concerned about the problem of promiscuous sex and intercourse among unmarried teenagers, they may not adopt this means of dealing with it. The Court holds that New York may not use its police power to legislate in the interests of its concept of the public morality as it pertains to minors. The Court's denial of a power so fundamental to self-government must, in the long run, prove to be a temporary departure from a wise and heretofore settled course of adjudication to the contrary.[113]

Notwithstanding this critique, Rehnquist's prediction about a restoration of legislative power in this area now seems wrong. Perhaps there was a touch of irony in his concluding words, but we have few reasons to believe that the Court will reconsider any of the three cases examined here. Furthermore, because of the ubiquity of contraceptives, a restoration of legislative power would now mean very little. Today, it is doubtful that any state legislature would propose laws like those at issue in *Eisenstadt* or *Carey,* and it is inconceivable that any state would now try to prevent married persons from buying or using contraceptives.

The Supreme Court is nonetheless culpable. Not only did it ignore the sound advice of Justice Holmes—who regularly warned about using the "broad words of the Fourteenth Amendment" to invalidate legislation enacted under the police power[114]—but the Court also endorsed some widely held prejudices among liberal intellectuals, prejudices that have led different interests of children to be regularly disregarded. Lest there be some misunderstanding as to how *Griswold, Eisenstadt,* and *Carey*

---

[113] Ibid., 718–719. Regarding the social problem of "children having children," William A. Galston has identified three important personal factors relating to poverty in the United States—specifically, completing high school, waiting until the age of twenty before marrying, and getting married before becoming a parent. Only 8 percent of the married couples who do these three things live in poverty with their child or children, while 79 percent of the families who fail to do all three live in poverty. Galston's conclusion is discussed in James Q. Wilson, *The Marriage Problem*, 10–11.

[114] See, for instance, his opinion in *Noble State Bank v. Haskell,* 219 U.S. 104, 110 (1910).

contributed to that development, let me offer a few more comments on the right to privacy.

If we took the words of Justice Brennan in *Eisenstadt* literally, we might suppose that the Commonwealth of Massachusetts had launched a sinister plot against some of its citizens. The precise formulation of the right to privacy—in Brennan's words, "to be free from unwarranted governmental intrusion into . . . the *decision* whether to bear or beget a child"—suggests that one of the parties to the suit was coerced into becoming a parent. But if we put aside cases of rape and most cases of incest, women must be assigned some responsibility when they become pregnant. And except in rare and bizarre circumstances, men become fathers only as a result of their freely chosen copulative acts.

Thus, as formulated in *Eisenstadt*, the "right to privacy" creates moral ambiguity where none exists. That is, no one in *Eisenstadt*—not the unnamed woman who received the Emko vaginal foam, and surely not William Baird—was denied the freedom to decide whether to bear or beget a child. Only if one assumes that all persons are free—nay, constitutionally "entitled"—to engage in nonmarital sexual relations does Brennan's statement on the expanded right to privacy become intelligible.

Even if one makes that assumption—an assumption Brennan later denied having made[115]—there is a further problem. When read in context, the precise formulation of the putative right seems to reflect Brennan's view that all contingencies in the realm of "contracepted" sex have been eliminated, and that any person (male or female?) who uses a contraceptive (what kind? one device or several?) will be spared the burden of an unintended pregnancy or an unwanted child. The alternative reading (sketched above) is that Brennan simply assigned to chance the domestic circumstances of those children who issued from sexual relations between single persons when contraception failed. Either reading should provoke reflection.

RIGHTS BEYOND CONTRACEPTION: ADULT SEXUAL FREEDOM AND THE WELL-BEING OF CHILDREN

Justice Brennan's thinking in *Eisenstadt* is representative of a generation of liberal scholars in law and other disciplines. In this mindset, the happiness or subjective satisfaction of adults is presumptively more important

---

[115] In *Carey v. Population Services International*, Brennan denied that the Constitution had ever been interpreted to protect private, consenting (hetero)sexual relations between adults (694 n. 17). But it seems that other justices on the Supreme Court later came to accept the reading of *Eisenstadt* being put forth here; see my remarks on *Lawrence v. Texas* (2003) below.

than the needs of children. The interests of the young are often little more than an afterthought, and sometimes they are not even that.

Aside from the evidence adduced in the last two chapters, what supports this claim? Consider the work of Judith Jarvis Thomson, Kenneth Karst, and John Robertson, three scholars who have done much to advance the aims of contemporary liberalism. Sophisticated and thought-provoking, their respective contributions to moral philosophy, constitutional law, and bioethics nonetheless attest to my thesis.

Thomson's influential essay "A Defence of Abortion" might seem to have nothing to do with the welfare of children. Her goal is to show that even if a fetus is a person (which she concedes it is from a very early stage), aborting it may in many cases be morally permissible. The central conceit of the essay is likening pregnancy to the burden a person would assume if he or she were required to act as a "dialysis unit" for a stranger with a life-threatening kidney ailment.[116]

Thomson sketches the following scenario: you awake one morning to discover that you have been abducted by members of the Society of Music Lovers, and a renowned violinist had been "plugged into" your circulatory system so that it may remove all the toxins from his blood.[117] When first presenting this analogy, Thomson states that being forced to allow the violinist the use of your kidneys for nine months would be akin to having to carry to term a child conceived as a result of rape.[118] Later, she applies this analogy (and others) to pregnancies arising from voluntary intercourse. She returns to the question of rape and concludes that "unborn persons whose existence is due to rape have no right to the use of their mothers' bodies."[119]

Thomson then asks whether a mother who has voluntarily called into existence the unborn child can kill it, even in self-defense. She notes that many opponents of abortion have overlooked "the special kind of responsibility" that a mother might have for the child because of the mother's voluntary action.[120] Yet Thomson is unwilling to say that abortion is permissible only in the cases of rape and incest, inasmuch as

> there are cases and there are cases, and the details make a difference. If the room is stuffy, and I therefore open a window to air it, and a burglar climbs in, it would be absurd to say, "Ah, now he can stay, she's given him a right to the use of her house—for she is partially responsible for his presence there, having

---

[116] Judith Jarvis Thomson, "A Defence of Abortion," in *The Philosophy of Law,* ed. Ronald M. Dworkin (New York: Oxford University Press, 1977), 112–128.

[117] Ibid., 113–114.

[118] Ibid., 114.

[119] Ibid., 121.

[120] Ibid.

voluntarily done what enabled him to get in, full knowledge that there are such things as burglars, and that burglars burgle." It would be still more absurd to say this if I had bars installed outside my windows, precisely to prevent burglars from getting in, and a burglar got in only because of a defect in the bars. It remains equally absurd if we imagine it is not a burglar who climbs in, but an innocent person who blunders or falls in.[121]

From this analogy, Thomson argues that there are at most some cases in which the unborn child has a right to the use of its mother's body. Having likened the bars in the window to an unidentified contraceptive, Thomson reasons that if a couple has

taken all reasonable precautions against having a child, they do not simply by virtue of their biological relationship to the child who comes into existence have a special responsibility for it. They may wish to assume responsibility for it, or they may not wish to.[122]

Regardless of whether this is a satisfactory position on the morality of abortion when contraception has failed, Thomson misses an implication of the principle above. If an unmarried couple disagrees about whether to have or to abort the child, Thomson has seemingly freed the man from any duties to the child if the mother elects to give birth. Since contraception has failed, the man has "no special responsibility for the child," and he may turn his back to the child and the child's mother.

Thomson might wish to change the words in the passage above to preclude my interpretation of it. She may not have intended the principle to have the implication that I think it has. Nevertheless, her failure to consider this scenario is revealing.[123]

Kenneth Karst's widely cited paper "The Freedom of Intimate Association" tries to extend the principles of *Griswold, Eisenstadt,* and *Carey* in several different directions.[124] Here is an effort to secure constitutional protection for the one-night stand, for no-fault divorce, for bigamy—and perhaps even for sibling incest:

One reason for extending constitutional protection to casual intimate associations is that they may ripen into durable intimate associations. Indeed, the value

---

[121] Ibid.

[122] Ibid., 126.

[123] After completing this section, I became aware of a scholarly essay that criticizes Thomson from the same perspective but proceeds further in the analysis. See Keith Pavlischek, "Abortion Logic and Paternal Responsibilities," in *The Abortion Controversy: A Reader,* ed. Louis P. Pojman and Francis J. Beckwith, 2d ed. (Belmont, Calif.: Wadsworth Publishing Co., n.d.). Pavlischek's article originally appeared in *Public Affairs Quarterly* in 1993.

[124] Karst, "The Freedom of Intimate Association," 624.

of commitment is fully realizable only in an atmosphere of freedom to choose whether a particular association will be fleeting or enduring.[125]

Coerced intimate association in the shape of forced childbearing or parenthood [an allusion to the respective policies of Connecticut, Massachusetts, and Texas, before *Griswold, Eisenstadt,* and *Roe*] is no less serious an invasion of the sense of self than is forced marriage or forced sexual intimacy.[126]

The most obvious practical consequences of *Griswold* and its successor decisions is to free couples—and especially women—to express themselves through sexual intimacy without the "chilling effect" of the risk of unwanted pregnancy.[127]

Many freedoms, few duties: that is the tenor of Karst's essay, which assumes that the state's interest in promoting favorable domestic circumstances for children merits little consideration when the happiness of adults is at stake. In Karst's article, putative rights multiply at dazzling speed: there is a right to have children and a right to avoid having them; there is a right to marriage and a corresponding right to enjoy all of its benefits while being spared its burdens; there is a more general right to association, including the right to the formal status of marriage, and there is also a broad right to "non-association," to be secured by easy access to contraceptives, abortion on demand, and no-fault divorce.[128]

Finally, there is John Robertson's *Children of Choice: Freedom and the New Reproductive Technologies.* Building on what he calls "the presumptive primacy of procreative liberty"—a notion derived from the Supreme Court cases examined here—Robertson conducts a wide-ranging discussion of issues such as abortion, maternal-fetal conflicts, and collaborative (i.e., noncoital) reproduction. He is ready to allow single persons and same-sex couples the freedom to use noncoital reproductive techniques—including artificial insemination, surrogacy arrangements, and in vitro fertilization—without asking whether such arrangements are consistent with basic interests of children.[129]

Another problem is a surprising omission. In his discussion of sperm and egg donation, Robertson proposes minimal state regulation. His judgment is that "as a matter of public policy, the question of secrecy or dis-

---

[125] Ibid., 633.

[126] Ibid., 641.

[127] Ibid., 654.

[128] Karst's discussion of parents' obligations to their children is perfunctory and weak. He focuses almost exclusively on material support, as if the mother or father who gives a child the most ingots is necessarily the best parent. He adds that "most children want and need parental discipline," a remark that might seem to suggest a good number of obligations, but that has little meaning in context.

[129] See Robertson, *Children of Choice,* ch. 2, esp. 38–39, and ch. 6, esp. 119–120.

closure [of such collaborative arrangements] is best left to the couple to resolve."[130] In view of the relatively small number of children conceived through such arrangements, that policy might seem sound. But Robertson admits that collaborative reproduction is becoming more popular. Its popularity might therefore create genetic and social problems of a high order, if a man or a woman were to make multiple donations of sperm or egg. Robertson's failure to discuss the potential problem of inbreeding—identified as early as 1979 in the *New England Journal of Medicine*—bears an alarming resemblance to the oversights of Thomson and Karst.[131]

Many things might be said about the mindset being described. As a historical and philosophic assessment, the following statement from Philip Rieff seems especially pertinent:

> In the culture preceding our own, the order of therapy was embedded in a consensus of "shalt nots." The best never lacked binding convictions, for they were the most bound, mainly by what they should not do—or even think, or dream. "Thou shalt" precipitated a sequence of operative "shalt nots." . . .
>
> What is revolutionary in modern culture refers to releases from inherited doctrines of therapeutic deprivation; from a predicate of renunciatory control, enjoining releases from impulse need, our culture has shifted toward a predicate of impulse release, projecting controls unsteadily based upon an infinite variety of wants raised to the status of needs.
>
> Difficult as the modern condition may be, I doubt that Western men can be persuaded again to the Greek opinion that the secret of happiness is to have as few needs as possible.[132]

---

[130] Ibid., 123.

[131] On note 10 of p. 255 of *Children of Choice*, Robertson describes the protocol in sperm banks, mentioning that they now "distribute lists of donors identified by height, weight, hair and eye color, race or ethnic background, education, and even hobbies, from which couples choose." The problem of inbreeding would most likely occur in a small- or medium-sized town or within an ethnic community in a larger town. See Martin Curie-Cohen, Lesleigh Luttrell, and Sander Shapiro, "Current Practice of Artificial Insemination by Donor in the United States," *New England Journal of Medicine* 300 (1979): 585.

The authors of this article express their fears: "Using a single donor for many recipients may result in inadvertent consanguinity or inbreeding. This complication could occur if two people mated who unknowingly shared the same genetic father (i.e., were half-sibs), or if a recipient was inseminated with the semen of a relative. Either may occur accidentally, since the identity of the semen donor is almost always concealed" (ibid., 588–589). The problem identified here is not beyond regulation, though in some environments—especially small towns—regulation may be difficult. But Robertson's failure to mention this potentially grave problem is another sign of contemporary liberalism's inattention to children.

[132] Philip Rieff, *The Triumph of the Therapeutic* (New York: Harper and Row, 1966), 15–17. By "ancient Greek opinion," Rieff seems to be referring to Stoicism; by "releases from inherited doctrines of therapeutic deprivation," he seems to imply that we now live in a post-Christian culture. (Note the allusion to Yeats's "Second Coming.")

Rieff's words accurately describe the changes documented in this chapter, and he is probably correct in saying that there is no turning back. The Supreme Court characterized a host of urges and desires as needs, designated them fundamental rights, and reaffirmed this "scheme of values" in *Planned Parenthood v. Casey* and, more recently, in *Lawrence v. Texas*. Academic liberals have been nearly unanimous in endorsing the project.[133]

In the face of this seemingly irreversible transformation, it might be considered sour grapes to point out that the victory of Justice Brennan and his allies is less than complete. But looking around the nation in the last decade or so, one sees signs that the new constitutional freedoms coexist with new assertions of authority. Evening curfews for minors, parental liability statutes, and *federal* child-support laws all suggest that what was seized by one hand of the body politic has been contested by the other.[134]

In this chapter, I have tried to document contemporary liberalism's inattention to the welfare of children when they are less than fully visible in a legal or social controversy. In the next chapter, I consider other leading decisions by the Supreme Court in which the interests of children are more directly asserted. The opinions in those cases contain some striking inconsistencies in their characterizations of children. If those inconsistencies are not further evidence of liberal indifference to children today, they at least show that there is real confusion in judicial circles about children's moral and developmental needs.

---

[133] On the basis of *Lawrence v. Texas,* 539 U.S. 558 (2003), I submit that the Court now reads *Eisenstadt* as having created a fundamental right for adults to engage in consenting, nonmarital intercourse. (Unsurprisingly, the majority opinion in *Lawrence* says nothing about the possible or likely social consequences of this freedom.) If I am correct, this would vindicate my interpretation of *Eisenstadt* above.

[134] On parental liability laws, see "Oregon Drafts Parents in War on Teen Crime," *Christian Science Monitor,* 12 September 1995, p. 1; Naomi R. Cahn, "Pragmatic Considerations about Parental Liability Statutes," *Wisconsin Law Review* (1996): 399; and Rhonda V. Magee Andrews, "The Justice of Parent Accountability: Voices in the Debate over Expanded Parental Liability," *Temple Law Review* 75 (2002): 375. On curfews for children and adolescents, see "Successes Reported for Curfews, but Doubts Persist," *The New York Times,* 3 June 1996, p. 1.

The situation being described here is hardly novel. Recall Claudio's words in *Measure for Measure,* 1.2.126–128: "As surfeit is the father of much fast / So every scope by the immoderate use / Turns to restraint."

CHAPTER FOUR

Conflicting Images of Children
in First Amendment Jurisprudence

THE SUPREME COURT'S invention of a broad right to sexual freedom and its failure to discuss any responsibilities attendant upon its exercise show that jurists as well as political theorists can adopt a morally reticent outlook on matters of great public consequence. The analysis in the last chapter also raises questions. We might ask, for example, whether the Court has been justified in constricting the police power in other cases, especially when the law was used to advance other interests of children.

In this chapter, I examine some legal controversies in which the interests of children are more conspicuous than they were in the cases involving the "right to privacy." My goal is to document a curious inconsistency in the characterization of children in different First Amendment cases. For reasons that are intelligible—though, in the end, hard to justify—the Supreme Court sometimes characterizes children as morally and psychologically fragile, and at other times depicts them as essentially indistinguishable from adults. These characterizations have, predictably, affected the outcomes in some cases.

What accounts for this inconsistency? I shall argue that the conflicting images are related to different ideas about freedom espoused by some of the justices. The point will soon become clear, but an overview of the relevant constitutional issues is first necessary.

In the contemporary era, some critics have faulted the Court for mandating "strict separation" between church and state and for adopting a highly permissive standard for obscenity. The decisions in *Engel v. Vitale,* *Lemon v. Kurtzman,* and *Miller v. California* provoked much debate, but unlike the "right to privacy," these cases involve explicit constitutional provisions, rather than unenumerated rights. Those provisions are found in the First Amendment, which reads: "Congress shall make no law respecting an establishment of religion or prohibiting the free exercise thereof; or abridging the freedom of speech, or of the press."[1]

[1] *Engel v. Vitale,* 370 U.S. 421 (1962) (holding that the daily recitation of a twenty-two-word nondenominational prayer in the public schools of New Hyde Park, New York, violated the Establishment Clause); *Lemon v. Kurtzman,* 403 U.S. 602 (1971) (invalidating programs in Pennsylvania and Rhode Island that used state funds to reimburse parochial schools for the cost of teachers' salaries, textbooks, and instructional materials in secular

The rulings in some First Amendment controversies have affected children and educational policy throughout the country. In *Abington School District v. Schempp,* the Warren Court held that the daily reading of ten biblical verses in the Pennsylvania public schools was unconstitutional.[2] More recently, in *Reno v. American Civil Liberties Union,* the Rehnquist Court invalidated the Communications Decency Act, which criminalized the "knowing transmission" of indecent stimuli to a minor over the Internet.[3]

To understand these controversies more fully, we must review the origins and history of the First Amendment. Despite their differences on many matters of interpretation, nearly all scholars agree that the words "shall make no law" were originally meant to bind only Congress. State legislatures were free to restrict speech and establish a religion, provided that such policies were consistent with their own constitutions. At least four states had established churches when the Bill of Rights was ratified in 1791, and obscenity prosecutions occurred regularly in state courts for much of the nineteenth and twentieth centuries.[4]

The Supreme Court confirmed that the Bill of Rights applied only to actions of the federal government in *Barron v. The Mayor and City Council of Baltimore* and *Permoli v. First Municipality of New Orleans.*[5] A central theme of these decisions was adumbrated in the previous chapter: the government of the United States is one of delegated or enumerated powers, whereas each individual state retains all powers not delegated to the federal government or prohibited to the states. Thus, the Bill of Rights was understood as a statement of principles about the freedom of individual citizens in relation to the new national government.[6]

---

subjects); *Miller v. California,* 413 U.S. 15 (1973) (setting forth a new test for obscenity prosecutions, and sustaining a conviction for the unsolicited mailing of "adult" materials, including pictures of men and women displaying their genitals and engaged in sexual acts).

[2] *Abington School District v. Schempp,* 374 U.S. 203 (1963). In *Murray v. Curlett,* the companion case to *Abington School District v. Schempp,* the Court struck down a rule by the Baltimore Board of Education requiring the recitation of the Lord's Prayer at the start of each school day.

[3] *Reno v. American Civil Liberties Union,* 521 U.S. 844 (1997). "Indecency" was understood by the sponsors of the legislation to mean depictions or descriptions of sexual or excretory activities or organs "in terms patently offensive as measured by contemporary community standards."

[4] With respect to the former point, see Leo Pfeffer, *Church, State, and Freedom,* rev. ed. (Boston: Beacon Press, 1967), 141; concerning the latter, see Leo M. Alpert, "Judicial Censorship of Obscene Literature," *Harvard Law Review* 52 (1938): 40; David M. Rabban, *Free Speech in Its Forgotten Years* (New York: Cambridge University Press, 1997); and the cases cited and discussed in the next section of this chapter.

[5] *Barron v. The Mayor and City Council of Baltimore,* 7 Pet. (32 U.S.) 243 (1833); *Permoli v. First Municipality of New Orleans,* 3 How. (44 U.S.) 589 (1845).

[6] Despite the holdings in *Barron v. Baltimore* and *Permoli,* the original (unamended) Constitution did contain important prohibitions on the states. See, for example, Article I, Section 10 ("No State shall . . . pass any Bill of Attainder . . . or grant any Title of Nobility").

In the decades following the Civil War, the common understanding of the Bill of Rights changed, and the Supreme Court affirmed that most of the provisions were binding on the states. According to the most influential historical interpretation, this change was effected by the passage of the Fourteenth Amendment, whose framers and ratifiers wished to "nationalize" the Bill of Rights (i.e., make its provisions binding on the states). This theory of nationalization, also known as "incorporation," is accepted by most, but not all, constitutional scholars. Disagreements concern the precise intentions behind the Fourteenth Amendment, the soundness of subsequent decisions, and the binding force of *stare decisis*.[7]

Notwithstanding this debate, the Supreme Court nationalized almost all of the provisions of the Bill of Rights by the 1960s. That development helps to explain some disputes relating to the Establishment Clause and Free Speech and Free Press Clauses, but the most heated arguments are due to the abandonment of the traditional interpretations of their provisions.

Since the late 1940s, the central question of Establishment Clause jurisprudence has been that of "nonpreferentialism." This theory holds that the clause prohibits a state religion (or a privileged status for any religion or sect), while permitting government aid to religion on a nonpreferential basis. Proponents of nonpreferentialism believe that the government has legitimate reasons for promoting religion. They often cite its role in fostering personal rectitude and argue that the state should lessen the "double burden" of parents who feel obliged to send their children to religious schools while still being required to support public schools through local taxes.[8]

---

[7] Leading contributions to the debate on the nationalization of the Bill of Rights include Howard J. Graham, "The 'Conspiracy Theory' of the Fourteenth Amendment," *Yale Law Journal* 47 (1938): 371; Charles Fairman, "Does the Fourteenth Amendment Incorporate the Bill of Rights?" *Stanford Law Review* 2 (1949): 5; William W. Crosskey, "Charles Fairman, 'Legislative History,' and the Constitutional Limitations on State Authority," *University of Chicago Law Review* 22 (1954): 1; Raoul Berger, *Government by Judiciary*, rev. ed. (Indianapolis, Ind.: Liberty Fund, 1997); Michael Kent Curtis, *No State Shall Abridge* (Durham, N.C.: Duke University Press, 1986).

[8] Two early and influential statements in defense of nonpreferentialism are Edward S. Corwin, "The Supreme Court as National School Board," *Law and Contemporary Problems* 14 (1949): 3; and John Courtney Murray, "Law or Prepossessions?" *Law and Contemporary Problems* 14 (1949): 23. See also Walter Berns, *The First Amendment and the Future of American Democracy* (New York: Basic Books, 1976), 1–32.

For my purposes, it is unnecessary for me to say whether the Fourteenth Amendment was intended to nationalize the Bill of Rights. But in accepting its nationalization as a historical fact, I encourage readers to think about what the notion means for the Establishment Clause. That is, if the clause is essentially a jurisdictional statement—meant to define the relationship concerning religion between the federal government and the states—then perhaps the Establishment Clause cannot be nationalized. Edward Corwin understood the clause in this way; see "The Supreme Court as National School Board," 19. See also the concurring opinion of Justice Clarence Thomas in *Elk Grove Unified School District v. Newdow*, 542 U.S. 1 (2004).

The alternative reading of the Establishment Clause is known as "high-wall separation." It is based on the account found in *Everson v. Ewing Township,* a case involving the constitutionality of bus-fare reimbursements for parents of children attending private schools (all of which were not-for-profit parochial schools). In the majority opinion, Justice Hugo Black cited Thomas Jefferson's letter to the Danbury Baptist Association (1802) as support for the following propositions:

> The "establishment of religion" clause of the First Amendment means at least this: Neither a state nor the Federal Government can set up a church. Neither can pass laws which aid one religion, aid all religions, or prefer one religion over another. Neither can force nor influence a person to go to or to remain away from church against his will or force him to profess a belief or disbelief in any religion. No person can be punished for entertaining or professing religious beliefs or disbeliefs, for church attendance or non-attendance. No tax in any amount, large or small, can be levied to support any religious activities or institutions, whatever they may be called, or whatever form they may adopt to teach or practice religion. . . . In the words of Jefferson, the clause against establishment of religion by law was intended to erect a "wall of separation between church and state."[9]

Many scholars have criticized these remarks and the Court's reliance on Jefferson's letter, but the interpretation of the Establishment Clause put forth in *Everson* has been highly influential.[10]

The debates regarding the Free Speech and Free Press Clauses and obscenity jurisprudence have been equally intense. In a period of just over one hundred years, the Supreme Court discarded the common-law test in *Regina v. Hicklin* (1868)—"whether the tendency of the matter charged as obscenity is to deprave and corrupt those whose minds are open to such immoral influences, and into whose hands a publication of this sort may fall"—and then tinkered with several other formulations before settling on a new standard in *Miller v. California* (1973).

The Supreme Court repudiated *Hicklin* in 1957 in both *Butler v. Michigan* and *Roth v. United States*.[11] Although *Hicklin* is not mentioned in *Butler v. Michigan,* the Michigan statute had language similar to the *Hicklin* test. The effect of the statute, according to Justice Felix Frankfurter's majority opinion, was to "reduce the adult population [of the state] to reading only what is fit for children." *Roth* expressly mentioned *Hicklin* and left no doubt that it was being overruled.

---

[9] *Everson v. Board of Education of Ewing Township,* 330 U.S. 1, 15–16 (1948).

[10] On the influence of the *Everson* decision and its reliance on Jefferson's letter, see the opinions in *Wallace v. Jaffree,* 472 U.S. 38 (1985).

[11] *Butler v. Michigan,* 352 U.S. 380 (1957); *Roth v. United States,* 354 U.S. 476 (1957).

In *Roth* and its companion case *Alberts v. California,* the Supreme Court ruled that obscene materials are constitutionally unprotected, remarking that "all ideas having even the slightest redeeming social importance . . . have the full protection of the guaranties."[12] Elsewhere in Justice William Brennan's majority opinion, the test for obscenity was defined as "whether to the average person, applying contemporary community standards, the dominant theme of the material taken as a whole appeals to the prurient interest."[13] Brennan nonetheless stressed that "sex and obscenity are not synonymous." Obscene material appeals to a person's "prurient interest" in sex, but a sexual theme is "not itself sufficient reason to deny material the constitutional protections of freedom of speech and press."[14]

After *Roth* and *Alberts,* the Supreme Court continued to revise its obscenity standard before adopting a new one in *Miller v. California* in 1973. The *Miller* standard, still valid today, adjudges materials obscene if three conditions obtain:

> (a) whether "the average person, applying contemporary community standards" would find that work, taken as a whole, appeals to the prurient interest . . . ; (b) whether the work depicts or describes, in a patently offensive way, sexual conduct specifically defined by the applicable state law; and (c) whether the work, taken as a whole, lacks serious literary, artistic, political, or scientific value.[15]

Defenders of the *Miller* test often say that it is a defensible standard because of the categorical words in the First Amendment ("shall make no law . . .") and the nationalization of the Bill of Rights. These persons argue that the Free Speech and Free Press Clauses now require the protection of words, images, and publications that many others find offensive or revolting. For different reasons, most scholars who hold this view believe that courts are mainly responsible for offering such protection.

From one standpoint, these developments have significantly enlarged individual freedom. Democratic power has been scaled back. The range of individual choice—in literature, film, and less elevated media—is also much greater now than at any time before the Second World War.

Something similar might be said about the disappearance of religious exercises in public schools. If freedom is understood as unhindered choice among alternatives, then the absence of organized prayer or Bible readings in public schools could make a child or an entire community more receptive to other faiths and thus lead to an increase in religious liberty.

---

[12] *Roth v. United States,* 484.
[13] Ibid., 489.
[14] Ibid., 487.
[15] *Miller v. California,* 24.

To make this argument, we probably need to assume that children have some capacity to make informed choices and that their freedom is diminished if there is pressure to participate in such exercises. According to one perspective, the pressure need not be overt, and the Supreme Court's view has been that if a substantial number of a student's classmates participate, he or she may feel "coerced" to join in.

While proponents of "negative" freedom usually regard the greater number of choices as evidence of greater freedom, those who endorse the "positive" concept see things differently. They would suggest that, in at least some circumstances, the expansion of choice and the exercise of certain choices can lead to a loss of freedom. To this way of thinking, much depends on the choices facing a person and the correct understanding of "freedom."

The elements of this outlook were presented in Chapter One, and the same considerations apply here. Today, many of the allegedly private pursuits subsumed under the Free Speech and Free Press Clauses implicate interests of children. Boundaries have been set up to keep these pursuits, involving words and images, beyond the reach of the law and (at the same time) outside the purview of the young. Those boundaries, however, seem less and less secure. We shall soon consider the evidence, but let us first ask what risks are incurred if children are exposed to such stimuli.

In "Two Concepts of Liberty," Berlin wrote that "conceptions of freedom directly derive from views of what constitutes a self, a person, a man."[16] Many texts in political theory support this idea, and canonical texts often draw a fundamental distinction between adults and children. The distinction reflects judgments embodied in law, political theory, and everyday life about the capacities and susceptibilities of children vis-à-vis adults. Amidst the deep differences that characterize Western political thought, the amount of agreement on this set of issues is surprising.

To simplify, we could say that rationality and self-control must be cultivated in children since they are driven by appetites, including a large appetite for prompt gratification. Being so inclined, they are often blind to other matters, such as a proper regard for the welfare of others, their own latent rationality, and their own long-term interests. None of these concerns can be given its due unless children acquire a measure of self-control and reflectiveness, allowing them to see beyond immediate wants and inclinations.

What texts support these ideas? In book 1 of the *Nicomachean Ethics*, Aristotle writes that a young man "lives and pursues every object in obedience to passion."[17] A similar idea is found in book 4 of the *Republic*,

---

[16] Berlin, "Two Concepts of Liberty," 134.

[17] Aristotle *Nicomachean Ethics* 1095a, trans. John Warrington (London: J. M. Dent, 1963), 5.

where Plato observes that some young persons never become sufficiently rational (in relation to the spirited part of the soul), "while the majority do so quite late."[18] Centuries later, John Locke warned that giving a child "an unrestrain'd Liberty" before the faculty of reason is properly developed is "to thrust him out amongst Brutes, and abandon him to a state as wretched and as much beneath that of a Man, as theirs."[19] William Blackstone echoes Locke, predicting that the child who is denied education and culture will grow up "like a mere beast . . . [and] lead a life useless to others, and shameful to himself."[20]

These ideas can be further specified, as illustrated by Aristotle's remarks on the virtue of temperance in book 3 of the *Nicomachean Ethics:*

> Children in fact live according to the dictates of appetite, and in them the desire for what is pleasant is strongest. Now if that desire is not going to be obedient and subject to the governing principle, it will know no bounds. For in an irrational being the desire for pleasure is insatiable, no matter how many springs of gratification it may tap; and the exercise of appetite increases its innate urge, and if appetites are strong and violent they even drive out the power of ratiocination. They should therefore be moderate and few, and . . . just as the child ought to live according to the direction of his tutor, so also should the appetitive element of the soul follow the guidance of the rational principle.[21]

The pleasures Aristotle has in mind are those of taste and touch, which, because they are shared by other animals, "appear slavish and beastly."[22]

More than 2,000 years later, Hegel revisited Aristotle's moral pedagogy. For Hegel, "children are *potentially* free, and their life directly embodies nothing save potential freedom."[23] Education must therefore aim to raise children "out of the instinctive, physical level on which they are originally, to self-subsistence and . . . to the level on which they have power to leave the natural unity of the family."[24] Elsewhere, Hegel defines two pedagogical tasks as breaking down the child's "self-will" and eradicating "his purely natural and sensuous self."[25]

Given the Hegelian and Aristotelian accounts of children as sensuous, pleasure-seeking beings—accounts that are in important ways congruent with the views of Plato, Locke, and Blackstone—how should we understand a child's interest in being spared exposure to pornography and other

---

[18] Plato *Republic* 441a–b.

[19] Locke, *Second Treatise,* ch. 6 ("Of Paternal Power"), sec. 63.

[20] William Blackstone, *Commentaries on the Laws of England,* vol. 1, ch. 16 ("Of Parent and Child").

[21] Aristotle *Nicomachean Ethics* 1119b, trans. Warrington, p. 68.

[22] Ibid., 1118b, trans. Warrington, 65.

[23] Hegel, *Philosophy of Right,* sec. 175 (emphasis added).

[24] Ibid.

[25] Ibid., "Addition" to sec. 174.

indecent stimuli? An answer is found in Immanuel Kant's "Conjectural Beginning of Human History."

In this essay, Kant reads the Genesis narrative philosophically to understand our emergence from the natural state and to discern the meaning of the "forbidden fruit" and the fig leaf. One of Kant's claims is that covering the genitals was not so much a sign of shame (after an act of disobedience) as a manifestation of reason over impulse. He provides the grounds to argue that all persons—children *and* adults—have an interest in being spared exposure to pornography:

> In the case of animals, sexual attraction is merely a matter of transient, mostly periodic impulse. But man soon discovered that for him this attraction can be prolonged and even increased by means of the imagination—a power which carries on its business, to be sure, the more moderately, but at once also the more constantly and uniformly, the more its object is removed from the senses. By means of the imagination, he discovered, the surfeit was avoided which goes with the satisfaction of mere animal desire. The fig leaf (3:7), then, was a far greater manifestation of reason than that shown in the earlier stage of development [when humans consumed the "forbidden fruit," representing the first action not urged upon them by instinct]. For the one shows merely a power to choose the extent to which to serve impulse; but the other—rendering an inclination more inward (*inniglich*) and constant by removing its object from the senses—already reflects a certain degree of mastery of reason over impulse. *Refusal* was the feat which brought about the passage from merely sensual (*empfundenem*) to spiritual (*idealischen*) attractions, from mere animal desire gradually to love, and along with this from the feeling of the merely agreeable to a taste for beauty.[26]

If Kant is correct, then modern societies should be wary of pornography, and the adult who regularly consumes it jeopardizes a host of goods. The likely consequences for young persons are graver still, since such stimuli confirm or validate their innate tendencies. Pornography thus makes it harder for them to develop their distinctly human faculties (because pornography valorizes impulse as it disparages reason and jeopardizes "spiritual attractions") and to develop truly human relationships with the other sex (because its members are mainly seen as sources of physical gratification).

Some readers might dismiss Kant's analysis as being "unscientific" or "impressionistic." But such a response is unfair in expecting (or demanding) the same precision we find in mathematics or the natural sciences. As

[26] Immanuel Kant, "Conjectural Beginning of Human History," trans. Emil L. Fackenheim, in Immanuel Kant, *On History*, ed. Lewis White Beck (Indianapolis, Ind.: Bobbs-Merrill, 1963), 57.

Aristotle noted long ago, a developed mind expects only as much precision from an inquiry as the relevant discipline allows.

Here we should consider a contemporary perspective. We might compare Kant's views about the fig leaf, heterosexual desire, and the development of culture with the following statement by political theorist Harry M. Clor:

> Productions deserving to be called pornographic are characterized by graphic and detailed portrayal of sex acts without love or affection and with the result that the erotic life is reduced to its grosser physical or animal elements. The passion depicted and solicited is a thoroughly *depersonalized* sexuality, a desire for possession of bodies without regard for the personalities inhabiting them. Human beings, women especially, are vividly portrayed as objects to be used. The life depicted and celebrated in the pornographic world is devoted to uninhibited accumulation of a mass of pleasurable sensations.[27]

To the preceding, let us add that pornography rarely, if ever, makes persons mindful of the responsibilities attendant upon sexual relations. (If pornography had this quality, it would not be pornography.) Thus, when viewed by young persons, it typically makes them forget that the sexual act is often fraught with consequences, such as the creation of new life or the transmission of disease.

The worries of the philosophers quoted above are real. They believe that, without proper education, persons may remain in that state of unfreedom which characterizes childhood in our species. Lest any reader think that those worries had no bearing on public policy, similar language is found in leading obscenity cases from the nineteenth century.

That fact does not mean that the old standard for obscenity prosecutions must be restored. But the similar characterizations of children help us to understand the bases for state and federal legislation and the federal judiciary's adherence to the *Hicklin* test for decades.[28]

There is another matter relevant to the theme of freedom and human nature, and it has implications for debates about the Establishment Clause. Because many adults regard religious observance as vital to their efforts to lead morally upright lives, we can understand why they want their children to share such observance. In "Two Concepts of Liberty," Berlin admits that many people regard religion as a source of freedom, at times identifying it

---

[27] Harry M. Clor, "The Death of Public Morality?" *American Journal of Jurisprudence* 45 (2000): 33, 36. See also Clor's *Obscenity and Public Morality* (Chicago: University of Chicago Press, 1969), esp. ch. 6, "Definitions of Obscenity and the Nature of the Obscene."

[28] The similarities in the characterizations of children are even more striking if we recall some of the disagreements among thinkers such as Plato, Aristotle, Locke, Blackstone, and Hegel (e.g., on the morality of slavery, including the question of "natural-born" slaves, and the related question about the capacities and status of women).

with their "higher" and more rational selves.[29] This tendency worries Berlin, but his admission is noteworthy, not least because he recognizes the limited relevance of negative freedom for children's welfare.

Many liberals will accept Berlin's view that equating religious observance with any kind of freedom is potentially dangerous and perhaps dishonest. Yet the same liberals would shun the negative concept of freedom when other interests of children are at stake. If, for example, children were at liberty to skip school or to remain wholly unschooled—like the youths who frolicked in the Land of Toys in Collodi's *Pinocchio*—then most liberals would say that a spurious notion of freedom had gained currency. Such "freedom," they will point out, leads to a harsh servitude, as Pinocchio and his friend Lampwick discovered when they began to bray like asses. Because of such scenarios, liberals will likely agree with Hegel in regarding compulsory schooling as a form of "liberation."

If I am correct, then liberals should extrapolate from the example. They should be able to understand why some parents resist the idea that the public school should be a "religion-free" zone. From diverse perspectives, a purely secular moral code may prove feasible for adults who have developed habits of self-discipline and respect various boundaries in their lives. Yet the same secular morality may not only clash with the tenets of the parents' religion (or religions), it may in some instances harm children, especially if this moral code aims to maximize personal freedom, with freedom understood in the negative sense.

There is more to consider. The idea of achieving freedom through religious devotion or obedience to religious law has a long history in the West. This is freedom in the positive sense, a notion expressed in sacred texts (Gospel of John 8:23, "If you continue in my word, you are truly my disciples, and you will know the truth and it shall make you free"), poetry (John Donne's "Batter My Heart"), and hymns ("In the Lord's Service There Is Perfect Freedom"). Given this heritage, it is unsurprising that some parents believe that voluntary religious exercises in public schools may have a morally "freeing" effect on children.[30]

Although the Supreme Court does not use the terms "negative" and "positive" freedom, it has been required to characterize various needs of children to define the interests in some cases. The Court has also described the moral propensities of children. Such theoretical engagements help to

---

[29] *Four Essays on Liberty,* xliv. See also the discussion in Chapter One of this book.

[30] It would be an error to suppose (on the basis of the excerpts here) that the idea of becoming free through religious devotion or obedience to religious law is exclusively a Christian notion. Recall the remarks of Rabbi Harold S. Kushner quoted in Chapter One. It would also be an error to suppose that the moral teachings of a particular religion can never be justified independent of that religion.

explain some common judicial distinctions. The Court distinguishes between children and adults, remarking in one case that "the power of the state to control the conduct of children reaches beyond the scope of its authority over adults."[31] As evidence of that greater authority, we could cite the cases *Ginsberg v. New York* and *New York v. Ferber*. In the former, the Court sustained a prohibition on the sale of pornographic materials to minors even though adults were free to purchase the same items; in the latter, it designated child pornography a category of expression unprotected by the First Amendment.[32]

In *Ginsberg,* the Court ruled that it was constitutionally permissible for the State of New York to employ "variable concepts" of obscenity. The statute in question adjusted the definition of obscenity to minors, taking account of their susceptibilities and the appeal of certain materials to them. In the majority opinion, Justice Brennan wrote that "we cannot say that the statute invades the area of freedom of expression constitutionally secured to minors."[33] The Court added that the legislation was rationally related to the goal of safeguarding minors.[34]

As a general matter, the Supreme Court has maintained that a state's interest in protecting "the physical and psychological well-being of a minor" is "compelling."[35] Despite the gravity of these words and the holdings in *Ginsberg* and *Ferber,* the Court sometimes fails to take concern for children to heart. While recognizing a host of new and controversial First Amendment rights for adults, its solicitude toward the young has waned. By now this development should be historically intelligible. As with the "right to privacy," we see the Court accepting the idea of negative freedom and giving little attention to interests that can be subsumed under the rubric of freedom in the positive sense.

This imbalance is reflected in an odd inconsistency in First Amendment cases. When deciding a case in which children are "incidentally" exposed to pornography or other "adult" stimuli, the Supreme Court sometimes assumes that the young are morally resilient beings whose welfare is not going to be unduly affected by coarse language, gratuitous nudity, or hardcore pornography. In places, the Court seems to assume that children are little Stoics and just as adept as adults at "managing their impressions" and "averting their eyes." Yet when deciding cases involving young persons and a state-sponsored religious exercise, the Court has characterized children very differently, depicting them as frail and impressionable and

---

[31] *Prince v. Massachusetts,* 170.

[32] *Ginsberg v. New York,* 390 U.S. 629 (1967); *New York v. Ferber,* 458 U.S. 747 (1982).

[33] *Ginsberg v. New York,* 637.

[34] Ibid., 642–643.

[35] *Globe Newspaper Co. v. Superior Court,* 457 U.S. 596, 607 (1982).

likely to suffer real (though unspecified) psychological damage from the "peer pressure" to participate in the exercise.[36]

I wish to avoid a misunderstanding. I am *not* saying that the Court deems religion more harmful to children than the various indecencies they might encounter in our liberal society. I *am* saying that the inconsistency reveals the extent to which the Court wants to affirm the negative concept of freedom and shun the positive concept, at least with respect to noneconomic liberties. The inconsistency is telling, and it suggests that the Court is confused about some crucial matters relating to children's development.

In documenting this inconsistency, I show the Supreme Court's indifference to some legitimate interests of children. I also argue that the Court's recent obscenity jurisprudence is hard to defend on both constitutional and philosophic grounds.

Some readers might say that my critique of the new obscenity jurisprudence (culminating in the three-part test of *Miller v. California*) requires me to offer a new judicial standard for obscenity. Without accepting that duty, I will say that a good standard would leave a high degree of authority to determine obscenity to legislatures and the ordinary workings of courts and juries. (I say more about this topic in the next chapter.)

The plan of this chapter is as follows. In the next section, I provide a historical summary of federal obscenity jurisprudence until the middle of the twentieth century. This summary will show the judiciary's acceptance of the traditional understanding of the vulnerability of children when the *Hicklin* test was the constitutional standard for obscenity. During those years, various federal (and state) judges relied on the traditional account as a way of justifying the *Hicklin* test. At the end of the next section, I briefly look at the changes in judicial thinking that led to the new standard for obscenity in *Miller v. California*. Thereafter, I document the phenomenon of "incidental exposure" as discussed above.

Later in the chapter, I focus on the Court's psychological and moral characterization of children in a series of well-known school-prayer cases. Though I say less about school prayer than obscenity as a constitutional issue, I hope that even opponents of religious exercises in public schools will see the importance of the inconsistency described above. I conclude the chapter with remarks on the Supreme Court's practice of judicial review and the curious inconsistency that has emerged.

---

[36] By "incidental exposure" to pornography and other indecent stimuli, I mean the exposure that is likely to occur (and often does occur) when adults "consume" or "produce" such stimuli and children are nearby. As we shall see, the fact or likelihood of incidental exposure was acknowledged in all three of these cases reviewed later in the chapter.

OBSCENITY JURISPRUDENCE FROM 1868 TO 1957: AN OVERVIEW

From any standpoint, the *Hicklin* test was highly restrictive. When the Supreme Court repudiated the test in 1957, Justice Felix Frankfurter wrote that it had the effect of reducing "the adult population . . . to reading only what is fit for children."[37] Frankfurter failed to ask whether this may have been the purpose of the test; if that was its purpose, his remark would lose some of its force.

I raise this as a question, not as a criticism of Frankfurter, because elements of the *Hicklin* test remain unclear. Although the test was allegedly based on a bill passed in Parliament in 1857, doubts remain about whether Lord Chief Justice Cockburn's criteria for adjudging materials obscene were faithful to that legislation. Known as "An Act for more effectually preventing the Sale of Obscene Books, Pictures, Prints, and other Articles,"[38] the legislation empowered magistrates and justices of the peace to issue special warrants for the seizure and destruction of obscene materials. The term "obscene," however, was undefined in the legislation.[39]

In *Hicklin,* Lord Chief Justice Cockburn referred to the parliamentary act of 1857 and then gave his "test" for obscenity: "Whether the tendency of the matter . . . is to deprave and corrupt those whose minds are open to such immoral influences, and into whose hands a publication of this sort may fall."[40] In retrospect, *Hicklin* seems novel for singling out the most vulnerable members of society, since most obscenity cases in the United Kingdom and various American states referred to the corruption of public morals (or to the corruption of youth *as well as* "divers other citizens") as the standard.[41] Yet as early as 1699, a British court characterized obscenity as that which tends to corrupt youth,[42] and when *Hicklin*

[37] *Butler v. Michigan,* 383. See also *Roth v. United States,* discussed below.

[38] 20 and 21 Victoria, ch. 83 (25 August 1857).

[39] Questions also remain about whether Lord Chancellor Campbell, the bill's sponsor in Parliament, was being forthright in endorsing it. According to some sources, the Lord Chancellor opposed censorship, especially literary censorship, yet he may have felt that the legislation was necessary to stem the circulation of pornographic prints and postcards. See Alpert, "Judicial Censorship of Obscene Literature," 40, 50–52. See also Sidney S. Grant and S. E. Angoff, "Massachusetts and Censorship," *Boston University Law Review* 10 (1930): 36, 52–56.

[40] *Regina v. Hicklin,* L.R. 3 Q.B. 360, 371 (1868).

[41] See, notably, *Commonwealth v. Sharpless,* 2 Serg. & Rawle (Pa.) 91 (1815), and *Commonwealth v. Holmes,* 17 Mass. 335 (1821). See also *Knowles v. State of Connecticut,* 3 Day (Conn.) 103 (1808); *State v. Appling,* 25 Mo. 315 (1857); and *Willis v. Warren,* 1 Hilton (N.Y.) 590 (1859).

[42] See *Rex v. Hill,* Mich 10 W. 3 (1699), which is summarized in *Rex v. Curl,* 2 Strange 789 (K.B. 1727).

was decided in 1868, that notion found expression in the laws of at least two American states.[43]

Within ten years of *Hicklin*, American judges began citing the decision in a series of cases involving congressional power to ban obscene materials from the mails. In some of these cases, the test was used to clarify the meaning of the word "obscene" in congressional legislation such as the "Comstock Act" of 1873. That law made it a crime to mail any "obscene, lewd, or lascivious" writing, picture, or instrument. Contraceptives and abortifacients, and information about their procurement and manufacture, fell within this prohibition.[44]

During the era of the Comstock Act, most cases involving printed matter were uncomplicated. The central question—whether certain materials were obscene—was one of fact, not law. Juries decided whether something was obscene, lewd, lascivious, or indecent in the ordinary sense of these words. Because these words have similar meanings, judges sometimes provided dictionary definitions to the jury.[45]

Some readers may wonder how this federal legislation survived constitutional challenge. Granting that Congress has the power to establish and regulate a postal system (under Article I, Section 8 of the Constitution), readers might ask how this legislation was reconciled with the First Amendment. The answer adds further complexity to the history and philosophy of personal freedom in the West.

Before the twentieth century, the Free Speech and Free Press Clauses were understood only as prohibitions on the *prior restraint* or censorship of speech and the press. This was the common-law understanding of freedom of speech and the press, and penalties could be assigned to persons who

[43] As a result of the movement to enact comprehensive penal codes in the American states, the concept of a "common-law crime" began to disappear in this country in the nineteenth century. Legislation passed in Massachusetts in 1835 made it a crime to import or distribute indecent writings, prints, pictures, and figures. The test for indecency was "manifestly tending to the corruption of the morals of youth." See Grant and Angoff, "Massachusetts and Censorship," 147, 148 (the second of a two-part article), and *Commonwealth v. Tarbox*, 1 Cushing (Mass.) 88 (1848). A Texas statute, also passed before *Hicklin*, was similar to the Massachusetts law; see *State v. Charles Hanson*, 23 Texas Rep. 233 (1859).

[44] Federal cases that refer to the *Hicklin* test include *United States v. Bennett*, 24 Fed. Cases 1093 (1879); *United States v. Williams*, 3 Fed. Rep. 484 (1880); *United States v. Britton*, 17 Fed. Rep. 730 (1883); *United States v. Bebout*, 28 Fed. Rep. 522 (1886); *United States v. Clarke*, 38 Fed. Rep. 732 (1889); and *United States v. Harmon*, 45 Fed. Rep. 414 (1891). This is not a complete list. The Comstock Act was prefigured in the Tariff Act of 1842, and was regularly amended after 1873. See Rev. Stat. 3893 (1873); 19 Stat. 90 (1876); 25 Stat. 496 (1888); 35 Stat. 416 (1908); 35 Stat. 1129 (1909); 36 Stat. 1339 (1911); 18 U.S. C. 334 (1934).

[45] See, for instance, *United States v. Britton*, 733; *United States v. Bebout*, 28 Fed. Rep. 522 (1886), 523; *United States v. Clarke*, 733.

used these freedoms in ways detrimental to the public interest. The core issue was the "tendency" of one's spoken or written words. The law distinguished between the responsible and the irresponsible exercise of freedom, and persons were accountable for their words as well as their deeds.[46]

This history has gained nearly universal acceptance. Even contemporary scholars who follow Justices Douglas and Black in their "absolutist" or "exceptionless" readings of the Free Speech and Free Press Clauses concede that the "no prior restraint" doctrine and the "bad tendency" test lived for many years in American constitutional law.

The use of the "bad tendency" standard, including the *Hicklin* test, helps to explain the greater legislative and judicial solicitude afforded to children from roughly 1875 to 1930. Several cases illustrate the greater solicitude, though some persons today may be unable to identify the "bad tendency" in various controversies. The aims of the defendants might even seem praiseworthy—as they did to a small number of persons a century ago.

Yet it was risky to construct a defense on that basis, as *Hicklin* itself shows. In this case, the defendant was convicted for distributing copies of an obscene pamphlet, despite his professed desire to advance the public weal. Containing extracts from Roman Catholic theologians on the practice of auricular confession, the pamphlet attacked the practice for its alleged immorality. The full title conveys the author's grievance: *The Confessional Unmasked; shewing the depravity of the Romish priesthood, the iniquity of the Confessional, and the questions put to females in confession.* The publisher of the pamphlet was a group called "The Protestant Electoral Union," whose aims were "to protest against those teachings and practices which are un-English, immoral, and blasphemous, [and] to maintain the Protestantism of the Bible and the liberty of England."[47]

In upholding this conviction, Lord Chief Justice Cockburn showed that the pamphleteer's argument was self-undermining. If the author believed that some questions in auricular confession are immoral, he should have realized that reproducing them in a pamphlet would be equally odious.[48] And even assuming that the defendant had a laudable object in view (an assumption made solely for the purpose of argument), the court concluded that "the old sound and honest maxim that you shall not do evil that good may come is applicable in law as well as morals."[49]

---

[46] One case involving a prosecution under the Comstock Act in which the "bad tendency" test was invoked is *United States v. Harmon.* Two cases involving other legislation in which this test was used are *Schenck v. United States,* 249 U.S. 47 (1919), and *Abrams v. United States,* 250 U.S. 616 (1919). The use of the "bad tendency" test is discussed in several places in Rabban, *Free Speech in Its Forgotten Years.*

[47] *Regina v. Hicklin,* 362.

[48] Ibid., 371.

[49] Ibid., 372.

After *Hicklin,* this "sound and honest maxim" was followed in federal obscenity cases in the United States. Courts had different reasons for adhering to this principle, but one important reason was the fear that disseminating such materials would corrupt the young.

The application of the *Hicklin* standard in various federal cases shows public solicitude toward children. This solicitude came at a cost, and even before *Hicklin* was overruled, some considered it an intolerably high cost. But unless we are to assume that children have *no* interest in being spared exposure to such stimuli and that today's thinking on the subject is indubitably correct, a review of these matters seems imperative.

Three important federal cases involving the Comstock Act were *United States v. Bennett* (1879), *United States v. Clarke* (1889), and *United States v. Harmon* (1891). Each case was often cited in other jurisdictions, and each contains important statements about the nature of obscenity and the social interests at stake.

In the first case, Deboigne M. Bennett had been convicted for mailing a copy of *Cupid's Yokes, or The Binding Forces of Conjugal Life,* a pamphlet written by Ezra Heywood. The text called for "sexual self-government," while polemicizing against "scandal-begetting clergymen and bribe-taking statesmen." It provided information about birth control and contained reports of sexual misconduct, though, according to one scholar, variations on the theme of sexual "self-government" were more common than instances of sexual muckraking.[50]

After being convicted, Bennett appealed, requesting a new trial and asking that the verdict be set aside. He averred that the statute was unconstitutional, that the indictment was defective because it lacked specificity, and that he should be acquitted because he did not know that the pamphlet was obscene when mailing it.[51] In denying Bennett's requests, Circuit Judge Blatchford responded to each of the preceding points.

On the constitutionality of the Comstock Act, Blatchford cited the Supreme Court's decision in *Ex Parte Jackson* as controlling. *Jackson* involved the scope of congressional power to establish a postal system under Article I, Section 8 of the Constitution. In upholding Section 3894 of the Revised Statutes—which made it a crime to advertise illegal lotteries in the mail—the Supreme Court ruled that congressional power embraces regulation of the entire postal system. Accordingly, "the right to designate what shall be carried necessarily involves the right to determine what shall

---

[50] The *Bennett* case is discussed in Rochelle Gurstein, *The Repeal of Reticence* (New York: Hill and Wang, 1996), 66–67. Based on the analysis in the last chapter, readers should understand why Heywood's advocacy of sexual "self-government" was thought to implicate interests of children.

[51] *United States v. Bennett,* 1094–1095.

be excluded."[52] Near the end of its opinion, the Supreme Court likened the legislation under review to the Comstock Act, saying that it had "no doubt" about the constitutionality of either. In *United States v. Bennett,* Judge Blatchford said that the Supreme Court's views in *Ex Parte Jackson* "apply fully to the present case."[53]

Most of Blatchford's opinion in *Bennett* focused on the alleged defects of the indictment. Bennett claimed that the publication said to be obscene— or at least those sections singled out as obscene—should have been set forth *in haec verba* (i.e., verbatim) in the indictment. This claim was based on the right of the accused to be presented with a precise statement of the alleged offense.

After analyzing more than a dozen obscenity cases from different states, Judge Blatchford concluded that "no case in the United States has been cited where an indictment in form like the one in this case . . . has been held defective."[54] Because of the nature of the charges, Bennett's complaint was baseless:

> The indictment proceeds on the ground, that, if . . . the publication of an inde-
> cent character is so indecent that the same would be offensive to the court and
> improper to be placed on the records thereof, and that, therefore, the jurors do
> not set forth the same in the indictment, it is not necessary to set forth in haec
> verba the book or publication or the obscene or indecent parts of it relied on,
> provided the book or publication is otherwise sufficiently identified in the in-
> dictment for the defendant to know what book or publication is intended.[55]

Regarding the last of Bennett's three claims—that he should be acquit-ted because he did not know the publication was obscene—Judge Blatch-ford hinted that Bennett was playing games. The statute made it a crime for a person to "knowingly deposit" into the mail any material designated "non-mailable." This last term referred to pamphlets, pictures, prints and writings that were "obscene, lewd, or lascivious." But it was for *the jury* to determine whether something was "non-mailable"—again, in the or-dinary sense of "obscene, lewd, or lascivious."[56]

---

[52] *Ex Parte Jackson,* 96 U.S. 727, 732 (1877).

[53] Ibid., 737; *United States v. Bennett,* 1095.

[54] *United States v. Bennett,* 1097.

[55] Ibid., 1095. The Supreme Court of the United States affirmed the soundness of this view in *Rosen v. United States,* 161 U.S. 29 (1896). The majority opinion, written by Jus-tice John Marshall Harlan, relied heavily on Judge Blatchford's analysis in *Bennett.*

[56] "If the defendant knew what the book was which he was depositing . . . it is of no con-sequence that he may not have known or thought it to be obscene and so non-mailable": *United States v. Bennett,* 1099. That Bennett mailed the book in question was not contested in the trial court (ibid., 1101), but in other cases from this era, juries were also required to determine whether the defendant knowingly mailed the matter alleged to be "non-mailable."

Perhaps the most important aspect of the *Bennett* case, at least for my purposes, involved the trial judge's instructions to the jury on the test for obscenity. Judge Blatchford saw "no error" in those instructions:

> Now, gentlemen, I have given you the test: it is not a question whether it would corrupt the morals, tend to deprave your minds or the minds of every person; it is a question whether it tends to deprave the minds of those open to such influences and into whose hands a publication of this character might come. It is within the law if it would suggest impure and libidinous thoughts to the young and the inexperienced. There has been some comment on the fact, that, in many libraries you may find books which contain more objectionable matter, it is said, than this book contains. It may be so; it is not material here. When such books are brought before you, you will be able to determine whether it is lawful to mail them or not.[57]

A similar statement is found in *United States v. Clarke*. In this case, the defendant admitted that he mailed multiple copies of a brochure and other papers on the causes and treatment of venereal diseases. The opinion in the case, written by Judge Thayer, casts doubt on the defendant's status as a duly licensed physician, even though he identified himself as one. (The title of the brochure was "Dr. Clarke's Treatise on Venereal, Sexual, Nervous, and Special Diseases.") During the trial, Thayer informed the jury that both standard medical works and a doctor's diagnosis of symptoms (in response to a patient's letter) would be exempt from prosecution, though neither of those conditions had been met.

In instructing the jury on the requirements for a conviction, Judge Thayer first explained the notion of obscenity in its ordinary sense. He then invoked the *Hicklin* test as a way of clarifying the purpose of the statute:

> There is to be found in every community a class of people who are so intelligent or so mature that their minds are not liable to be affected by reading matter, however obscene, lewd, or indecent it may be. Then there is another large class to be found in every community—the young and immature, the ignorant, and those who are sensually inclined—who are liable to be influenced to their harm by reading indecent and obscene publications. The statute under which this indictment is framed was designed to protect the latter class from harm.[58]

Judge Thayer also touched on another matter relevant to the Comstock Act. To show that the pamphlets in question were neither obscene nor lewd, the defendant's attorney drew comparisons by reading aloud selections from Shakespeare, Suetonius, and the Bible. Thayer later instructed

---

[57] *United States v. Bennett*, 1102.
[58] *United States v. Clarke*, 734.

the jury that it was not being asked to decide whether any of those works are obscene or whether they would be excluded from the mails if the defendant were found guilty. Such works, he told the jury,

> taken in connection with their context, may be, or may not be, obscene or indecent. . . . Of course, so far as your experience goes of [sic] the effect that Shakespeare's writings, or any other author's writings, have had on the world, notwithstanding certain passages that they contain, you have the right to resort to that experience in determining what will be the probable effect of the publications involved in this case.[59]

Most of the themes in *Clarke* were also treated in *United States v. Harmon* [sic], a case of some notoriety. Moses Harman was the editor and publisher of a newspaper known as *Lucifer, the Light Bearer*. Printed in Valley Falls, Kansas, the newspaper had about 1,500 subscribers throughout the United States. The edition of the newspaper dated 14 February 1890 included an article purportedly written by "Richard V. O'Neill, M.D.," of New York City. The article was an account of dark pathologies in family life, such as spousal abuse, homosexual incest, and bestiality, "each described with an aura of scientific detachment though replete with sensational details."[60]

In his opinion in *Harmon*, Judge Phillips cited the *Hicklin* test while giving signs of dissatisfaction with it. The following passage, for example, acknowledges the presence of children in society, but the principle hinted at below appears to be some distance from *Hicklin*:

> Laws of this character are made for society in the aggregate, and not in particular. So, while there may be individuals and societies of men and women of peculiar notions or idiosyncrasies, whose moral sense would neither be depraved nor offended by the publication now under consideration, yet the exceptional sensibility, or want of sensibility, of such cannot be allowed as a standard by which its obscenity or indecency is to be tested. Rather, . . . the test . . . [is:] What is its probable, reasonable effect on the sense of decency . . . of society, extending to the family, made up of men and women, young boys and girls?[61]

---

[59] Ibid., 735. In response to a question from the jury foreman, Judge Thayer answered that, if the effect of the material "as a whole" would be to deprave and corrupt the minds of those into whose hands it might fall and whose minds are open to such influences, the material should be adjudged obscene. In the end, it was immaterial whether such effect "is produced by single passages or portions of the pamphlets and circulars, or by many passages or portions" (ibid., 736).

[60] Gurstein, *The Repeal of Reticence*, 75.

[61] *United States v. Harmon*, 417. This passage appears on the same page as the paragraph in which the *Hicklin* test was cited.

Even with a less restrictive standard, the article was grossly offensive to public decency and modesty. Judge Phillips added that

> it is not too much to say that no ordinary mind can subject itself to the repeated reading and contemplation of such subjects and language without the risk of becoming indurated to all sense of modesty in speech and chastity in thought. The appetite for such literature increases with the feeding. The more it is pandered to, the more insatiable its craving for something yet more vicious in taste.[62]

Judge Phillips also needed to determine whether Harman's motives should be grounds for exonerating him or reducing his punishment. He decided against such leniency, reasoning that, for certain offenses, the intention could be inferred from the act. Thus, although Harman may have published the article to direct attention to genuine social problems (as a precondition to solving them), its coarse language and prurient tone revealed other, discreditable motives.

Even if Harman acted in good faith and considered himself a social reformer, his views had disturbing implications:

> In short, the proposition is that a man can do no public wrong who believes that what he does is for the ultimate public good. The underlying vice of all this character of argument is that it leaves out of view the existence of the social compact, and the idea of government by law. If . . . there were no arbiter but the individual conscience of the actor to determine whether the means are justifiable, homicide, infanticide, pillage, and incontinence might run riot.[63]

Judge Phillips was not the first jurist to express such a fear, and other federal judges responded similarly when defendants asserted the purity of their motives and argued that they were heeding the demands of "conscience" in these matters.[64]

As noted, *Bennett, Clarke,* and *Harmon* were important federal cases. In different respects, they were also representative cases. Defendants in at

---

[62] Ibid., 418. Judge Phillips's dissatisfaction with the *Hicklin* test is evident in a few places in his opinion, but the less restrictive standard that was apparently applied in *Harmon* might have been due to something else. By mutual agreement, the federal government and the defendant chose not to have a jury trial, leaving Judge Phillips to try all the relevant matters of fact and law. Because of that development, Judge Phillips felt that "the court" should not evaluate the facts "as a judge," but should "try to reflect in its findings the common experience, observation, and judgment of the jury of average intelligence" (ibid., 418).

[63] Ibid., 422.

[64] Despite being the sole trier of law and fact in the case, Judge Phillips praised the institution of the jury, commenting that it was "assumed to be the best and truest exponents of the public judgment of the common sense" (ibid., 418). His perspective should be kept in mind, given subsequent developments in obscenity jurisprudence, contemporary liberalism's endorsement of those developments, and its wariness of "the public judgment of the common sense."

least six prosecutions under the Comstock Act charged that the indictment was defective because it lacked specificity.[65] Other defendants said that they did not know the material in question was obscene and that they should therefore be acquitted.[66] Finally, despite the decision of a unanimous Supreme Court in *Ex Parte Jackson*, still others attacked the constitutionality of the Comstock Act.[67]

I have pointed out these commonalties in federal litigation, even though this chapter is not meant to be a comprehensive history of obscenity law. Thus, readers who are interested in the many factors—social, political, intellectual—that led to the repudiation of the *Hicklin* test by the Supreme Court in 1957 must look elsewhere for the full story. Let me, however, briefly describe developments in the federal courts from about 1910 to 1957.[68]

As the opinion by Judge Phillips in *Harmon* suggests, some federal judges were critical of the *Hicklin* standard. One important and widely discussed critique was developed by Judge Learned Hand in *United States v. Kennerley* in 1913. This case involved a prosecution against Mitchell Kennerley, a publisher, for sending the novel *Hagar Revelly* through the mail. Kennerley was convicted, and Judge Hand overruled Kennerley's demurrer to the indictment (i.e., the conviction was declared valid).

In his opinion, Judge Hand wrote that the *Hicklin* test had been "accepted by the lower federal courts until it would be no longer proper for me to disregard it."[69] But Hand regretted that he was obliged to apply *Hicklin*, asking,

Should not the word "obscene" be allowed to indicate the present critical point in the compromise between candor and shame at which the community may have arrived here and now? If letters must, like other kinds of conduct, be subject to the social sense of what is right, it would seem that a jury in each case establish the standard much as they do in cases of negligence. To put thought in leash to the average conscience of the time is perhaps tolerable, but to fetter it by the necessities of the lowest and least capable seems a fatal policy.[70]

[65] Besides *United States v. Bennett*, see *United States v. Foote*, 25 Fed. Cases 1140 (1876); *Grimm v. United States*, 156 U.S. 604 (1895); *Rosen v. United States; Price v. United States*, 165 U.S. 311 (1897); and *Tyomies Publishing Co. v. United States*, 211 Fed. Rep. 385 (1914).

[66] See, for instance, *Rosen v. United States* and *Price v. United States*. The "good motives" argument and variations thereof were also made in other cases, e.g., *Knowles v. United States*, 170 Fed. Rep. 409 (1909), and *Lynch v. United States*, 285 Fed Rep. 163 (1922).

[67] See, for example, *Knowles v. United States* and *Tyomies Publishing Co. v. United States*.

[68] A concise history of obscenity jurisprudence from *Hicklin* to *Roth* is found in Clor, *Obscenity and Public Morality*, ch. 1.

[69] *United States v. Kennerley*, 209 Fed. Rep. 119, 120 (1913).

[70] Ibid., 121.

Within twenty years, more dissatisfaction with *Hicklin* was evident. In 1930, the United States Court of Appeals for the Second Circuit ruled that Mary Dennett's pamphlet *The Sex Side of Life* could not be banned from the mails. The defendant, a mother of two boys, wrote the pamphlet because she found existing treatments of the subject inadequate. Organizations such as the YMCA and the YWCA and the public-health departments of different states then ordered the pamphlet from Dennett.[71]

In overruling Dennett's conviction, Judge Augustus Hand voiced no doubts about the constitutionality of the Comstock Act. But the act was not intended to interfere with "serious instruction" regarding human sexuality, unless "the terms in which the information is conveyed are clearly indecent."[72] Judge Hand saw that the work "might arouse sex impulses" in its intended audience, but that was not its "general object."[73]

These developments within the Second Circuit reached their culmination in 1936. That year, in *United States v. Levine*, Judge Learned Hand declared that *Hicklin* was no longer valid within that circuit:

> The standard must be the likelihood that the work will so much arouse the salacity of the reader to whom it is sent as to outweigh any literary, scientific, or other merits it may have in the reader's hands; of this the jury is the arbiter.[74]

The developments just described all took place within the federal courts. Recall that before the Free Speech and Free Press Clauses were "incorporated," each individual state had the authority to pass its own laws relating to obscenity, consistent with its own constitution. *Hicklin* was cited in state obscenity trials, and, according to Leo Alpert, a modified version of the test was applied in New York and Massachusetts, the only two states in which prosecutions for obscene *literature* occurred.[75] Such prosecutions—for Theodore Dreiser's *American Tragedy,* D. H. Lawrence's *Lady Chatterly's Lover,* and Gustave Flaubert's *November,* among others—are now infamous. But it was only after "incorporation" and the

---

[71] *United States v. Dennett,* 39 Fed. Rep. 2d 564 (1930).

[72] Ibid., 569.

[73] "The statute we have to construe was never thought to bar from the mails everything which *might* stimulate sex impulses. If so, much chaste poetry and fiction, as well as many useful medical works would be under the ban. Like everything else, this law must be construed reasonably with a view to the general objects aimed at" (ibid., 568–569).

[74] *United States v. Levine,* 83 F 2d 156, 158 (1936). This case involved a prosecution for sending obscene advertisements through the mail. The advertisements were for books such as *Secret Museum of Anthropology* (containing photos of nude women in remote corners of the world), *Crossways of Sex* (allegedly a scientific treatise on sexual pathologies), and *Black Lust* (an erotic novel about an English girl captured at the fall of Khartoum and then kept in a harem).

[75] Alpert, "Judicial Censorship of Obscene Literature," 53.

Roth decision in 1957 that something approaching a uniform obscenity standard—for both state and federal prosecutions—emerged.[76]

CRACKS IN THE SHIELD: THE NEW OBSCENITY JURISPRUDENCE AND THE PROBLEM OF "INCIDENTAL" EXPOSURE

Having already described the leading cases in the new obscenity jurisprudence (specifically, *Butler v. Michigan, Roth v. United States,* and *Miller v. California*), I now discuss three cases in which the Supreme Court vindicated Free Speech claims for adults, while acknowledging the fact (or strong likelihood) of children being "incidentally" exposed to pornographic or other inappropriate stimuli. In my judgment, the three cases were wrongly decided, and the interests of children in each controversy became progressively higher. I nonetheless take some consolation from the spirited dissents in each case.[77]

In *Cohen v. California,* the Court reviewed a prosecution under a broad "disturbing-the-peace" statute. Police arrested Paul Robert Cohen in a corridor in the Los Angeles County Courthouse on 26 April 1968 for wearing a jacket bearing the words "F[**]k the Draft." According to the opinion of the Court of Appeals of California (Second Appellate District), the words on Cohen's jacket were "plainly visible," and women and children were in the corridor when Cohen was arrested. He was convicted for violating section 415 of the California Penal Code and sentenced to thirty days' imprisonment.[78]

Under the statute, it was a misdemeanor to disturb "the peace or quiet of any neighborhood or person, by loud or unusual noise, or by tumultuous or offensive conduct." The statute also made it a crime to use "vulgar, profane, or indecent language within the presence or hearing of women and children, in a loud and boisterous manner."[79] Cohen's conviction was based on the "offensive conduct" provision, and, in affirming his conviction, the California appellate court interpreted that phrase to mean "behavior which has a tendency to provoke *others* to acts of violence or in turn to disturb the peace." The same court added that it was

[76] Public concern about obscenity, including obscenity in literature, was shared by many persons during the years between the *Hicklin* and *Roth* decisions, including intellectual leaders of American society. Recall the composition of the New England Society for the Suppression of Vice, discussed in the last chapter.

[77] The main purpose of this section is to document the phenomenon of "incidental exposure." I offer some explanatory and critical remarks on the relevant cases, but more general comments on the "new" obscenity jurisprudence appear in the conclusion to this chapter.

[78] See *Cohen v. California,* 403 U.S. 15, 16 (1971).

[79] Ibid. (note 1).

"foreseeable" that Cohen's conduct might have led to acts of violence against him or to attempts to remove his jacket. Cohen appealed, arguing that the statute violated his right to freedom of expression under the First and Fourteenth Amendments.[80]

The key premise in the Supreme Court's analysis was that Cohen's conviction rested exclusively on speech. According to Justice Harlan's majority opinion, the "conduct" was "the fact of communication."[81] The Court then asked whether Cohen could be punished for the content of his message or for the manner in which he exercised his freedom.

For several reasons, the Court denied that he could. First, Cohen was not trying to incite disobedience or disrupt the draft. Second, his message lacked erotic content, so the case could not be designated an obscenity prosecution. Third, the words on Cohen's jacket were not "fighting words," since no individual could take them as a personal insult and no group could construe them as an incitement to physical conflict.[82]

Having resolved these matters, the Court still had one big question to face:

> Against this background, the issue flushed by this case stands out in bold relief. It is whether California can excise, as "offensive conduct," one particular scurrilous epithet from public discourse, either upon the theory of the court below that its use is inherently likely to cause violent reaction or upon a more general assertion that the States, acting as guardians of public morality, may properly remove this offensive word from the public vocabulary.[83]

Because the Court had noted that the words on the jacket were not "fighting words," it rejected the lower court's view that those words were "inherently likely to cause violent reaction."[84] The Court was then left to decide whether the state could criminalize the public use of this "scurrilous epithet."

The Court's willingness to consider this question was itself unusual. As always, the justices were required to accept the statutory construction rendered by the state court of last resort. This requirement should have

---

[80] Ibid., 17.

[81] Ibid., 18.

[82] Ibid., 19–20. Moreover, the Court dismissed the idea (presumably put forth by the state's attorney during oral argument) that the statute was meant to preserve decorum in the courthouse, since the statute was applicable throughout the state. See ibid., 19.

If the message on Cohen's jacket had been characterized as an obscene communication or as fighting words, the Court would have probably upheld his conviction, since both of those categories of speech are constitutionally unprotected, according to *Roth v. United States* and *Chaplinsky v. New Hampshire*, 315 U.S. 568 (1942).

[83] *Cohen v. California*, 22.

[84] Ibid., 22–23.

confined the Supreme Court's analysis to the "offensive conduct" portion of the statute. Why the Court went beyond that point is explained by Justice Harlan:

> The *amicus* urges, with some force, that this issue [i.e., the state's authority to purge the scurrilous epithet from public discourse] is not properly before us since the statute, as construed, punishes only conduct that might cause others to react violently. However, because the opinion below appears to enact a virtually irrebuttable presumption that use of this word will produce such results, the statute as thus construed appears to impose, in effect, a flat ban on the public utterance of this word. With the case in this posture, it does not seem inappropriate to inquire whether any other rationale might properly support this result.[85]

In finding that no other rationale supported Cohen's conviction, Justice Harlan offered his views on freedom of expression in contemporary society. Some scholars and activists now regularly quote a few of Harlan's remarks, and those remarks convey the basis of the Court's decision: "The constitutional right of free expression is powerful medicine in a society as diverse and populous as ours"; "That the air may at times be filled with verbal cacophony is . . . not a sign of weakness but of strength"; "It is . . . often true that one man's vulgarity is another's lyric."[86]

Besides answering the preceding questions, the majority resolved one other constitutional issue of importance. In oral argument, the state's attorney maintained that California had the authority to spare sensitive persons exposure to Cohen's "crude" and "distasteful" mode of expression. (The adjectives are Harlan's.) The Court rejected this claim as well, conceding that government may act to prevent unwelcome ideas and stimuli from intruding into one's *home,* while noting that we are often "captives" to offensive speech and stimuli outside that "sanctuary."[87]

This point is hard to dispute, but in view of the facts of the case, the Court's response was unsatisfactory:

> Persons confronted with Cohen's jacket were in a quite different posture than, say, those subjected to the raucous emissions of sound trucks blaring outside their residences [an allusion to *Kovacs v. Cooper*]. Those in the Los Angeles courthouse could effectively avoid further bombardment of their sensibilities simply by averting their eyes.[88]

Recalling that the statute penalized the use of coarse language (albeit in a "loud and boisterous manner"), and further recalling that children were

[85] Ibid., 23 (note 5).
[86] Ibid., 24–25.
[87] Ibid., 21–22.
[88] Ibid., 21. See also *Kovacs v. Cooper,* 336 U.S. 77 (1949).

in the same corridor as Cohen, I have difficulty accepting the two sentences above as a serious answer to a constitutional question. Even if many young persons in the corridor could not read or comprehend the message on Cohen's jacket, some could understand it.

What follows? It would be easy to say that nothing follows. The erotic content of this message was nil, and the likelihood of the message provoking a minor to violence was just above nil. Still, we cannot deny the ugliness of that verb (even today), especially in public. Here some readers might retreat to the notion that "words are often chosen as much for their emotive as their cognitive force,"[89] but only the most precocious adolescents could be expected to reflect on Cohen's "choice" of words.

To continue in this vein is to invite certain risks—charges of squeamishness, prudery, even neurosis. So perhaps I should only say that Harlan's expectation was unrealistic. Like other persons, however, I can only speculate as to how greater realism on Harlan's part might have affected the decision in the case.[90]

Some persons, including three of the dissenters (Justices Black and Blackmun and Chief Justice Warren), held that the correct decision in *Cohen v. California* depended on whether Cohen's method of communicating his sentiments was "speech" or "conduct." The distinction was important here, and for these dissenters it was dispositive, but in subsequent cases involving similar prosecutions it had little significance.[91] The same cannot be said of the Court's expectation that all persons, young and old alike, will "avert their eyes" to protect their sensibilities. In the context of Cohen's constitutional challenge, this was a curious, though secondary, issue. In *Erznoznik v. City of Jacksonville,* however, it became a more conspicuous and more worrisome matter.

Erznoznik involved an ordinance prohibiting drive-in movie theaters from showing any films containing nudity when the screen could be seen from a public place. On 13 March 1972, police charged Richard Erznoznik, the manager of the University Drive-In Theatre in Jacksonville, Florida, with violating the ordinance for showing the movie *Class of '74.* Against Erznoznik's contention that the ordinance violated his First Amendment rights, the trial court upheld the ordinance as a legitimate exercise of the city's police power, a ruling upheld by a Florida appellate court. The

---

[89] *Cohen v. California,* 26.

[90] Because the Supreme Court did not accept the California appellate court's interpretation of the statutory provision, the Court might have sustained Cohen's conviction on the ground that he had violated the "offensive conduct" provision of the statute, through his indecent language. Assuming the Court was justified in ignoring the California court's construction of the statute, I would have voted to uphold the conviction on this ground.

[91] See, for example, *Rosenfeld v. New Jersey,* 408 U.S. 901 (1972); *Lewis v. New Orleans,* 408 U.S. 913 (1972); and *Brown v. Oklahoma,* 408 U.S. 914 (1972).

Supreme Court of the United States agreed to hear the case after the Florida Supreme Court denied certiorari.[92]

The City of Jacksonville admitted that its ordinance banned the showing of films that were not obscene according to the criteria of *Miller v. California.* The ordinance had designated as a "nuisance" any movie containing nudity that could be seen from a public place. The city defended its designation primarily on two grounds: that it could protect all citizens against unwilling exposure to potentially offensive stimuli, and that it could more specifically protect minors against a certain type of stimulus.[93]

The Supreme Court concluded that the ordinance was a "content-based" restriction, since it prohibited only a certain class of movies from being shown at drive-in theaters. That characteristic distinguished it from valid "time, place, and manner regulations," which apply to all speech, regardless of content. Only in narrowly defined circumstances had the Court upheld content-based restrictions.[94]

As in *Cohen v. California,* the Court stressed that citizens in our society are often "captive audiences." In Justice Lewis Powell's majority opinion, the Court also affirmed, in three separate places, that citizens are free to "look away." Here is one such affirmation, a statement that captures the drift of the majority's thinking:

> The plain, if at times disquieting, truth is that in our pluralistic society, [because of] constantly proliferating new and ingenious forms of expression, "we are inescapably captive audiences for many purposes." Much that we encounter offends our esthetic, if not our political and moral, sensibilities. . . . Nevertheless, the Constitution does not permit government to decide which types of otherwise protected speech are sufficiently offensive to require protection for the unwilling listener or viewer. Rather, absent the narrow circumstances described above, the burden normally falls upon the viewer to "avoid further bombardment of [his] sensibilities simply by averting [his] eyes."[95]

[92] *Erznoznik v. City of Jacksonville,* 422 U.S. 205, 205, 206–207 (1975). According to the ordinance, "nudity" meant depictions of "the human male or female bare buttocks, human female bare breasts, . . . [and] human bare pubic areas" (ibid., 207).

[93] Ibid., 208–212 and 212–215.

[94] The "narrow circumstances" were when "the speaker intrudes on the privacy of the home" (citing *Rowan v. Post Office Department,* 397 U.S. 728, decided in 1970) and when "the degree of captivity makes it impractical for the unwilling viewer or auditor to avoid exposure" (citing *Lehman v. City of Shaker Heights,* 418 U.S. 298, decided in 1974). In *Rowan,* the Court upheld a federal statute allowing persons who received "pandering" advertisements to instruct the Postmaster General to notify the sender that such mail should stop being sent. In *Lehman,* the Court sustained a city's policy of forbidding political advertisements while permitting nonpolitical ads on local buses. The degree of "captivity" for a person on the bus was thought to be considerably greater than that of a person on the street.

[95] *Erznoznik v. City of Jacksonville,* 210.

Read in isolation, this passage seems uncontroversial, even platitudinous, at least with respect to most things that adults see and hear on the street. But the Jacksonville ordinance was concerned with something that adults rarely, if ever, encounter there.

Another problem is the Court's analysis of the ordinance as a measure to protect children. The Court first noted that a state or municipality had greater authority to restrict certain "communicative materials" to children than to adults. But the Court quickly changed direction by citing *Tinker v. Des Moines School District* and asserting that "minors are entitled to a significant measure of First Amendment protection."[96]

The Court then concluded that the ordinance was overbroad as it pertained to children. Because it categorically forbade nudity, it barred films that might contain "a picture of a baby's buttocks, the nude body of a war victim, or scenes from a culture in which nudity is indigenous."[97] In making this point, the Court referred to *Ginsberg v. New York,* where it ruled that not all nudity is obscene, even with respect to minors.[98]

The problems with the Court's interpretation may be grasped through Chief Justice Burger's dissenting opinion. Also signed by Justice Rehnquist, Burger's dissent focused solely on the first justification for the ordinance— that is, sparing adults exposure to potentially offensive stimuli. The analysis began with the proposition, taken from Justice Robert Jackson, that every medium of communication "is a law unto itself."[99] The uniqueness of the medium here distinguished this case from *Cohen v. California:*

> Whatever validity the notion that passersby may protect their sensibilities by averting their eyes may have when applied to words printed on an individual's jacket, . . . it distorts reality to apply that notion to the outsize screen of a drive-in movie theater. Such screens are invariably huge; indeed, photographs . . .

[96] Ibid., 212–213. In *Tinker v. Des Moines School District*, 393 U.S. 503 (1968), the Court recognized the right of three teenagers to wear black armbands in public school to protest the Vietnam War.

[97] *Erznoznik v. City of Jacksonville,* 213.

[98] *Ginsberg v. New York* was discussed above.

Readers should reflect on the overbreadth analysis here and the likelihood of an official prosecuting Erznoznik for showing a movie with a scene of a baby's (exposed) buttocks or a dead soldier, lying naked on the ground. Readers should also consider the likelihood of scenes such as those mentioned by the Court appearing on drive-in screens in the United States.

My remarks are prompted by the Court's decision in *New York v. Ferber,* in which the Court sustained a prosecution for the sale of child pornography. In denying that the First Amendment protects this class of materials, the Court asked whether some such materials might have redeeming social value (e.g., in clinical or psychiatric texts). The Court answered that the likelihood of that occurrence was extremely small, and it upheld the New York statute even though a state court voided the statute for overbreadth on these grounds.

[99] *Erznoznik v. City of Jacksonville,* 220, quoting the concurring opinion of Justice Jackson in *Kovacs v. Cooper,* 97.

show that the screen of petitioner's theater dominated the view from public places including nearby residences and adjacent highways. Moreover, when films are projected on such screens the combination of color and animation against a necessarily dark background is designed to, and results in, attracting and holding [sic] the attention of all observers.[100]

Burger then evaluated the First Amendment interests in the case, which he deemed "trivial at best." He contested the majority's view that the ordinance restricted the dissemination of ideas, because Erznoznik remained free to show (nonobscene) films containing nudity, provided that he shielded the screen from public view. Furthermore, persons outside the drive-in had no real First Amendment interests because they typically saw only fragments of a film and could not hear the dialogue. The "communicative value" of the films to such persons was therefore slight.[101]

Burger then drew an analogy with ordinances and statutes regulating nudity in public. If a serious drama or musical containing nudity is performed in a theater, a state or municipality still has the authority, as a straightforward exercise of the police power, to forbid its staging in a public park. The City of Jacksonville therefore has the authority to ban images of nude people projected onto oversized screens and visible from different vantage points.[102]

As mentioned, Chief Justice Burger said nothing about the city's interest in protecting children through the ordinance. All of the preceding points, however, could be extended to that theme. The communicative value of these films to youths outside the drive-in was even less than it was to adults there, because young persons are generally less capable of mentally assembling fragments of a film into a coherent whole. Finally, if Burger correctly assessed the unique qualities of a drive-in theater, and if the traditional account of the susceptibilities of children is also correct, then it was unrealistic for the Court to expect any kids to look away from nude images on Erznoznik's screen.

Because drive-in movie theaters are unknown in many parts of the United States, the ruling in *Erznoznik* may have directly affected only a modest percentage of American youths. Even so, readers should be mindful of the implicit meanings sometimes contained in a Supreme Court opinion. As we have seen, such messages may be more significant than the ruling itself.

The "message" of *Erznoznik*—that it is not unrealistic to expect children to look away from provocative images, or that their exposure to such images should be a matter of slight public concern—has surely gained

---

[100] *Erznoznik v. City of Jacksonville,* 220–221.
[101] Ibid., 222–223.
[102] Justice White wrote a separate dissenting opinion in *Erznoznik* on this ground.

currency in American society. How much? We can hazard a guess on the basis of the Court's ruling in *United States v. Playboy Entertainment Group, Inc.*

Decided on 22 May 2000, this case is more complex than either *Cohen* or *Erznoznik*. Despite its complexity, I include it here because it vividly shows the Court's willingness to countenance children's exposure to indecent and possibly obscene stimuli, even when the First Amendment rights of adults are secure.

United States v. Playboy Entertainment Group, Inc. involved the constitutionality of Section 505 of the Telecommunications Act of 1996. Because the justices disagreed about what Section 505 entailed, I have reproduced the relevant portions:

(a) Requirement
In providing sexually explicit adult programming or other programming that is indecent on any channel of its service primarily dedicated to sexually-oriented programming, a multichannel video distributor shall fully scramble or otherwise fully block the video and audio portion of such channel so that one not a subscriber to such channel or programming does not receive it.

(b) Implementation
Until a multichannel video programming distributor complies with the requirement set forth in subsection (a) of this section, the distributor shall limit the access of children to the programming referred to in that subsection by not providing such programming during the hours of the day (as determined by the Commission) when a significant number of children are likely to view it. [The allowable hours were set by administrative regulation between 10:00 p.m. and 6:00 a.m.]

(c) "Scramble" defined
As used in this section, the term "scramble" means to rearrange the content of the signal of the programming so that the programming cannot be viewed or heard in an understandable manner.[103]

As this excerpt suggests, Section 505 was meant to stop the problem known in the cable-television industry as "signal bleed." More specifically,

---

[103] These portions of Section 505 are included as an appendix to the majority opinion. See *United States v. Playboy Entertainment Group, Inc.*, 529 U.S. 803, 826–827 (2000). Readers should notice that subsection "a" is referred to as a "requirement" and that subsection "b" begins with the word "until." Despite the plainness of this language, Justice Anthony Kennedy's majority opinion wrongly suggests that cable operators had a choice of *either* scrambling or blocking (which is in fact the requirement of subsection "a") *or* "time channeling" (which is enjoined upon cable operators until they fulfill the requirement of subsection "a"). See, for example, ibid., 806, 808, 812, 821, and 826.

the law was to prevent children from seeing images or hearing dialogue from sexually explicit programs resulting from signal bleed.

Channel "scrambling" was used before Section 505 became law, because cable operators wanted to limit nonpaying customers' access to channels they might wish to see. But Congress enacted the statute because of imperfections in scrambling technology. Nonsubscribers were encountering sexually explicit images on their televisions, though the frequency of this occurrence was a matter of debate.[104]

To comply with the statute, and because of the cost of better scrambling technology, most cable operators offering sexually explicit programming restricted their broadcasts from 10:00 p.m. to 6:00 a.m. Thus, in the words of the majority opinion, "for two-thirds of the day no household in those service areas could receive the programming, whether or not the household or the viewer wanted to do so."[105] Playboy Entertainment Group, Inc., sued in federal district court, charging that Section 505 was a needlessly restrictive, content-based statute that violated the First Amendment.[106]

In March 1998, the district court held a full trial. It ruled that the government's interests were "compelling," but that those interests could be advanced in less restrictive ways. The district court singled out, as a plausible alternative to Section 505, Section 504 of the Telecommunications Act of 1996. Section 504 requires cable operators "upon request by a cable service subscriber . . . without charge, [to] fully scramble or otherwise fully block any channel the subscriber does not wish to receive."[107]

The district court ruled that, if sufficiently publicized, Section 504 would provide the same protection as Section 505. Section 504 also had the advantages of being "content-neutral" and less restrictive of Playboy's

[104] Ibid., 806–808.

[105] Ibid., 807.

[106] Ibid., 809. Section 505 was to become effective on 9 March 1996, thirty days after the Telecommunications Act was signed by the president. On 7 March 1996, Playboy Entertainment obtained a temporary restraining order and brought suit in a three-judge district court (United States District Court for the District of Delaware). In the suit, Playboy sought a declaration that Section 505 violates the Constitution and an injunction prohibiting the enforcement of the law. The district court denied Playboy a preliminary injunction, a judgment summarily affirmed by the Supreme Court. The temporary restraining order was lifted the following year, and the Federal Communications Commission said that it would begin enforcement of Section 505 on 18 May 1997.

Playboy Entertainment Group owns, produces, and distributes programs for adult television networks, including Playboy Television and the "Spice" Channel. Playboy retransmits its programs to cable-television operators, who in turn transmit it to their subscribers, through either monthly subscriptions or "pay-per-view" (ibid., 807). Playboy conceded that almost all of its programming consists of sexually explicit material.

[107] Ibid., 828. The text of Section 504 is also included in the appendix to the majority opinion.

First Amendment rights. The district court required Playboy to notify cable-television subscribers about the problem of signal bleed and the remedy afforded by Section 504. The means of providing adequate notice included inserts in the monthly billing statement, announcements on preview or "barker" channels, and advertisements on cable channels other than those carrying sexually explicit programs.[108]

On appeal, the Supreme Court affirmed the district court's decision. Section 505 was a content-based restriction, because it was concerned with signal bleed only from sexually explicit cable programming. The Court therefore applied the standard of "strict scrutiny" in reviewing the law. The use of that standard meant that even if the government's interest was "compelling," a less restrictive alternative would be obligatory if that alternative would serve the government's purpose(s). Much of the Court's majority opinion, written by Justice Anthony Kennedy, concerned the feasibility and effectiveness of Section 504 as an alternative to Section 505.[109]

Here is how Justice Kennedy saw the situation:

> When a plausible, less restrictive alternative is offered to a content-based restriction, it is the Government's obligation to prove that the alternative will be ineffective to achieve its goals. The Government has not met that burden here. In support of its position, the Government cites empirical evidence showing that Section 504, as promulgated and implemented before trial, generated few requests for household-by-household blocking. Between March 1996 and May 1997, while the Government was enjoined from enforcing Section 505, Section 504 remained in operation. A survey of cable operators determined that fewer than 0.5% of cable subscribers requested full blocking during that time.[110]

This datum could be interpreted in several ways. Kennedy first suggested that cable subscribers were indifferent to the problem of signal bleed and responded to Section 504 as a possible solution "with a collective yawn."[111] A few pages later, he acknowledged three other plausible explanations for the lack of individual blocking requests: (1) individual blocking might not be an effective alternative, because of technological shortcomings; (2) Section 504 had been insufficiently publicized between March 1996 and May 1997; (3) the actual incidence of signal bleed might be less common than the government initially supposed.[112]

Kennedy and the majority ruled that Section 505 could be sustained, as the government urged, only if the first of these three possibilities was true. But that condition seemingly did not obtain. According to the district

---

[108] Ibid., 809–810.
[109] See, in general, part 2 of the majority opinion.
[110] Ibid., 816.
[111] Ibid.
[112] Ibid., 818–819.

court's opinion, which Kennedy cited, the first and third possibilities were "equally consistent" with the record. As for the second possibility, it was unclear whether the remedy afforded by Section 504 had been sufficiently publicized. "The case," Kennedy concluded, seemed to be "a draw," and unless the district court had badly erred, "the tie goes to free expression."[113]

The remainder of the majority opinion considered whether the district court had badly erred. In trying to answer that question, the Supreme Court canvassed each of the three possible explanations for the lack of individual blocking requests between March 1996 and May 1997. The majority and the dissenters disagreed about basic facts and their larger meaning.

How widespread was signal bleed? The district court had ruled that the federal government had failed to show its pervasiveness, a point Kennedy and the majority accepted. Although both parties to the dispute submitted videotapes to the Court—some of which showed static or "snow," some of which showed explicit signal bleed—Kennedy found it difficult to generalize from the evidence.[114] Using spreadsheets, one expert estimated that 39 million homes with 29.5 million children were potentially exposed to signal bleed, but Kennedy faulted the government for not verifying this information through surveys or field tests. Kennedy also found the legislative record unhelpful, and he expected that many more complaints would have been filed if signal bleed were as common as alleged. Finally, Kennedy emphasized that signal bleed is itself an amorphous term, encompassing fuzzy and fleeting images as well as clear and uninterrupted programming (and many points between these two poles).[115]

Was there any basis for opposing Section 504 as a less restrictive alternative to Section 505? The attorneys for the United States expressed skepticism about the success of the proposed solution. The attorneys challenged the district court's recommendation of a "hypothetical, enhanced version of Section 504" as a way of meeting the federal government's interests. To this complaint, the Supreme Court replied that the district court was not obliged to repair the statute fully or to predict the success of the proposed alternative: "It was for the Government," Kennedy wrote, "presented with a plausible, less restrictive alternative, to prove the alternative to be ineffective, and Section 505 to be the least restrictive available means."[116]

The attorneys for the United States also submitted that if Section 504 were sufficiently publicized, the cost to Playboy of installing "blocking

---

[113] Ibid., 819.
[114] Ibid.
[115] Ibid., 819–822.
[116] Ibid., 823.

devices" (in response to individual requests) would exceed the revenues from distributing its programming and lead to the company's insolvency. The Court's response was that the record failed to support the assumption here, namely, "that a sufficient percentage of households, informed of the potential for signal bleed, would consider it enough of a problem to order blocking devices."[117]

Finally, what of technology? Would Section 504 eliminate signal bleed? Or would it be at least as effective as the arrangements mandated by Section 505? Even Kennedy's defenders should admit that he did not face this issue squarely. He seemed to say that, in theory, Section 504 could work better than Section 505, since the former would allow any parents troubled by signal bleed to have it wholly eliminated (whereas under Section 505, signal bleed might still occur between 10:00 p.m. and 6:00 a.m., the "safe harbor" period).[118] But Kennedy played down the gap between theory and practice, adding that "it is no response that voluntary blocking requires a consumer to take action, or may be inconvenient, or may not go perfectly every time."[119]

Further complexities in Kennedy's opinion should be noted. He recognized that exposure to sexually explicit images could affect young children, but he repeated those familiar words from *Cohen v. California*— that all persons in our polity are expected to "avert their eyes" when they encounter offensive stimuli.[120] Finally, as mentioned, Kennedy stressed the indefiniteness of the term "signal bleed." Notwithstanding these complexities, Kennedy and the majority concluded that the district court was not seriously in error, and the Supreme Court affirmed the lower court's ruling.

Before considering the dissenting opinion, we should notice Justice Kennedy's reference to Section 505 as a "prohibition" of speech. Here is how Kennedy tried to justify that reference. Since most cable operators were complying with Section 505 by "time channeling," it meant that constitutionally protected speech was being "silenced" for two-thirds of the day, "regardless of the presence or likely presence of children or the wishes of the viewers."[121] Kennedy also cited the district court's finding that 30 to 50 percent of all adult programming is viewed by households before 10 p.m. Kennedy further contended that it mattered little that Section 505 did not impose a complete prohibition, because the distinction between laws burdening speech and laws banning speech was merely a

---

[117] Ibid., 824.
[118] Ibid., 825–826.
[119] Ibid., 824.
[120] Ibid., 813.
[121] Ibid., 812.

matter of degree: content-based "burdens" must be subjected to the same scrutiny as content-based prohibitions.[122]

The dissenting opinion in *Playboy Entertainment Group, Inc.* was written by Justice Stephen Breyer and joined by Chief Justice Rehnquist and Justices Sandra Day O'Connor and Antonin Scalia. It challenged the two principal claims of the majority opinion. The dissenters argued, first, that the record before the Court revealed that signal bleed is a significant, nationwide problem, and second, that the government had shown that Section 504 was not an equally effective alternative to Section 505.

On the scope of the problem, Breyer declared that the majority was "flat-out wrong."[123] To substantiate this, he cited evidence unmentioned in the majority opinion, while building on points contained therein. Breyer first noted that both parties to the dispute admitted that basic scrambling technology does not scramble the audio portion of a program. Perhaps because of this shortcoming, Playboy Entertainment conducted a survey to establish what percentage of cable operators had fully complied with Section 505 (meaning no discernible audio or video bleed). Only 25 percent of the operators indicated their full compliance.[124]

Taking this datum, Breyer applied it to the estimate given by the government expert on the number of American children likely to be affected by signal bleed from adult programming. The revised figure was 22 million children.[125]

Breyer also tried to show that the majority opinion suffered from illogic. He posed a question: If most cable operators had switched to nighttime hours to comply with Section 505—a point granted by the majority—how could anyone say that signal bleed was not a pervasive problem? Economic factors were also at work, but Breyer reasoned that if daytime signal bleed was making cable operators "skittish" about a prosecution, then large numbers of children were being exposed to sexually explicit images.[126]

After defining the scope of the problem, Breyer weighed the likely effectiveness of Section 504 as an alternative to Section 505. His analysis began by noting the different objectives of these two sections:

> Section 504 gives parents the power to tell cable operators to keep any channel out of their home. Section 505 does more. Unless parents explicitly consent, it inhibits the transmission of adult cable channels to children whose parents may be unaware of what they are watching, whose parents cannot easily supervise

[122] Ibid.
[123] Ibid., 839.
[124] Ibid.
[125] Ibid., 839–840.
[126] Ibid., 840.

television viewing habits, whose parents do not know of their Section 504 "opt-out" rights, or whose parents are simply unavailable at critical times.[127]

Breyer then cited some facts unmentioned in the majority opinion. According to the United States Department of Education, 28 million school-age children have either both parents or their only parent in the work force, and at least 5 million children are left alone at home without supervision each week. Section 505 thus served a valuable purpose: it helped parents by preventing minors from being exposed to sexually explicit materials in the absence of parental supervision.[128]

By contrast, Section 504 did nothing to promote the same end, unless parents initiated the process. Here again Breyer took account of social realities. He wrote that the "opt-out" rights in Section 504 worked only when parents

(1) become aware of their Section 504 rights, (2) discover that their children are watching sexually explicit signal "bleed," (3) reach their cable operator and ask that it block the sending of its signal to their home, (4) await installation of an individual blocking device, and, perhaps (5) (where the block fails or the channel number changes) make a new request.[129]

Better publicity, as required by the district court, might help with respect to number (1), but the district court's solution would not help parents with respect to numbers (2) through (5).[130]

Breyer's judgment was that Section 505 was a *burden* on adult speech: it was not a prohibition. Men and women remained free to watch Playboy's programming, even if "time channeling" created some inconveniences for them. Those inconveniences might require them to record the programming, watch it at night, or subscribe to digital cable with a better blocking system. But they were still free to watch it.[131]

---

[127] Ibid., 841–842. Breyer likened Section 505 to policies that prohibit children from seeing X-rated movies and attending cabarets in theaters. This seems slightly wrong, since under Section 505, unsupervised children might still see images and hear audio resulting from signal bleed (i.e., between 10:00 p.m. and 6:00 a.m.). Nevertheless, under the original statutory scheme, conscientious parents (if a child is lucky enough to have them) could take advantage of Section 504 to prohibit signal bleed even from 10:00 p.m. and 6:00 a.m. This task might, however, require much persistence on the parents' part. On this last point, see below.

[128] Ibid., 842.

[129] Ibid., 843.

[130] Justice Breyer also contested the conclusion regarding the costs associated with Section 504 as an alternative to Section 505. Citing the district court's opinion, he wrote: "Even if better notice did adequately inform viewers of their Section 504 rights, exercise of those rights by more than 6% of the subscriber base would itself raise Playboy's costs to the point that Playboy would be forced off the air entirely" (ibid., 844).

[131] Ibid., 838. In *Erznoznik*, dissenting Chief Justice Burger did not distinguish between a burden and a prohibition on speech. But his dissent in that case seems to be based on such

Near the end of his opinion, Breyer remarked that the Court's decision was difficult to reconcile with "foundational cases" such as *Ginsberg v. New York*.[132] The remark has some truth to it, but the decision in *United States v. Playboy Entertainment Group, Inc.* provides further evidence that the Supreme Court is disinclined to take account of the distinct needs of the young when adults assert their free-speech rights. This development may seem acceptable, since few adults now want to live in a society where they may view only programs appropriate for children. But if Breyer was correct about the distinction between a burden on speech and a ban on speech (as I think he was), then even civil libertarians should reflect on the larger meaning of this case.[133]

Perhaps the most distressing thing about the majority opinion in *Playboy Entertainment Group, Inc.* is its insouciance: its rather thoughtless repetition of that phrase from *Cohen* ("avert their eyes") and its sometimes cavalier indifference toward the vulnerability of the young. (Justice Kennedy's line from above—"It is no response that voluntary blocking requires a consumer to take action, or may be inconvenient, or may not go perfectly every time"—stands out.) The disturbing prospect is that the Court will more often assume that the moral faculties of children are indistinguishable from those of adults. A more recent case—*Ashcroft v. American Civil Liberties Union*—provides further evidence of this tendency.[134]

This prospect should not surprise us. While the realism of Justice Breyer's dissent in *Playboy Entertainment Group, Inc.* should be applauded, it is anomalous in the contemporary era. Let me explain.

Whatever one's view of the *Hicklin* standard, it at least took account of the *possibility* that the free circulation of pornography among adults might lead to such materials falling into the hands of children. Such realism is absent in the standards of *Roth* and *Miller*. The assumption in those

---

a distinction. He remarked that Erznoznik was still free to show films containing nudity, providing that he put up a shield to prevent passersby from seeing the screen.

[132] Ibid., 847.

[133] The social interests at stake in *Playboy Entertainment Group, Inc.* were greater than those in *Erznoznik* or *Cohen*, mainly because of the pervasiveness of the medium and the stimuli being purveyed. In March 2005, the Kaiser Family Foundation reported that 37 percent of American youths have access to cable television in their bedrooms. According to other studies, the average school-age child watches roughly twenty-seven hours of television weekly. See Sandra G. Boodman, "Solo Viewing, Bad Endings," *Washington Post*, 11 April 2006, F1.

[134] In *Ashcroft*, the Court invalidated the Child Online Protection Act, which sought to limit minors' access to commercial pornography sites on the Internet. The Court struck down the legislation because it did not employ the "least restrictive means" to further its interest. In fact, the legislation imposed only a very modest burden (namely, having some form of positive identification) on adults wishing to visit commercial pornography sites. Justice Kennedy wrote the majority opinion in the case, and Justice Breyer again wrote a strong dissent: *Ashcroft v. American Civil Liberties Union*, 124 S. Ct. 2783 (2004).

two cases is that all adults will act responsibly: that the magazines and movies will always be kept away from young and curious eyes. The assumption was unwarranted, and, given the proliferation of salacious materials in recent decades, it has become easier for the Court to think that children will be unaffected by programming on the Spice Channel. By itself, this criticism cannot fully account for the decision in *United States v. Playboy Entertainment Group, Inc.*, but it helps us to understand the intellectual and social context better.

COERCING THE COERCIBLE? CHILDREN AND STATE-SPONSORED RELIGIOUS EXERCISES

In view of the developments just described, the Supreme Court's Establishment Clause jurisprudence contains a surprise. Instead of positing moral self-sufficiency or moral resiliency in the young, the Court often assumes that they are psychologically and morally fragile. That assumption typically means that they are deemed incapable of deciding whether they truly wish to take part in a religious exercise on school grounds. Considered in isolation, the Court's thinking on this subject is plausible, but the picture of the psychologically fragile child is hard to reconcile with that of the morally self-sufficient child.[135]

The image of the psychologically fragile child originated in *Minersville School District v. Gobitis* and *West Virginia State Board of Education v. Barnette,* two cases involving the constitutionality of a mandatory flag salute in the public schools.[136] As a civic exercise, the flag salute was genuinely compulsory, with students facing expulsion if they refused to participate. *Gobitis* and *Barnette* are thus important reference points because the notion of "compulsion" in cases involving school prayer has been so contestable.

In both *Gobitis* and *Barnette,* children affiliated with Jehovah's Witnesses had refused to salute the flag on the ground that such a gesture is forbidden by Scripture (Exodus 20:3–5). Lillian and William Gobitis of Minersville, Pennsylvania, were removed from the public school to avoid expulsion, but the children's father objected to the financial burden of private schooling. He sued in his own behalf and on behalf of his children, contending that the compulsory salute violated his children's freedom of conscience. In West Virginia, authorities expelled children from public

---

[135] In this section, I am more interested in the overall image of children presented by the Court than with the soundness of its decisions in these controversies. I shall have a bit more to say about the decisions themselves in the conclusion to this chapter.

[136] *Minersville School District v. Gobitis,* 310 U.S. 586 (1940); *West Virginia State Board of Education v. Barnette,* 319 U.S. 624 (1943).

schools and prosecuted their parents for causing delinquency. A group of parents then sought to restrain enforcement of the relevant laws.

In *Gobitis,* a seven-member majority held that Lillian and William Gobitis (aged twelve and ten, respectively) could not be relieved from "obedience to a general law not aimed at the promotion or restriction of religious beliefs."[137] In the majority opinion, Justice Felix Frankfurter wrote that the ordinance was meant to promote national unity, a governmental interest "inferior to none in the hierarchy of legal values."[138] As the sole dissenter in the case, Justice Harlan Stone argued that the compulsory salute violated both the Free Speech and the Free Exercise Clauses of the First Amendment.[139]

Frankfurter at one point designated the flag salute a form of "conduct."[140] This designation made it easier for the majority to uphold the ordinance. Citing cases and historical sources, Frankfurter tried to show that the Free Exercise Clause did not allow the judiciary to exempt an individual from conduct required by a law of general applicability not targeted at a specific faith or sect. Frankfurter's opinion acknowledges public hostility toward Jehovah's Witnesses, yet stresses the purely civic character of the flag salute and the limited competence of the judiciary to invalidate legislation:

> The wisdom of training children in patriotic impulses by those compulsions which necessarily pervade so much of the educational process is not for our independent judgment. Even were we convinced of the folly of such a measure, such belief would be no proof of its unconstitutionality. . . . Perhaps it is best, even from the standpoint of those interests which ordinances like the one under review seek to promote, to give the least popular sect leave from conformities like those here in issue. But the courtroom is not the arena for debating issues of educational policy. It is not our province to choose among competing considerations in the subtle process of securing effective loyalty to the traditional ideals of democracy. . . . So to hold would in effect make us the school board for the country. That authority has not been given to this Court, nor should we assume it.[141]

Throughout his dissenting opinion, Justice Stone referred to the flag salute as a form of speech or expression. His formulations were roughly the same: "coerc[ing] a sentiment"; "compelling belief"; "bear[ing] false

---

[137] *Minersville School District v. Gobitis,* 594.

[138] Ibid., 595.

[139] Justice McReynolds concurred in the result but did not write a separate opinion in *Gobitis.*

[140] Ibid., 595.

[141] Ibid., 598. Frankfurter could justifiably refer to the flag salute as "purely civic" because the Pledge of Allegiance at this time contained no reference to our nation being "under God." Congress added that phrase in 1954.

witness to . . . religion"; and "compel[ling] public affirmations which violate . . . religious conscience." Stone said little about the governmental interest in the case, but he denied that any such interest could justify a mandatory flag salute.[142]

Stone's dissent contains some historical remarks worthy of mention. He wrote that the ordinance sustained by the majority was unique in Anglo-American legislation because it forced children to express a sentiment alien to them. About halfway through his opinion, he took a broader view of the subject:

> History teaches us that there have been but few infringements of personal liberty by the state which have not been justified, as they are here, in the name of righteousness and the public good, and few which have not been directed, as they are now, at politically helpless minorities.[143]

Reflections such as these are even more prominent in *Barnette*. Decided in the middle of the Second World War, *Barnette* was essentially the same controversy as *Gobitis*. This time, however, the Supreme Court ruled in favor of the Jehovah's Witnesses.

The lingering and still pivotal question in *Barnette* was whether the flag salute should be characterized as speech or conduct. Frankfurter stuck to the latter view, whereas Justices Black and Douglas, who signed the majority opinion in *Gobitis*, abandoned that view and now wrote a concurring opinion. (They likened the salute to a test oath and held that it violated the Free Exercise Clause.[144]) Justices Owen Roberts and Stanley Reed, dissenting in *Barnette*, announced that they adhered to the views in the majority opinion in *Gobitis*, but they did not join Frankfurter's dissenting opinion.

Like Justice Stone in *Gobitis*, Justice Robert Jackson injected historical themes into the majority opinion in *Barnette*. References to "governmental pressure toward unity," "officially disciplined uniformity," and "the coercive elimination of dissent" remind us of the intellectual preoccupations of a generation at war, concerns that have persisted beyond 1945.

Some might complain that Jackson's historical judgments are pat or superficial, but his opinion must be deemed a rhetorical success, regardless of whether the majority was correct on the constitutional question. Passages such as the one below were a novelty in constitutional law, and they must have caused some Americans to think about their attitudes toward different minorities:

> Struggles to coerce uniformity of sentiment in support of some end thought essential to their time and country have been waged by many good as well as by

---

[142] Ibid., 604.
[143] Ibid.
[144] *West Virginia State Board of Education v. Barnette*, 643–644.

evil men. . . . Ultimate futility of such attempts to compel coherence is the lesson of every such effort from the Roman drive to stamp out Christianity as a disturber of its pagan unity, the Inquisition as a means to religious and dynastic unity, the Siberian exiles as a means to Russian unity, down to the fast failing efforts of our present totalitarian enemies. Those who begin coercive elimination of dissent soon find themselves exterminating dissenters. Compulsory unification of opinion achieves only the unanimity of the graveyard.[145]

The solicitude shown to the children of Jehovah's Witnesses in *Barnette* set a precedent. In time, the Court was asked to decide the constitutionality of exercises that could not be described as "purely civic." And in declaring Bible readings and nondenominational prayers repugnant to the Establishment Clause, the Court tried to adopt the perspective of the outsider, the boy or girl who, for any number of reasons, might be a minority within the classroom.

To mention this is different from saying that the Court was authorized to make the outsider's perspective dispositive in resolving those cases. The school-prayer decisions are controversial for many reasons, and some would say that the Court's sympathy for the outsider became an integral element of a dubious constitutional doctrine.

Whatever the truth of that matter, the majority opinion in *Barnette* revealed that the Court's self-perception was changing. Frankfurter's words in both *Gobitis* and *Barnette* are pleas for judicial self-restraint, made rhetorically more effective by his opposition to compulsory flag salutes as a matter of policy.[146]

Jackson's arguments in *Barnette* for a broader understanding of the judicial function were no doubt necessary to overrule *Gobitis,* but his opinion went beyond the requirements of that task. According to Jackson, the Bill of Rights was "to withdraw certain subjects from the vicissitudes of political controversy," and it was the judiciary's duty to take the "majestic generalities" of the first eight amendments and "establish them as legal principles."[147]

---

[145] Ibid., 640–641. For a brief account of popular prejudices against Jehovah's Witnesses at this time, see Alpheus Thomas Mason, *Harlan Fiske Stone: Pillar of the Law* (New York: Viking Press, 1956), 525–532 and 599–605.

[146] See the beginning of Frankfurter's dissent in *Barnette:* "One who belongs to the most vilified and persecuted minority in history is not likely to be insensible to the freedom guaranteed by our Constitution. Were my purely personal attitudes relevant I should wholeheartedly associate myself with the general libertarian views in the Court's opinion, representing as they do the thought and action of a lifetime" (ibid., 646–647).

[147] Moreover, in Jackson's words, "we act in these matters not by authority of our competence but by force of our commissions. We cannot, because of modest estimates of our competence in such specialties as public education, withhold the judgment that history authenticates as the function of this Court when liberty is infringed" (ibid., 640).

Before turning to the school-prayer cases, we should briefly review two other Establishment Clause cases that helped to promote the image of the psychologically fragile child. In *McCollum v. Board of Education* and *Zorach v. Clauson,* the Court assessed the constitutionality of "released-time" programs in the public schools.[148] Such programs, affecting roughly two million American students around 1950, involved releasing students from regular classes to receive religious education. Parents who wanted their children to participate notified the public school, after which students began attending the religious-education class.

In *McCollum,* the Court invalidated the released-time program of School District Number 71 in Champaign, Illinois. In the majority opinion, Justice Hugo Black wrote that the public-school system was being used to promote various faiths. The use of school property for the classes and the close cooperation between the school authorities and a local religious council violated the Establishment Clause.[149]

Despite the appellant's claim that the mere existence of the released-time program pressured students to enroll in it, the majority opinion says nothing about the claim.[150] But the issue was explored in a long concurring opinion written by Justice Frankfurter and signed by Justices Robert Jackson, Wiley Rutledge, and Harold Burton.

Frankfurter compared the Champaign program with the earliest version of released time, developed in Gary, Indiana, in 1914. In the Gary program, the religious instruction took place on church property during a recess period in the public school. Administrators in the public school had no supervisory role in the program; only the children's parents and religious instructors could discipline students for nonattendance.

These features distinguished the program in Gary from the one in Champaign. In Champaign, the superintendent of schools was authorized to decide whether it was practical for a new religious group to offer instruction in the program. Religious education was offered in classrooms in the public school while other students received instruction in secular subjects. (The teachers for the religious-education classes were paid by the religious council and were not employees of the public school.) Finally,

---

[148] *McCollum v. Board of Education,* 333 U.S. 203 (1947); *Zorach v. Clauson,* 343 U.S. 306 (1951).

[149] The local religious council was made up of representatives of the Catholic, Protestant, and Jewish faiths.

In the penultimate paragraph of the majority opinion, Black wrote: "The State also affords sectarian groups an invaluable aid in that it helps to provide pupils for their religious classes through the use of the State's compulsory machinery" (*McCollum v. Board of Education,* 212).

[150] See *McCollum v. Board of Education,* 207, note 1.

in Champaign, public-school officials assumed some responsibility for student truancy from the religious-education classes.[151]

Taking those factors into account, Frankfurter concluded that students were under pressure to participate in the released-time program:

> Religious education so conducted on school time and property is patently woven into the working scheme of the school. The Champaign arrangement thus presents powerful elements of inherent pressure by the school system in the interest of religious sects. . . . That a child is offered an alternative may reduce the constraint; it does not eliminate the operation of influence by the school in matters sacred to conscience and outside the school's domain. The law of imitation operates, and non-conformity is not an outstanding characteristic of children.[152]

Frankfurter saw another problem. The Champaign program was sure to promote a "feeling of separatism" among some students. This was simply a matter of demographics, because not all of the sects in Champaign were able to provide teachers for the program.[153]

Just over five years after *McCollum,* the Supreme Court reviewed another released-time program in *Zorach v. Clauson.* The most conspicuous difference between the New York City program upheld in *Zorach* and the Champaign program was the location of the religion classes: in the New York program, students left the grounds of the public school. Apart from that difference, the New York and Champaign programs had much in common. Students in New York were released for one hour a week (and only on the written request of their parents), during which time other students stayed in their regular classes. The religious institutions made weekly attendance reports to the schools, but the *Zorach* opinions lack a clear statement on what disciplinary role (if any) the public school played in the event of truancy.[154]

Writing for the majority in *Zorach,* Justice Douglas held that the New York City public schools "do no more than accommodate their schedules to a program of outside religious instruction."[155] He dismissed the notion

---

[151] Ibid., 222–227.

[152] Ibid., 227.

[153] Ibid. In the end, Frankfurter found the Champaign program unconstitutional because it was "sponsoring and effectively furthering religious beliefs by its educational arrangement" (ibid., 231).

The sole dissenter in *McCollum* was Justice Reed, who, in a lengthy opinion, worried that a rule of law was being derived from a figure of speech (i.e., "wall of separation"). He urged the other justices not to "bar every friendly gesture between church and state" (ibid., 256).

[154] On this matter, see the first two pages of the majority opinion, including the first footnote.

[155] *Zorach v. Clauson,* 315.

that the program itself or the school authorities put any kind of pressure on students to enroll in released time. And since there was no "claim of coercion," there was no basis for saying that the program violated either the Establishment Clause or the Free Exercise Clause.[156]

To the three dissenters—Justices Black, Jackson, and Frankfurter, each of whom wrote a separate opinion—Douglas's analysis was unpersuasive. The key issue, as they saw it, was that students were required to be in an academic setting. This requirement effectively channeled students into the released-time program. The dissenters apparently believed (but without directly saying so) that some students would take part in the released-time program just to do something different or to get out of school for an hour. Based on the dissenters' reading of the Establishment Clause—which, in their eyes, has always demanded strict neutrality between "religion" and "irreligion"—this situation gave "religion" an unfair advantage.[157]

Justice Jackson also worried that the classes in the public school were coming to a standstill while the religious classes were going on. He seemed to take this as a sign that participation in the released-time program was the "default" position.[158]

Looking at the opinions in *Gobitis, Barnette, McCollum,* and *Zorach,* we might say that the Supreme Court's decisions in the school-prayer cases came as no surprise. Because of the holding in *Barnette* and the ideas about indirect coercion put forth in *McCollum* and *Zorach,* the outcomes in *Engel v. Vitale* and *Abington School District v. Schempp* may, in retrospect, have seemed inevitable. Yet even with solid majorities in those two cases, the decisions were and remain controversial.

In *Engel v. Vitale* (1962), the Court held that the daily recitation of a "denominationally neutral" prayer in New Hyde Park, New York, violated the Establishment Clause. Composed by the state's Board of Regents, the prayer was read at the beginning of each school day by a teacher or a pupil chosen by the teacher. Students could be excused from saying the prayer with a written parental request.

A majority of the Court concluded that the daily recitation of the prayer amounted to a "religious program" carried out by the government. In Justice Black's words:

> We think that the constitutional prohibition against laws respecting an establishment of religion must at least mean that in this country it is no part of the

---

[156] Ibid., 311–312.

[157] See, for instance, Justice Black's reference to the Court's "exaltation of the orthodox and its derogation of nonbelievers" (ibid., 319). In some places, Black and the other dissenters in *Zorach* seemed to forget that children could participate in the released-time program only with parental permission.

[158] Ibid., 324–325.

business of government to compose official prayers for any group of the American people to recite. . . .

It is a matter of history that this very practice of establishing governmentally composed prayers for religious services was one of the reasons which caused many of our early colonists to leave England and seek religious freedom in America.[159]

To Black and the majority, it mattered little that students could be exempted from saying the prayer, because the Establishment Clause does not depend on showing "direct governmental compulsion."[160] Black left no uncertainty about his position:

When the power, prestige, and financial support of government is placed behind a particular religious belief, the indirect coercive pressure upon religious minorities to conform to the prevailing officially approved religion is plain.[161]

Near the end of Black's opinion, he asserted that nothing in the majority's view called into question the constitutionality of civic exercises containing references to God or Providence, such as reciting the Declaration of Independence or singing the national anthem. To Black, those patriotic or ceremonial occasions were easily distinguished from "the unquestioned religious exercise" that the State of New York was sponsoring. Furthermore, no constitutional problems arose if students and other persons were "officially encouraged" to participate in those civic exercises.[162]

As the lone dissenter in *Engel v. Vitale*, Justice Potter Stewart questioned the soundness of Black's distinction and the relevance of historical disputes about the Book of Common Prayer. Because England has had an established church for several centuries, references to those disputes were "unenlightening."[163] In a manner that today might seem folksy, Stewart asked how an official religion could be established by allowing children to say a prayer that they freely chose to recite. To take away that choice was "to deny them the opportunity of sharing in the spiritual heritage of our Nation."[164]

What did Stewart mean? His dissent concluded with a sizable list of public pronouncements and ceremonies that include divine invocations (e.g., a presidential inauguration, the daily Sessions of both the House of Representatives and the Senate). Most of these ceremonies and proclamations involved national political offices, prompting Stewart to ask whether

---

[159] *Engel v. Vitale*, 425–427.
[160] Ibid., 430.
[161] Ibid., 431.
[162] Ibid., 435 (note 21).
[163] Ibid., 445.
[164] Ibid.

the Court means to say that the First Amendment imposes a lesser restriction upon the Federal Government than does the Fourteenth Amendment upon the States. Or is the Court suggesting that the Constitution permits judges and Congressmen and Presidents to join in prayer, but prohibits school children from doing so?[165]

To some scholars, Stewart's questions have never been satisfactorily answered.[166]

The 1963 case known as *Abington School District v. Schempp* actually involved disputes in two states. A Pennsylvania statute required that at least ten verses from the Bible be read, without comment, at the opening of the school day. In Maryland, the City of Baltimore had adopted a rule pursuant to state legislation similar to Pennsylvania's. The local rule required that the school day begin with the "reading, without comment, of a chapter in the Holy Bible and/or the use of the Lord's Prayer." In both Pennsylvania and Baltimore, any student could be excused from these exercises upon the written request of his or her parents.[167]

Both parents and students challenged the constitutionality of the Pennsylvania statute and the Baltimore rule. Roger and Donna Schempp were students at Abington Senior High School in Pennsylvania. With their parents, they attended a Unitarian Church in Germantown, a section of Philadelphia. William J. Murray III went to a public school in Baltimore, and his mother was a taxpayer there. Both William and his mother were atheists.[168]

In striking down the Pennsylvania statute and the Baltimore rule, the Court returned to familiar themes. Citing *Everson,* it reminded readers that "this Court has rejected unequivocally the contention that the Establishment Clause forbids only governmental preference of one religion over another."[169] And citing *Engel v. Vitale,* it maintained that "the fact that individual students may absent themselves upon parental request . . . furnishes no defense to a claim of unconstitutionality under the Establishment Clause."[170]

---

[165] Ibid., 450 (note 9).

[166] Responding to the argument in Justice Douglas's concurring opinion that the daily prayer in New Hyde Park was unconstitutional because the state was financing a religious exercise, Stewart pointed out that public monies are used to pay the chaplains of the military, the Congress, and the federal and state prisons (ibid., 449 [note 9]).

[167] *Abington School District v. Schempp,* 205–207 and 211–212. According to Justice Tom Clark's majority opinion, four versions of the Bible were used in Abington Senior High School, including the Hebrew Bible (ibid., 207). In Baltimore, students could use either the King James or the Douay version of the Christian Bible (ibid., 211, text and note 4).

[168] According to the district court opinion, William Murray was fourteen years old. See *Murray v. Curlett,* 179 A. 2d 698, 699 (1962).

[169] *Abington School District v. Schempp,* 216.

[170] Ibid., 224–225.

Abington School District v. Schempp is noteworthy for several developments, three of which help to explain its unusual length: (1) In the majority opinion, the Court reproduced "expert testimony" (given in the first trial) on different aspects of the Pennsylvania exercises. In his long concurring opinion, Justice Brennan cited nearly a dozen studies by social scientists on social conformity in groups and "peer-group norms" among children and adolescents. These studies were said to show the likelihood of indirect coercion in voluntary religious exercises in the public schools.[171] (2) Perhaps because of public controversy over *McCollum* and subsequent cases, the Court put forth a two-prong test to determine whether legislation violates the Establishment Clause (namely, "to withstand the strictures of the Establishment Clause there must be a secular legislative purpose and a primary effect that neither advances nor inhibits religion").[172] To the argument that the exercises had important secular purposes—for example, "the promotion of moral values [and] the contradiction to the materialistic trends of our times"—the Court responded that the "place of the Bible as an instrument of religion cannot be gainsaid." (The Court reasoned that if the secular purposes were the principal goals of the legislation, then students should not have been able to obtain an exemption from the exercises.)[173] (3) In his concurring opinion, Justice Brennan provided a history of devotional exercises in American schools (both public and private) to clarify the constitutional problem facing the Court. Brennan also responded to criticisms of recent Establishment Clause decisions (by both scholars and dissenting justices) and tried to anticipate future developments in this area.[174]

Despite its inability to persuade other members of the Court, Justice Potter Stewart's dissenting opinion in *Abington School District* cannot be ignored. Stewart believed that the judicial record contained gaps that precluded the Court from making a responsible decision. He therefore proposed that the two discrete cases be remanded to obtain additional

---

[171] The majority opinion includes the testimony of Dr. Solomon Grayzel and Dr. Luther A. Weigle, but the opinion nowhere explains why either was asked to testify (ibid., 209–210). In the federal district court, Dr. Grayzel was identified as an ordained rabbi and an editor at the Jewish Publication Society in Philadelphia. Dr. Weigle was identified as Dean Emeritus of the Yale Divinity School and an ordained Lutheran minister. See *Schempp v. School District of Abington Township,* 177 Fed. Sup. 398, 401–402 (1959).

For the social-science research cited by Justice Brennan, see *Abington School District v. Schempp,* 287–292 and note 68. For Brennan's other remarks on the susceptibility of children to peer pressure, see ibid., 261–264.

[172] *Abington School District v. Schempp,* 222.

[173] Ibid., 223–224.

[174] Because of the dearth of public schools when the First Amendment was framed and ratified, Brennan wrote that "on our precise problem the historical record is at best ambiguous" (ibid., 237). The central question for him thus became: Did the practices here challenged threaten those consequences which the Framers feared?

evidence.[175] This proposal was based on Stewart's view that the Court had a duty to interpret the provisions "so as to render them constitutional if reasonably possible."[176]

Such a comment might suggest that Stewart was imputing bad motives to his brethren. He was not, but he disagreed with them about the meaning of state neutrality toward religion. As he did in *Engel v. Vitale*, Stewart criticized the "wall of separation" metaphor, while pointing out that in some situations "a doctrinaire reading of the Establishment Clause leads to an irreconcilable conflict with the Free Exercise Clause."[177] This was such a situation, and Stewart held, contrary to the other justices, that the central religious value in the First Amendment is "the safeguarding of an individual's right to free exercise of his religion."[178] He recognized a "substantial" free-exercise claim on the part of those who desired to have the school day open with the reading of select passages from the Bible.[179]

Stewart admitted the possibility of coercion in both controversies, though he had difficulty finding evidence of it. His candor on this point amounted to a criticism of the other justices for concluding that "indirect" coercion was present in the classroom:

> It is clear that the dangers of coercion involved in the holding of religious exercises in a schoolroom differ qualitatively from those presented by the use of similar exercises or affirmations in ceremonies attended by adults. Even as to children, however, the duty laid upon government in connection with religious exercises in the public schools is that of refraining from so structuring the school environment as to put any pressure on a child to participate in the exercise; it is not that of providing an atmosphere in which children are kept scrupulously insulated from any awareness that some of their fellows may want to open the school day with prayer, or of the fact that there exist in our pluralistic society differences of religious belief.[180]

In concluding, Stewart repeated that the Constitution protects the freedom of everyone, "Jew or Agnostic, Christian or Atheist, Buddhist or Freethinker, to believe or disbelieve, to worship or not worship, to pray or keep silent, . . . uncoerced and unrestrained by government."[181] This

---

[175] Ibid., 308–309, 318–320.

[176] Ibid., 315.

[177] Ibid., 309.

[178] Ibid., 312.

[179] Ibid.

[180] Ibid., 316–317. As noted, Stewart saw no evidence in either case that students were being coerced to participate in the religious exercises. (See ibid., 314–315 and 319.) Despite seeing no evidence that students were being coerced, he concluded that the only responsible thing to do was to remand the cases in an effort to learn whether coercion had occurred.

[181] Ibid., 319–320.

meant that public schools deserved much latitude in accommodating students who felt the need or desire to pray during the school day. Allowing for the good will and resourcefulness of the parties, Stewart hoped that such accommodation could take place without any coercion, thereby minimizing the need for judicial involvement.[182]

After *Abington School District v. Schempp*, almost thirty years passed before the Supreme Court again considered the constitutionality of an indisputably religious exercise in a public school. During those three decades, the Court was engaged with other Establishment Clause controversies, and its rulings in a few of those cases shaped the opinions in *Lee v. Weisman*, decided in 1992.[183]

It is fitting to end this section with a discussion of *Lee v. Weisman* because the case touches on nearly every issue considered thus far. The image of the psychologically fragile child is again present, though the dissenting justices argued that the image was wholly inappropriate in this context.

The controversy began to take shape a few days before Deborah Weisman's graduation in June 1989 from the Nathan Bishop Middle School in Providence, Rhode Island. Acting for himself and his daughter, Deborah's father sought a temporary restraining order in the United States District Court. Daniel Weisman wanted the court to prohibit school officials from including an invocation or benediction in the graduation ceremony. The court denied the motion because it lacked time to consider the issues. One month later, Daniel Weisman filed an amended complaint, seeking a permanent injunction that would bar school officials from inviting clergy to deliver invocations and benedictions at future graduations, including Deborah's high-school graduation.[184]

---

[182] Stewart owned that there are situations that would amount to coercion, such as denying students an opportunity to be excused from the religious exercise or scheduling the exercise so that it was a far more attractive option than any others facing the students (ibid., 318).

[183] Establishment Clause cases decided after *Abington School District v. Schempp* and relevant to the themes being discussed here include *Stone v. Graham*, 449 U.S. 39 (1980) (invalidating, in a per curiam opinion, a Kentucky policy that required the posting of a copy of the Ten Commandments in each public-school classroom); *Wallace v. Jaffree*, 472 U.S. 38 (1985) (striking down an Alabama law authorizing a one-minute period of silence in all public schools "for meditation or voluntary prayer"); and *Marsh v. Chambers*, 463 U.S. 783 (1983) (upholding the Nebraska Legislature's practice of beginning each of its sessions with a prayer by a chaplain who was remunerated with state funds). The controversy in *Wallace v. Jaffree* is less pertinent to these inquiries than a reader might suppose, but the opinions in that case contain important statements on the historical meaning of the Establishment Clause. The Court's decision in *Marsh v. Chambers* was clearly relevant to the controversy in *Lee v. Weisman*.

[184] The Supreme Court of the United States heard oral argument in *Lee v. Weisman* on 6 November 1991; the case was decided on 24 June 1992. At that time, Deborah Weisman

The invocation and benediction at the ceremony at Nathan Bishop Middle School were given by Rabbi Leslie Gutterman, who was invited by the school's principal, Robert Lee. Before the ceremony, the principal gave Rabbi Gutterman a pamphlet titled "Guidelines for Civic Occasions," prepared by the National Conference of Christians and Jews. The principal advised Rabbi Gutterman that the invocation and benediction should be nonsectarian. The majority opinion in *Lee v. Weisman* suggests that Rabbi Gutterman's prayers could be reasonably described as "nonsectarian."[185]

In ruling in favor of the Weismans, the Supreme Court again stated that Establishment Clause may be violated even without direct coercion. According to Justice Anthony Kennedy's majority opinion, the state's involvement in religion in this case was "pervasive, to the point of creating a state-sponsored and state-directed religious exercise in a public school."[186] By meeting with Rabbi Gutterman, supplying him with the pamphlet, and advising him that the invocation and benediction should be nonsectarian, the principal "directed and controlled the content of the prayers."[187]

Justice Kennedy's opinion also noted that graduation ceremonies are an important rite of passage, and for that reason, participation in them is "in a fair and real sense obligatory."[188] Because students so rarely absent themselves from these ceremonies, the school placed them in an untenable position. On this subject, Justice Kennedy tried to impart historical insight to his readers:

> The lessons of the First Amendment are as urgent in the modern world as in the 18th century when it was written. One timeless lesson is that if citizens are subjected to state-sponsored religious exercises, the State disavows its own duty to guard and respect that sphere of inviolable conscience which is the mark of a free people. To compromise that principle today would be to deny our own tradition and forfeit our standing to urge others to secure the protections of that tradition for themselves.[189]

Kennedy knew that some persons might contest the idea that citizens were being "subjected" to a state-sponsored religious exercise, so he tried to describe what took place. By supervising the graduation ceremony, the

---

was enrolled as a student at Classical High School in Providence, Rhode Island. According to the Court, it appeared "likely, if not certain, that an invocation and benediction will be conducted at her high school graduation": *Lee v. Weisman*, 505 U.S. 577, 584 (1992).

[185] Ibid. See esp. the Court's remarks at 589.
[186] Ibid., 587.
[187] Ibid., 588.
[188] Ibid., 586.
[189] Ibid., 592.

school district put pressure on students to become participants in the invocation and benediction. That pressure was compounded by adolescent peer pressure, which is said to promote conformity, especially in "matters of social convention." Both types of pressure, wrote Kennedy, "can be as real as any overt compulsion."[190]

Kennedy also tried to spell out the choices facing the student who could not endorse or embrace what Rabbi Gutterman was saying. Such a student could "stand . . . or . . . maintain respectful silence."[191] Kennedy, however, worried that either gesture might be taken as an endorsement of the prayers or a sign of participation in the exercise. "A reasonable dissenter," he mused, might have grounds for thinking that classmates would (mis)interpret standing or maintaining a respectful silence as an endorsement of Rabbi Gutterman's prayers.[192]

The dissenting opinion in *Lee v. Weisman* challenges all of these points. Written by Justice Antonin Scalia and signed by Justice Thomas and Chief Justice Rehnquist, it attacks the theory of "indirect coercion" and argues that American history and tradition are "replete with public ceremonies featuring prayers of thanksgiving and petition."[193] There is also a "more specific tradition of invocations and benedictions" at graduation exercises at public schools.[194]

Another problem, in Scalia's eyes, was the majority's attempt to explain the choices facing the "dissenting" student. More precisely, the Court erred when it tried to explain the *meaning* of those choices. The dissenting student had the option of *sitting* in "respectful silence," a point that the majority seemed willing to concede, though it did not expressly say so. But if this choice were openly acknowledged, the majority's analysis might fall apart:

> [The] notion that a student who simply *sits* in "respectful silence" during the invocation and benediction (when all others are standing) has somehow joined—or would somehow be perceived as having joined—in the prayers is nothing short of ludicrous. We indeed live in a vulgar age. But surely "our social conventions" . . . have not coarsened to the point that anyone who does

---

[190] Ibid., 593. Kennedy (ibid.) wrote that "research in psychology" shows the influence of adolescent peer pressure, and he cited four studies to that effect. He also sought to distinguish prayer at the opening of a state legislative session (the constitutionality of which was affirmed in *Marsh v. Chambers*) from prayer in a public-school graduation ceremony. In the former, adults are "free to enter and leave with little comment and for any number of reasons" (ibid., 597; see also 585–586).

[191] Ibid., 593.

[192] Ibid.

[193] Ibid., 633.

[194] Ibid., 635–636.

not stand on his chair and shout obscenities can reasonably be deemed to have assented to everything said in his presence.[195]

This passage should be read in conjunction with Scalia's views on the second option for the "dissenting" student. Quoting the majority opinion, he wrote that standing might mean "adherence to a view or simple respect for the views of others."[196] Scalia held that the latter is much more common than the former in our society. On that basis, he concluded that the analysis in the majority opinion was wrong: the dissenter who chose to stand had little reason to believe that this action "signified her own participation [in] or approval [of]" the group exercise.

The more general problem was the Court's theory of psychological or indirect coercion. Scalia proposed that the concept of "coercion" be restricted to acts "backed by the threat of penalty."[197] Such threats were nonexistent here, and he found it curious that the majority applied the theory of indirect coercion to high-school seniors. He asked: "Many graduating seniors, of course, are old enough to vote. Why, then, does the Court treat them as though they were first-graders?"[198]

To strengthen his argument, Scalia conceded that some element of coercion may have been present in *Engel v. Vitale* and *Abington School District v. Schempp*. But he did not regard those cases as controlling for two reasons: first, school instruction is different from a public ceremony, even when that ceremony relates to education; and second, students must attend school, whereas attendance at this graduation ceremony is truly optional (notwithstanding the majority's view to the contrary).[199]

In sum, Scalia believed that the majority had uncritically accepted and extended the idea of indirect coercion. In places, his dissent mocks the Court's "psycho-journey," asserting that the relevant distinctions on the subject of coercion should be plain to those "who have made a career of reading the disciples of Blackstone rather than of Freud."[200] Whatever one thinks of Scalia's critique, it seems correct in supposing that the decision in *Lee v. Weisman* depended crucially on the theory of indirect coercion.

This completes my attempt to document the picture of the psychologically fragile child. Apart from my comment on *Lee v. Weisman*, I leave it

[195] Ibid., 637.
[196] Ibid., 638, quoting the majority opinion at 593.
[197] Ibid., 642.
[198] Ibid., 639. See also ibid., 641.
[199] Ibid., 643. Justice Scalia also chided the majority for its view that school officials were directing a religious exercise and were in effect composing prayers: "The Court identifies nothing in the record remotely suggesting that school officials have ever drafted, edited, screened, or censored graduation prayers, or that Rabbi Gutterman was a mouthpiece of school officials" (ibid., 640).
[200] Ibid., 642.

to readers to determine the importance of this imagery in resolving each of the cases considered here.

Conflicting Images of Children: The Search for a Justification

The inconsistency described at the outset of the chapter should now be clear. On the one hand, the Supreme Court tells us that children are morally and psychologically vulnerable and highly susceptible to peer pressure and "indirect" coercion. On the other hand, the Court believes that it is not unrealistic to expect children to "avert their eyes" from various types of adult stimuli. This is a large inconsistency, and one wonders whether it can somehow be justified.

One justification that suggests itself is surprisingly direct. It takes issue with my analysis and contends that the only real freedom is freedom in the negative sense. As noted in Chapter One, this position is sometimes attributed to Isaiah Berlin, though he did not hold it. Yet passages in Berlin's writings lend support to it.

As we have seen, the idea of negative freedom typically corresponds to a theory of the human person. In most instances, such theories emphasize the following themes: the ever-present possibility of personal transformation; the nearly universal capacity for independent moral judgment in individual men and women; and the paramount importance of respecting the dictates of conscience.

This account, which might be called the "liberal-individualist" account of the human person, has much in common with the dominant perspective on the Supreme Court in its Establishment Clause jurisprudence. (One might compare the first section of Berlin's "Two Concepts of Liberty" with Justice Kennedy's views on freedom of conscience in his majority opinion in *Lee v. Weisman*.) The similarity between these two positions is significant. It shows that the Supreme Court also subscribes to the liberal-individualist account of the human person, at least in this area of constitutional law.

When the Court, for example, expresses its worries about the pressure children might feel to participate in the recitation of a prayer, it is making a judgment about the indignity of compulsion in matters of conscience. This perspective has a long history in the West, stretching back to the wars of religion in the sixteenth and seventeenth centuries and Locke's *Letter Concerning Toleration*. Motives count for little here. Even if someone deems personal salvation the highest good and wants to secure it for others, the claims of individual conscience command respect.

The point can be amplified. Though we rarely speak of minors undergoing religious "conversions," young persons sometimes take an interest in religion and then affiliate with a particular faith. From the standpoint of most liberal theory, this is unproblematic. Consider a boy or girl growing up in a family indifferent to religion, with neither favorable nor unfavorable views toward any faith. Most liberals, I think, would find it unobjectionable if this youth took an interest in a friend's religion and became involved in it—say, by regularly attending services. This example suggests that liberal opposition to religious exercises on school property rests mainly on the possibility of compulsion or coercion there, rather than on opposition to religion per se.

The liberal position on the free exercise of religion seems to have two views implicit in it: (1) a religious exercise conducted under state auspices in some sense means that the state endorses the ideas of that religion; (2) the state's endorsement is more likely to diminish "free choice" than is any endorsement of the same religious practice or set of ideas within society. These two views are surely plausible, and as a descriptive statement, the second view may hold true in different settings. A child who grew up in a religiously nonobservant family, for example, might be much more influenced by a daily religious exercise in the public school than by sporadic encounters with religiously devout neighbors.[201]

What about the problem of "incidental exposure"? Does the liberal-individualist account of the human person help us to understand why the Court has allowed children to be exposed to adult stimuli? Though the connection might be obscure at first glance, the answer to this question is also "yes."

As in the Establishment Clause cases discussed above, the key variable is the notion of "conscience." The Supreme Court has extended this notion beyond religion into new realms involving matters related to intimate or private life, such as contraception, abortion, pornography, and homosexuality. We saw how this development took root, and we should note the connections between the expanded and traditional notions of conscience. As Rochelle Gurstein's valuable study shows, the expanded notion has affinities with the traditional notion, since both are related to the realm of private life, the realm that, historically, sheltered activities pertaining to the body.

---

[201] Conceding the plausibility of these two views does not imply that something occurring under the auspices of the state always exerts a greater influence. Consider the controversies examined here. Is one supposed to believe that Rabbi Gutterman's two short prayers would *necessarily* have a greater influence on an adolescent than would a few minutes of the "Spice" Channel or similar programming? This is one reason why the question of "endorsement" needs to be kept separate from the question of "influence."

To avoid the charge of evasiveness, let me say that as a matter of *policy*, I oppose religious exercises in public schools if they are structured like those in *Engel v. Vitale* or *Abington School District v. Schempp*. Nevertheless, Justice Stewart's dissenting opinion in the latter case strikes me as very important.

Relying on works by Hannah Arendt and the anthropologist Mary Douglas, Gurstein argues that the private realm, as the realm of biological necessity, was regarded with contempt in the ancient world, a judgment that still prevails in some "traditional" societies. Somewhat paradoxically, in the ancient world the private realm was also "a sanctuary for deeply venerated mysteries," because it is the site of reproduction, birth, sustenance, and death—processes that have never been fully comprehensible to ordinary mortals.[202] One aim of Gurstein's book is to show how, in the last 150 years, the status of private life was transformed from the sphere "in which people are least individuated" to "the locus of freedom and individuality."[203]

The Supreme Court's enlargement of the notion of "conscience" has been controversial, and many resist the idea that the new claims of conscience deserve the same respect as the old claims. Nevertheless, the expanded notion of conscience helps to understand the problem of "incidental exposure." Here is why. When the notion of conscience is understood so broadly, liberal anxiety about "compulsion" can be invoked to oppose almost any laws pertaining to the regulation of pornographic or indecent stimuli, including those laws needed to shield children. Over time, such opposition has resulted in a growing indifference toward children's exposure to pornographic and other indecent stimuli. More than a few sources support this historical interpretation.[204]

As children's exposure to all kinds of pornography has increased, the effects have been predictable. Adolescents are now widely seen as sexual beings in their own right and, in the view of some scholars and activists, as deserving of the same panoply of rights that the Supreme Court has given to adults.[205]

---

[202] Gurstein, *The Repeal of Reticence*, 9–10.

[203] Ibid., 10–14. Anyone who doubts the importance of the private realm to the traditional notion of conscience—and, by extension, its importance to religions such as Judaism and Christianity—should reflect on the conspicuous place this realm occupies in the foundational texts of those religions, e.g., the creation narrative in the Book of Genesis, the birth of Isaac to Sarah, and the birth of Jesus to Mary. Recall, too, the strictures in each religion relating to diet and sexuality. Thus, "following the dictates of conscience" can refer to different aspects of religious observance, such as a person's refusal to salute a flag, an obligation to dress in a certain manner, and the requirement to consume or abstain from certain foods.

[204] See esp. *Eisenstadt v. Baird*, 453, and *Planned Parenthood v. Casey*, 851 ("At the heart of liberty is the right to define one's own concept of existence, of meaning, of the universe, and of the meaning of human life"). Justice Harry Blackmun's dissenting opinion in *Bowers v. Hardwick*, 478 U.S. 186 (1986), might be read in conjunction with these cases. See also cases such as *Roth v. United States* (discussed above) and *Stanley v. Georgia*, 394 U.S. 557 (1969) (holding that the First and Fourteenth Amendments prohibit states from criminalizing the private possession of obscene materials in one's home). For a survey of the relevant matters, see Gurstein, *The Repeal of Reticence*.

[205] See, for instance, Marjorie Heins, *Not in Front of the Children: "Indecency," Censorship, and the Innocence of Youth* (New York: Hill and Wang, 2001). It is distressing to

These developments were not inevitable, because the expanded notion of conscience was put forth and rejected as the basis of unenumerated constitutional rights in cases such as *State v. Nelson* (discussed in Chapter Three) and *United States v. Harmon* (discussed in this chapter). But after the Supreme Court's decision in *Griswold v. Connecticut,* the expanded notion of conscience took shape in *Eisenstadt v. Baird, Roe v. Wade,* and *Planned Parenthood v. Casey.*

For many reasons, these newer claims of "conscience" do not merit the same solicitude as the older claims. But prominent scholars and jurists have endorsed the newer claims, and the endorsement could explain why the odd inconsistency documented here has not been seen as problematic.

Some readers might consider these theoretical and historical matters a distraction. They might simply want to know: Can the inconsistency be justified on constitutional grounds? That is, does the Constitution, correctly interpreted, yield this inconsistency or double standard?

The First Amendment issues are difficult, but to make a stronger case for the inconsistency, I shall assume that all the Establishment Clause cases discussed here were correctly decided. I shall further assume that the overall characterization of children in those cases is correct. We are thus left to consider the direction of obscenity and jurisprudence since 1957.

I begin with the obvious. My dissatisfaction with the rulings in *Cohen, Erznoznik,* and *Playboy Entertainment Group, Inc.* is plain. But I know why some persons think that the new obscenity jurisprudence has brought us closer to the "plain" or "true" meaning of the relevant clauses in the First Amendment.

To understand why I resist this doctrine, consider what it presupposes. As we saw above, the words in the Free Speech and Free Press Clauses were long interpreted to mean only that government was forbidden to put "prior restraints" on speech and the press. For more than 150 years, the key variable was the "tendency" of one's words, spoken or written. Is that a defensible interpretation of the two clauses? To say that it was an indefensible interpretation would be bold, inasmuch as it held sway for the first 150 years of the nation's history. (This legal doctrine can thus be distinguished from "liberty of contract" in the *Lochner* era in that the latter emerged roughly a century after the Constitution was ratified.)

---

note that the "principles" championed by Heins could easily be extended to preteens. Her book might therefore serve as a valuable resource for those seeking to lower the age of sexual consent and to decriminalize child pornography.

As American society further sexualizes children, some minors are now setting up Web cameras and opening their own "for-pay" pornography sites. For the details on one thirteen-year-old boy's odyssey, see Kurt Eichenwald, "Through His Webcam, a Boy Joins a Sordid Online World," *The New York Times,* 19 December 2005, A1.

In fact, the "bad tendency" standard was still being applied as late as 1948. That year, in *Winters v. New York*, the Supreme Court struck down a New York law penalizing the distribution of printed matter "made up of news or stories of criminal deeds of bloodshed or lust so massed as to become vehicles for inciting violent and depraved crimes." In his dissent, Justice Felix Frankfurter argued that statutes like the one being struck down were indispensable to representative democracy, since the very purpose of instituting government is to avoid conditions of lawlessness and violence. Accordingly, established societies have an interest in not making lawlessness and violence attractive, especially to impressionable persons.[206]

But suppose someone continues to point to the "plain words" of the clauses. Hard questions remain, because almost everyone acknowledges at least a few unprotected categories of speech. What are they? Disagreement persists, but the lists of many scholars still include fighting words, "true threats," obscenity, and child pornography (as a separate category from obscenity).

Ardent libertarians might challenge some of these categories, but no sensible person would challenge all of them. But to acknowledge the existence of unprotected categories of speech is a large concession. It makes the "majestic generalities" of the Bill of Rights somewhat less majestic.

Moreover, the existence of unprotected categories means that the "bad tendency" standard has not been wholly repudiated. We can still make moral judgments about what people say, print, and write, and in some circumstances, the law can and should promote other social interests. But if this point is granted, we are entitled to question the dramatic changes in obscenity law in the last fifty years.

Is such questioning necessary? The decision in *United States v. Playboy Entertainment Group, Inc.* suggests that it is. Canonical political theorists and many federal jurists working before 1957 would understand our fears. Such fears, however, are trivialized by Justice Kennedy's suggestion that all persons, including the young, should simply look away when they encounter sexually explicit images on television. (If the Court revisits *Lee v. Weisman* or decides a similar controversy soon, one wonders whether Justice Kennedy might—in the interest of consistency—advise the aggrieved students to look away and cover their ears during the invocation and benediction.)[207]

---

[206] *Winters v. New York*, 333 U.S. 507 (1948). Roughly twenty states in 1948 had statutes like the one struck down in *Winters*.

[207] Notice also that Justice Kennedy takes account of the moral impressionability of minors in other cases, such as *Roper v. Simmons*, 125 Sup. Ct. 1183 (2005). In this case, the Court ruled that executing juvenile murderers between the ages of sixteen and eighteen violates the Eighth Amendment. In his majority opinion, Justice Kennedy stressed that minors between these ages lack the maturity of adults and "are more vulnerable or susceptible to negative influences and outside pressures."

As a final point, I want to correct a misconception. There is a widespread notion, perhaps traceable to Justice Jackson's opinion in *Gobitis*, that the Bill of Rights was supposed to place certain controversies "beyond the vicissitudes" of everyday politics. The related notion is that the amendments represent the supra-democratic will of the people, and that when the Court strikes down a law, the people, in a sense, have authorized the Court's action. Thus, with respect to pornography, indecent stimuli, and the problem of "incidental exposure," one might be tempted to say that the nation put these matters beyond the reach of ordinary politics.

But history reveals something else. For more than a century, the question as to how the unprotected category of obscenity relates to the Free Speech and Free Press Clauses has largely been answered for us by nine eminent lawyers. Consider the record. We took note of the adoption of the *Hicklin* test by the federal judiciary in the 1870s, its abandonment in 1957, and the adoption of a new standard in *Miller v. California*. Many persons are happy with the way this jurisprudence has evolved; many others decry the evolution. Whatever one's position, it is hard to maintain that the current law of obscenity somehow reflects the will of the people.

We would do well to face up to that. And because of the difficulties in characterizing the new obscenity jurisprudence as an expression of the people's will, the strange inconsistency documented here seems even harder to justify.

CHAPTER FIVE

Looking Backwards and Forward

THIS CHAPTER INCLUDES further thoughts on where American liberalism has been in recent decades and a slightly hopeful projection about where it might be going. The trends documented in this book may continue, but contemporary liberalism has some of the resources needed to resist them. This chapter may therefore be understood as an attempt to nudge liberal political and legal theory in a more promising direction.

I begin with a familiar theme. I have defended the view that freedom in the positive sense remains a morally valid idea. We ought to mention, however, that some scholars—including Ronald Dworkin, perhaps the foremost liberal legal philosopher of this era—embrace the contrary view. In *Freedom's Law: The Moral Reading of the American Constitution*, Dworkin criticizes the idea of freedom in the positive sense and suggests that history has essentially stripped the idea of its moral validity. In this chapter, I examine Dworkin's efforts to justify controversial civil liberties.

I defend two propositions: (1) Although the essays in *Freedom's Law* and elsewhere help to explain the emergence of our permissive obscenity standard and the "right to privacy," Dworkin's arguments in defense of those developments are unpersuasive, because he says so little about the welfare of children. Given the premises of his work, this is regrettable, and it provides further evidence of the same tendencies within contemporary liberalism. (2) Despite his apparent desire to develop a cogent social philosophy that relies exclusively on the idea of freedom in the negative sense, Dworkin's failure in this task suggests the futility of this enterprise. Any political or legal theory that aspires to be comprehensive in the way that Dworkin's does needs to incorporate both ideas of freedom—if only to ensure that basic interests of children are not routinely slighted.[1]

Dworkin's views on liberty emerge as he presents his theory of constitutional interpretation, which I will review.[2] My account of Dworkin's interpretative theory is largely based on the Introduction to *Freedom's Law,*

---

[1] Like most contemporary liberals, Dworkin objects to the wholesale application of the idea of negative freedom to economic life, arguing that it gives rise to a callous laissez-faire system. But as in other chapters, my focus here is on applications of the ideas of negative and positive freedom outside the realm of economics.

[2] Ronald Dworkin, *Freedom's Law: The Moral Reading of the American Constitution* (Cambridge, Mass.: Harvard University Press, 1996).

and other essays in that book and elsewhere. The Introduction is an important theoretical statement, which is then applied to different controversies. In discussing Dworkin's work, I do not enter fully into scholarly debates about constitutional interpretation. Dworkin's theory may or may not be more attractive than its competitors, but it still suffers from serious weaknesses. I aim to show the weaknesses, and should also say why I am focusing on Dworkin.

The last two chapters considered significant counterarguments to the positions I defended. Still, some readers might say that fairness requires me to consider the work of a prominent legal theorist to justify those developments in civil-liberties jurisprudence. Dworkin's prominence and his spirited polemics make him a good choice. Among Dworkin's books, *Freedom's Law* merits special attention because it engages so many questions relating to civil liberties. The book also reflects the mainstream of American liberal thinking on civil liberties.[3]

DEFENDING PORNOGRAPHY AND "PRIVACY": DWORKIN, CIVIL LIBERTIES, AND AMERICAN CHILDREN

As its subtitle suggests, *Freedom's Law* advocates a specific method of interpreting the Constitution. To evaluate Dworkin's liberalism, we must take account of that method. The "moral reading" refers to a set of interpretative principles to guide scholars and jurists when considering real constitutional cases.

How does the method work? Its departure point is the open-ended or abstract language of certain constitutional provisions, such as those found in the First Amendment. Such provisions, according to Dworkin, reflect moral judgments about "political decency and justice," and because of the abstractness of the language, they might be interpreted in different ways.[4] When a constitutional provision is ambiguous, "fresh moral judgment" is often required to resolve a case. When there is no ambiguity (as, for example, in the plain language of the Third Amendment, which forbids the quartering of troops in peacetime), such moral judgments are rarely necessary, and constitutional interpretation is less difficult and less contentious.[5]

---

[3] In this chapter, I am especially interested in Dworkin's attempts to justify the "right to privacy" and the Supreme Court's obscenity jurisprudence since 1957. I concentrate on writings published in the 1990s and after. I do not know what Dworkin would say about the inconsistency documented in the last chapter, because he has written little on Establishment Clause jurisprudence.

[4] Ibid., 2; 7–11.

[5] Ibid., 7–9.

The moral reading is allegedly democratic, and its simplicity and directness are said to be among its chief attractions.[6] All citizens may use it, and Dworkin says that it is neither a liberal nor a conservative strategy for interpreting the Constitution.[7] Nonetheless, judges have a special role in this enterprise. Without discussing the matter deeply, Dworkin submits that the "authoritative" interpretation of the Constitution belongs to judges generally, and the justices of the Supreme Court in particular.[8]

Some persons might worry that this function gives the judiciary too much power. Dworkin tries to allay this worry by emphasizing that both liberal and conservative judges use the moral reading. Conservative judges use it when they argue that the Fourteenth Amendment (if properly interpreted) forbids affirmative-action programs. Liberal judges use it in controversies such as those discussed in the last two chapters. In places, Dworkin suggests that political parity exists on the American judiciary and that worries about an "imperial judiciary" are unfounded. Yet he elsewhere admits that since 1945, liberal judges have used the moral reading more often than conservative judges have.[9]

Like any theory of interpretation, the moral reading is better understood alongside its competitors. Dworkin cites the method known as "originalism" as the moral reading's main rival. Both originalism and the moral reading try to elucidate obscure or ambiguous constitutional provisions, but their methods are fundamentally opposed.

"Originalism" describes the theory of constitutional interpretation advocated by Justice Antonin Scalia and former federal judge Robert Bork, among other jurists. The theory holds that judges must try to discern the original meaning of a constitutional provision when deciding a case. That is, they are obliged to establish how specific provisions were understood when ratified. This does not mean that one generation is held captive to the values of a bygone era, because the Constitution permits changes in policy through regular elections and through the creation of a federal system.[10]

An example will illustrate these points. The Eighth Amendment forbids the imposition of cruel and unusual punishments. Because "cruel and unusual" can be interpreted in many ways, how can we know whether the death penalty is constitutionally permissible?

---

[6] Ibid., 12–15.

[7] Ibid., 3.

[8] Ibid., 2. See also 12–13 and 34–35. For a very different view, see Mark Tushnet, "*Marbury v. Madison* and the Theory of Judicial Supremacy," in *Great Cases in Constitutional Law,* ed. Robert P. George (Princeton: Princeton University Press, 2000).

[9] Ibid., 3.

[10] For a fuller account of Scalia's theory, see his essay "Originalism: The Lesser Evil," *Cincinnati Law Review* 57 (1989): 849.

For originalists, the answer is simple. Capital punishment was widely used in the United States when the Bill of Rights was ratified. Its use is also implicitly recognized in several provisions (e.g., Section 1 of the Fourteenth Amendment), and no amendment speaks directly to the use of this punishment. For these reasons, the death penalty is constitutional; states may abolish it or use it as they see fit. (The federal government may also use the death penalty for crimes over which it has jurisdiction.) A judge's personal opposition to the death penalty—as bad or unjust or immoral policy—should have no bearing on his or her assessment of the punishment's constitutionality.[11]

We will soon be able to gauge Dworkin's response to the preceding, but let us consider the moral reading using an example from *Freedom's Law*. The Equal Protection Clause of the Fourteenth Amendment provides that no state shall "deny to any person within its jurisdiction the equal protection of the laws." Even though knowledge of American history tells us something about the purposes of this clause and the amendment, the language admits of several interpretations. How, then, should judges interpret the clause when adjudicating claims under it?

Dworkin's first point is that the clause enacts a *moral* principle, which ought to be recognized as "a very general principle."[12] The clause does not specify any concrete applications, and the Fourteenth Amendment and the rest of the Constitution contain few hints about the correct application of this clause to real cases.

Here we see the importance of historical knowledge. Those who enacted the Equal Protection Clause (the "framers") surely had some ideas about its applications in view of the Fourteenth Amendment's larger objectives. Those objectives related to the status of recently freed slaves, as both the Thirteenth and the Fifteenth Amendment show. Dworkin advises us to keep those objectives in mind when trying to interpret the clause. Only this approach allows us, for example, to make sense of a landmark case such as *Brown v. Board of Education*,[13] which held that racially segregated public schools are unconstitutional. Nonetheless, if we want to understand why *Brown* was correctly decided, we require something beyond knowledge of the general aims of the Fourteenth Amendment.

Dworkin argues that the Supreme Court had two ways of proceeding in 1954. The Court could have taken note of the language of the Equal Protection Clause and then tried to determine whether racially segregated

---

[11] Because my analysis in the last two chapters was based on originalism, readers have already seen how that theory can be applied to other controversies, including cases involving putative rights not expressly mentioned in the Constitution.

[12] Dworkin, *Freedom's Law,* 9.

[13] *Brown v. Board of Education,* 347 U.S. 483 (1954).

schools were deemed consistent with the clause when it was ratified. Alternatively, the *Brown* Court could have interpreted the clause through its knowledge of American history and through a fresh judgment about what the moral principle in the clause demanded in 1954. Of these two approaches, Dworkin endorses the second.

The first approach, which Dworkin associates with originalism, leads to a problem. Because racially segregated schools existed in the District of Columbia when the Fourteenth Amendment was being drafted, Dworkin concludes that the framers of the amendment believed that such schools did not violate the Equal Protection Clause. (The assumption here is that Congress authorized such schools in discharging its duties as a government of general jurisdiction for the District of Columbia.) Thus, if the Court had followed the interpretative method of originalism, racially segregated schools would have been upheld in *Brown*, an outcome that scarcely anyone could abide today. The *Brown* decision therefore shows the unsoundness of originalism. In Dworkin's words: "We are governed by what our lawmakers said—by the principles they laid down—not by any information we might have about how they themselves would have interpreted those principles or applied them in concrete cases."[14]

Because it turns on the interpretation of a specific constitutional clause, *Brown* involves an enumerated constitutional right. To see how the moral reading is applied to cases involving unenumerated rights, consider Dworkin's attempt to derive a right to physician-assisted suicide from the more general right of "constitutional privacy." Although he does not discuss the reasoning in the case, Dworkin approves of Justice Douglas's opinion in *Griswold*, and he applauds the High Court's use of the "common-law"

---

[14] Dworkin, *Freedom's Law*, 10. See also 8–9 and 12–13. Other scholars, including some who endorse originalism, read *Brown* in the same way and agree that it presents significant problem for originalism as an interpretative theory. But this view has not gone unchallenged. Notably, Michael McConnell argues that *Brown* can be justified on originalist grounds. For McConnell, a crucial issue is that at no time after the Fourteenth Amendment was proposed and ratified did Congress vote to segregate schools in the District of Columbia (though Congress appropriated funds for segregated schools already there). Moreover, McConnell documents substantial opposition to segregation in the congressional debates preceding the Civil Rights Act of 1875, with these debates also serving as debates about the meaning of the Fourteenth Amendment. He points out that majorities in both the House and the Senate from 1870 to 1875 supported the desegregation position, though that version of the bill failed to pass because some members of the House invoked procedural rules relating to filibusters and dilatory motions. Because of those rules, the legislation required a two-thirds majority to pass, which it narrowly missed. See Michael McConnell, "Originalism and the Desegregation Decisions," *Virginia Law Review* 81 (1995): 947, and "The Originalist Case for *Brown v. Board of Education*," *Harvard Journal of Law and Public Policy* 19 (1996): 457.

method. In this view, the Supreme Court (and lower appellate courts) should extend the principles of past cases to new and qualitatively different controversies in civil liberties.[15]

To be sure, the very existence of unenumerated rights and questions about their scope are among the most contested matters in American constitutional law. Which interpretative theory is sounder? Let us concede that through his analysis of the *Brown* decision, Dworkin *may have* identified a genuine problem with originalism. But has he established the superiority of the moral reading vis-à-vis originalism? For several reasons, he defends the moral reading as intellectually sound and far superior to originalism.

First, Dworkin stresses that the moral reading is not a moral free-for-all. Judges are constrained in different ways when interpreting the abstract language of certain provisions. Conservative judges will agree with Dworkin on the need for judicial self-restraint in the following respects:

> Judges may not read their own convictions into the Constitution. They may not read the abstract moral clauses as expressing any particular moral judgment, no matter how much that judgment appeals to them, unless they find it consistent in principle with the structural design of the Constitution as a whole, and also with the dominant lines of past constitutional interpretation by other judges.[16]

On a related note, Dworkin admits that judges can abuse their power. Some judges act in good faith, others in bad faith. So we should not fault the moral reading if jurists who profess loyalty to it disregard its principles.[17]

The other reason why Dworkin favors the moral reading is its compatibility with democracy. This is a complex matter, with Dworkin presenting his views on different notions of freedom, especially as they relate to democratic theory.

In Dworkin's view, if we take account of the actual language of the Constitution, the only significant objection against the moral reading "is that it offends democracy."[18] Against this criticism, he holds that a proper understanding of democracy will show that the charge is baseless.

Dworkin develops this argument in the section called "The Majoritarian Premise" in the Introduction to *Freedom's Law*. The "majoritarian premise" is a key element in what he considers an indefensible (though widely held) conception of democracy. Dworkin embraces an alternative account of democracy, which he says is compatible with the moral reading.

---

[15] See Dworkin, *Freedom's Law*, ch. 5 ("Do We Have a Right to Die?"). Dissenting in *Griswold*, Justice Hugo Black strongly criticized the use of the "common-law" method in constitutional law (akin to the method endorsed by Dworkin).

[16] Ibid., 10.

[17] Ibid., 11.

[18] Ibid., 15.

Before we examine that alternative, let us look at the majoritarian premise and the corresponding conception of democracy.

Consider, as a starting point, the system of parliamentary democracy in Great Britain. While all citizens in Britain have rights, Parliament determines the content of those rights. As Dworkin notes, there are "understandings" about laws that Parliament should not enact, but the political community defers to the majority's judgment (acting through Parliament) about the substance of different rights and their enforcement. British courts generally lack the power to invalidate legislation, including laws affecting individual rights. According to Dworkin, one reason for this has been that "the majoritarian premise . . . and the majoritarian conception of democracy it produces . . . have been more or less unexamined fixtures of British political morality for over a century."[19]

Using this account, Dworkin develops several theses about the majoritarian premise and democratic theory. First, democracy means designing political procedures so that "the decision that is reached is the decision that a majority or plurality of citizens favor, or would favor if it had adequate information."[20] Second, the majoritarian premise reflects the view that something morally regrettable occurs *whenever* a political majority or plurality cannot have its way.[21]

If Dworkin is correct about these matters, we can understand his fears. Persons who accept the majoritarian premise would have to countenance some morally repugnant scenarios, such as the wholesale exclusion of a religious or racial minority from public office.[22] But is Dworkin correct about these matters?

One peculiarity in his initial account of the majoritarian premise is that Dworkin fails to identify a single scholar who espouses it. He refers to it as an enduring feature of British political morality, yet he also fails to cite a single public figure in Great Britain who endorses it.[23] (Later in *Freedom's Law,* Dworkin hints that Judge Robert Bork flirted with the majoritarian premise before his nomination to the Supreme Court, but Dworkin does not cite the relevant writings by Bork.[24]) We might therefore ask what Dworkin achieves here.

---

[19] Ibid., 16. The facts mentioned in the beginning of this paragraph still hold even after the Human Rights Act (1998), which incorporated the European Convention on Human Rights into British law. The important point is that Parliament can repeal that legislation as it can repeal other legislation.

[20] Ibid.

[21] Ibid., 16–17.

[22] Ibid., 17.

[23] Ibid., 15–16.

[24] Ibid., 274.

In any event, it is questionable whether leading jurists in Great Britain understand the doctrine of majority rule as Dworkin says they do. Consider the perspective of Lord Reid:

> It is often said that it would be unconstitutional for the United Kingdom to do certain things, meaning that the moral . . . [or] other reasons against doing them are so strong that most people would regard it as *highly improper* if Parliament did these things. But . . . if Parliament chose to do any of them the courts could not hold the Act . . . invalid.[25] (Emphasis added.)

To judge from this excerpt, Lord Reid rejects the view that Dworkin puts forth above.

Perhaps because few persons actually subscribe to the majoritarian premise, Dworkin is sometimes imprecise about its content. In one passage, he describes the majoritarian premise as the view that a "defining goal of democracy [is] that collective decisions *always or normally* be those that a majority or plurality of citizens would favor if fully informed and rational" (emphasis added).[26] The difference between "always" and "normally" here is enormous, and one would like to know what Dworkin really meant to say.

Let us now consider Dworkin's alternative to the majoritarian conception of democracy, which he calls the "constitutional" conception. We might suppose that the constitutional conception merely precludes political outcomes that morally reflective persons would find intolerable. But Dworkin wants to describe democracy in such a way that it is associated with liberty in the negative sense. That is, he wants democracy to be understood as *liberal* democracy, with a strong emphasis on the adjective.

This might seem unobjectionable, since our representative democracy is a limited democracy and we justify many limits on democratic power with reference to individual rights. (The same can be said of Great Britain, despite structural differences.) Dworkin's point, however, is not merely conceptual. He wants democracy to be characterized so that his readers are favorably disposed to the regular exercise of judicial review, especially as it occurred during the "halcyon" days of the Warren Court.[27]

Consider the following contrast. When Dworkin first introduces the constitutional conception of democracy, he cites the equal status of citizens as one feature that distinguishes it from the majoritarian conception:

---

[25] *Madzimbamuto v. Lardner-Burke*, [1969] 1 A.C. 645, 723 (P.C. 1968) (appeal taken from S. Rhodesia), cited in Lord Irvine of Lairg, "Sovereignty in Comparative Perspective," in *The Unpredictable Constitution*, ed. Norman Dorsen (New York and London: New York University Press, 2002), 316.

[26] Dworkin, *Freedom's Law*, 17.

[27] The adjective is Dworkin's: *Freedom's Law*, 3.

The constitutional conception of democracy . . . takes the following attitude to majoritarian government. Democracy means government subject to conditions— we might call these the "democratic" conditions—of equal status for all citizens. When majoritarian institutions provide and respect the democratic conditions, then the verdicts of these institutions should be accepted by everyone for that reason. But when they do not, or when their provision or respect is defective, there can be no objection, in the name of democracy, to other procedures that protect and respect them better. The democratic conditions plainly include, for example, a requirement that public offices must in principle be open to members of all races and groups on equal terms. If some law provided that only members of one race were eligible for public office, then there would be no moral cost—no matter for moral regret at all—if a court that enjoyed the power to do so under a valid constitution struck down that law as unconstitutional. That would presumably be an occasion on which the majoritarian premise was flouted, but though this is a matter of regret according to the majoritarian conception of democracy, it is not according to the constitutional conception.[28]

After drawing this basic contrast between the majoritarian and constitutional conceptions of democracy, Dworkin adds detail to each, and the contrast grows starker. Its growing starkness can be explained by Dworkin's desire to give flesh to the idea of the equal status of all democratic citizens. Besides the meaning given in the excerpt above, Dworkin assigns other, roughly synonymous meanings to the idea of equal status, including the requirement that each citizen be treated with "equal concern and respect" by the political community. Such treatment is part of what he calls the "conditions of moral membership" in that community.[29]

When we examine the content of those conditions, it becomes apparent that Dworkin frames several issues in a debate so that the outcomes he favors are preordained. He argues that full moral membership in a political community requires that each person be given "a *part* in any collective decision, a *stake* in it, and *independence* from it."[30] These requirements seem uncontroversial, but the applications Dworkin derives from them are highly controversial.

Consider the notion that each citizen must have a part (or voice) in any decision made by the political community. This idea will mean different things to different people. Some would accept Dworkin's view that the idea should be interpreted to guarantee freedom of speech and expression in both political life and "the informal life of the community."[31] Others,

[28] Ibid., 17–18.
[29] Ibid., 17–18 and 23–24.
[30] Ibid., 24.
[31] Ibid., 25.

however, will resist that broad interpretation, which (according to Dworkin) entails that under the rubric of "political participation," a state must give citizens wide freedom to buy, produce, and distribute pornography.

Still others might dispute Dworkin's contention that a genuine political community must be "a community of independent moral agents."[32] They might have further reasons for resisting the idea, since Dworkin holds that on matters of political, ethical, and moral judgment, citizens are to arrive at their beliefs "through their own reflective and finally individual conviction."[33] This assertion is meant to be more than a truism, and, among its other implications, it would deny the capacity of American states to promote public morals through the exercise of the police power, a topic about which Dworkin says nothing in *Freedom's Law*. (Similarly, one searches in vain for a reference to the Tenth Amendment in *Freedom's Law*, and the amendment is nowhere cited in the book's index.)

All of these ideas about the equal status of citizens, the conditions of moral membership in a polity, and the distinction between the majoritarian and constitutional conceptions of democracy converge. From the outset, Dworkin espouses a liberal-individualist account of the human person and the corresponding idea of freedom (meaning "negative" freedom). He wants to extend the notions of "conscience" and "compulsion" to new realms and to fortify their position in those realms where the judiciary has recently accepted them.

With respect to the "right to privacy," Dworkin applies the notion of conscience to the constitutional debate about abortion.[34] Given the theoretical views in the Introduction to *Freedom's Law* and the Court's language in cases such as *Eisenstadt, Roe,* and *Casey,* this attempt is understandable. But notice what he omits. Dworkin's analysis of *Roe* begins with the premise that *Griswold, Eisenstadt,* and *Carey* are not merely correct, but indisputably correct.[35] Often grouping the three cases together (as though he wants to efface the differences in the relevant laws), Dworkin devotes only a sentence to the purposes of the statutes. Moreover, he does not mention the possibility of a jurist being opposed to a policy while recognizing a state's power to enact it—the position of both Justice Black and Justice Stewart in *Griswold*.[36]

---

[32] Ibid., 26.

[33] Ibid.

[34] See esp. the views expressed at ibid., 110–112.

[35] Ibid., 12–13, 103, 124, 141.

[36] Dworkin summarizes the rulings in these three cases in note 12 to chapter 1 of *Freedom's Law* (on p. 354). In note 7 to chapter 2 (p. 356), he discusses the rationale of the Connecticut statutes in a single sentence, writing only that the two Connecticut laws aimed to discourage extramarital sexual relations.

Dworkin's analysis of the three contraception cases in his book *Life's Dominion* (New

In all likelihood, Dworkin avoids analyzing *Griswold, Eisenstadt,* and *Carey* because the use of contraceptives has become so common in the United States. Owing to their widespread use, he might assume that his readers do not need to understand the distinction between the desirability of a policy and a state's authority to enact it. Yet that distinction is crucial. If it is forgotten, ignored, or obscured in this context, it becomes much easier to argue for a constitutional right to abortion. This approach simplifies Dworkin's work as he tries to vindicate the putative right to abortion, but astute readers will see that he takes the easy way out. Such readers will not be lulled into thinking that the widespread use of contraceptives today provides a post hoc justification for the decisions in *Griswold, Eisenstadt,* and *Carey.*

The three contraception cases illustrate a large problem with the moral reading. If judges who use it must take constitutional structure, text, and precedent seriously, the grand project of "procreative autonomy" (i.e., the "right to privacy") would never get off the ground. The established jurisprudence of the police power, extending more than 150 years, would preclude that.[37]

Regarding the Supreme Court's obscenity jurisprudence, Dworkin says little about the *content* of changing obscenity standards before and after *Roth v. United States.* (He briefly discusses the doctrine of "no prior restraint" and considers its repudiation a great victory.[38]) Using the same liberal-individualist account of the human person, he defends an even more permissive obscenity standard than that promulgated in *Miller v. California.*[39] And he misleads his readers by writing that "modern democracies" chose to give pornography as much protection as political speech, as if the current law of obscenity resulted from a referendum or sustained legislative deliberation or a constitutional convention.[40]

In pointing out its shortcomings, I do not mean to deny the value of Dworkin's book. *Freedom's Law* helps us to understand the mindset of an influential liberal jurist, and we can read the book as a "phenomenology" of a certain idea of freedom. This comment applies especially to the essays on the Free Speech and Free Press Clauses. The moral reading might well

---

York: Vintage Books, 1994) is no more satisfying than that in *Freedom's Law. Life's Dominion* lacks a sustained analysis of any of the three cases, and the index reveals that *Griswold* is cited on only six pages (none of them consecutive) in a book exceeding 250 pages.

[37] This point deserves to be stressed, since Dworkin believes that the widely observed distinction between enumerated and unenumerated rights is "bogus" (*Freedom's Law,* 72). Space considerations prevent me from evaluating this startlingly bold claim.

[38] Dworkin, *Freedom's Law,* 196–198.

[39] See esp. chapter 8 ("Why Must Speech Be Free?") and chapter 9 ("Pornography and Hate") in *Freedom's Law.*

[40] Ibid., 221.

be an accurate *descriptive* account of Supreme Court's approach to these clauses in the twentieth century. Nonetheless, the Court's decisions in this area are not as principled as Dworkin supposes. They are more accurately described as a hodgepodge, characterized by sudden shifts and stops, often to salvage moral decency.

Dworkin, however, wants to affirm a categorical principle, arguing that "we are a liberal society committed to individual moral responsibility, and *any* censoring on grounds of content is inconsistent with that commitment."[41] The longing for simplicity and neatness is understandable, but this is a careless formulation, and it contradicts what Dworkin writes elsewhere. Sensible scholars will insist that some categories of expression—above all, child pornography—must remain unprotected.

An error like this is unsurprising, because *Freedom's Law* contains very few references to children. The dearth of references undermines Dworkin's desire to be philosophically rigorous. It also conflicts with his goal of having each citizen treated with "equal concern and respect."

Let me elaborate. Despite Dworkin's desire to be philosophically rigorous, *Freedom's Law* is often philosophically deficient. Its deficiencies are evident in both what Dworkin says and what he fails to say. One large problem is Dworkin's failure to probe the moral limits of negative freedom. The limits should be intelligible to those who have studied Isaiah Berlin closely. But Dworkin seems more interested in using Berlin's work for his own predefined purposes than in reflecting on Berlin's ideas.

His writings on Berlin illuminate little, and some of his assertions about positive freedom are flatly wrong or highly misleading. When first defining the term, for example, Dworkin equates the idea with Constant's notion of ancient freedom, that is, the right to participate in politics. But this oversimplifies. Freedom in the positive sense plays a role in democratic theory (e.g., Rousseau's *Social Contract*), but the meaning is broader than Dworkin suggests. Dworkin fails to explore the broader meaning and relevant applications, yet he follows Berlin in invoking the specter of totalitarianism. So Dworkin's readers might conclude that all of the other applications are morally discreditable.[42]

Dworkin's inattention to children is also hard to reconcile with his principle that government must treat all citizens with equal concern and respect. What lies behind this principle? The image of the human person in his writings is a rational and reflective adult, someone unafraid to challenge convention and tradition and unexamined prejudice in different settings. It

---

[41] Ibid., 205 (emphasis in original).

[42] See the "Introduction" and chapter 9 ("Pornography and Hate") in *Freedom's Law.* Chapter 9 first appeared (with a different title) in Edna and Avishai Margalit, eds., *Isaiah Berlin: A Celebration.*

is in some respects an attractive image, undoubtedly based on chapters in twentieth-century U.S. history. That imagery makes it easier for some to accept Dworkin's view that governments are obliged to respect the choices of dissenters and nonconformists of every stripe.

The notion of "equal concern and respect" is the foundation of Dworkin's political and legal theory, but his understanding of equality is curious because (at least in *Freedom's Law*) it is mainly about personal freedom. With respect to noneconomic liberties, "equal concern and respect" encompasses the freedom for adults to behave eccentrically or coarsely, whatever the consequences. Dworkin writes that freedom in the negative sense must encompass "the tawdry as well as the heroic,"[43] and he has worked for years to give the tawdry its due.

Others, however, might legitimately ask how much certain "lifestyle" choices of adults should count when those choices implicate interests of children. I already explained how Dworkin fails to do this with respect to *Griswold, Eisenstadt,* and *Carey.* Now let me say a bit more about obscenity.

Dworkin knows that children lack the capacity to make truly informed choices about matters such as sexuality. On that basis (and despite a contradictory formulation elsewhere), he accepts the Supreme Court's view that child pornography is an unprotected category of expression.[44] On the same grounds, he would likely accept strictures on the sale of pornography to minors.

These conclusions are significant, and we can say that Dworkin's analysis of obscenity jurisprudence in *Freedom's Law* should have gone further. Because children lack the capacity to make truly informed choices about their sexuality, Dworkin should have more thoroughly analyzed the changing obscenity standards in the nineteenth and twentieth centuries. Specifically, he should have explored what the changing standards have meant for children. The idea of "equal concern and respect" would seem to require nothing less.

As we saw, obscenity was at one time defined as that which tends to corrupt youth. (In this formulation, children were deemed among the most vulnerable members of society.) Later, according to the *Roth* decision, the test was "whether to the average person, applying contemporary community standards, the dominant theme of the material taken as a whole appeals to the prurient interest." Sixteen years later, this test from *Roth* was supplemented by two other requirements in *Miller v. California:* (1) the material must portray or describe, "in a patently offensive way," the sexual conduct defined by the relevant state law; and (2) the material,

---

[43] Dworkin, *Freedom's Law,* 219.
[44] Ibid., 232–233. (Compare with ibid., 205.)

considered as a whole, must lack "serious literary, artistic, political, or scientific value."

During the hundred years separating the *Hicklin* test from *Miller v. California*, the federal courts stopped taking the susceptibilities of the young into account. This is not hyperbole. Children gradually disappeared from the obscenity equation, and the Supreme Court confirmed the point in *Pinkus v. United States*,[45] ruling that the idea of "community" in the first part of the *Miller* test (in the reference to "community standards") excludes children.

Dworkin's defenders might say that I omit something important. They might point to the decision in *Ginsberg v. New York* and say that the concept of "variable obscenity" can still be used to prohibit direct sales of certain adult materials to youths. *Ginsberg* remains valid law, but the ruling is less important now than it was before. Today, young persons do not need to buy pornography in stores or at newsstands, because they can obtain it freely elsewhere.

It is worth recalling the Supreme Court's role in this development. The Court made it much easier for minors to view and obtain pornography through its decisions in *Reno v. American Civil Liberties Union, United States v. Playboy Entertainment Group, Inc.*, and *Ashcroft v. American Civil Liberties Union*. These cases sent a clear message: the Court will not permit the vulnerabilities of the young to hinder adults wanting easy access to pornography on cable television and the Internet. And easy access for adults means easy access for children.

So even while the Court describes the interest in protecting minors from certain adult stimuli as "compelling," it enjoins the government to employ the "least restrictive means" to advance that interest (as noted in all three of the cases just cited). As a practical matter, this requirement is almost impossible to meet, and, as a result, the tawdry gets much more than it is due.

Dworkin evidently thinks that this is what his principle of equal concern and respect mandates. Is he right? Without knowing precisely what the principle requires, I am sure that it demands something else. "Equal concern and respect" can be interpreted in different ways, but it cannot be taken seriously as an overarching principle if it excludes children altogether.

Perhaps the obscenity standard closest to the spirit of Dworkin's principle is the *Roth* test, which was prefigured in Judge Learned Hand's opinion in the *United States v. Levine* case. The test calls for a judgment about the value of the material in question while requiring us to take account of its potentially corrupting effects. The material is assessed from

---

[45] *Pinkus v. United States*, 436 U.S. 293 (1978).

the standpoint of the "average person" (rather than the most vulnerable class of persons), which might strike many as a reasonable compromise.[46] (It strikes me as a reasonable compromise, though other questions on the subject of obscenity and the welfare of children still deserve attention— e.g., whether anyone should follow Justice Anthony Kennedy in equating modest burdens on speech with prohibitions of speech.)

In response, Dworkin might say that adopting the standpoint of the average person promotes the social conformity that his ideas of moral independence and ethical individualism are meant to foil. That may be so, but ethical individualism applies to adults. It cannot apply to children, as even Dworkin indirectly concedes.

Alternatively, Dworkin might reply by saying that I overstate the difficulty of the problem. In one passage, he quotes Justice William J. Brennan's dissenting opinion in *Paris Adult Theatre v. Slaton* as it relates to the search for a "workable" obscenity standard.[47] In this case, Justice Brennan announced a change in his views on obscenity jurisprudence. Because of a measure of ambiguity in all previous attempts to define the obscene, he urged the Supreme Court to abandon those efforts. As an alternative, Brennan proposed that all consenting, adult activities pertaining to sexuality be decriminalized. In other words, "in the absence of distribution to minors or obtrusive exposure to unconsenting adults,"[48] governments should not suppress any materials as obscene. Dworkin endorses this change in Brennan's thinking, but without noticing that the criterion in Brennan's *Paris Adult Theatre* dissent is question-begging. If we acknowledge the basic differences between adults and children, and if we grant that *some* materials or stimuli are inappropriate for children, we will *always* need a definition of obscenity to establish which types of distribution to minors should be prohibited. The need remains even if we accept the idea of variable concepts of obscenity.[49]

To judge from essays published before *Freedom's Law*, Dworkin at one time better understood the social interests behind the law of obscenity. In

[46] Again, Judge Hand's obscenity standard required the jury to decide whether "the work will so much arouse the salacity of the reader . . . as to outweigh any literary, scientific, or other merits it may have" (*United States v. Levine*, 158).

[47] See Dworkin, *Freedom's Law*, 207.

[48] *Paris Adult Theatre v. Slaton*, 49.

[49] *Paris Adult Theatre v. Slaton* and *Miller v. California* were decided together, and in his dissents, Justice Brennan wrote that the circumstances of those cases made it unnecessary for him to elaborate on the problems of distribution of sexual materials to minors and exposure to unconsenting adults. I am uncertain whether Brennan ever returned to this problem, but Dworkin should have been able to see that Brennan's purported solution begs the question.

"Do We Have a Right to Pornography?" he admits that the broad recognition of such a right would

> sharply limit the ability of individuals consciously and reflectively to influence the conditions of their own and their children's development. It would limit their ability to bring about the cultural structure they think best, a structure in which sexual experience generally has dignity and beauty.[50]

This is a big concession, but there is more. Three of the essays in *Freedom's Law* are about pornography. In them, Dworkin considers the possible effects of pornography on the social position of American women, while arguing that our society can resist the crude and debasing ideas of pornography through intellectual opposition (i.e., "through more speech").

Regardless of whether this is a satisfactory remedy, Dworkin believes that his principle of "equal concern and respect" requires him to look at pornography from the standpoint of women. I agree that the principle requires this assessment, but his analysis is incomplete. If the principle requires him to evaluate pornography from the standpoint of women, how can he disregard children? Why is there not even a gesture in this direction in *Freedom's Law?*

It would not be difficult for Dworkin to identify the relevant matters for analysis. When obscenity was defined as that which corrupts the young, "corruption" referred, among other things, to a diminished sense of the responsibilities associated with human sexual relations. This idea persisted longer than many people might suppose. It finds expression, for example, in the surprisingly traditional outlook in Justice Brennan's opinion in *Ginsberg v. New York*. So even though Dworkin says little about these matters, we are entitled to ask what he thinks about them. Would he, for example, recognize any of the social interests reflected in the pre-*Miller* obscenity standards as legitimate?

The answer is not clear. What is clear is that Dworkin wants to use the principle of equal concern and respect to give lexical priority to negative freedom. His defenses of the new obscenity jurisprudence and the "right to privacy" are crucial evidence. Like Justice Brennan, whom he admires so much, Dworkin reads the Constitution mainly as a charter of individual freedoms. That is one reason the structural foundations of our system hold little interest for him, despite his occasional references to the importance of "structural design" in constitutional interpretation.[51]

---

[50] Ronald Dworkin, "Do We Have a Right to Pornography?" in *A Matter of Principle* (Cambridge, Mass.: Harvard University Press, 1985), 349.

[51] It would be instructive to compare Brennan's general understanding of the Constitution with the Introduction to *Freedom's Law*. Dworkin's views are theoretically more sophisticated than Brennan's, but similarities are apparent. See esp. William J. Brennan, Jr.,

Dworkin might go on the offensive here. He might say that accepting my viewpoint means that certain interests of children will always trump the putative right or liberty of adults. The result would be restrictions on contraceptives and the restoration of the *Hicklin* standard. Even the "softest" pornography could be banned, if it would lead some adolescents to adopt a frivolous attitude toward sexuality and parenthood.

But this is not my position. My desire to draw attention to certain interests of children does not mean that such interests must have anything like "lexical priority." To my mind, all of the interests of children canvassed in this book are legitimate, but other political and social interests are in competition with them. My overriding goal has been to document contemporary liberalism's inattention to different interests of children; for the most part, I am not recommending any precise allocation of political values.

Even in the highly unlikely event that the Supreme Court restored legislative authority to the states (i.e., if the Court reversed the rulings in *Griswold* and *Eisenstadt*), I would not advocate restrictions on the sale or use of contraceptives (to or by adults). Our present milieu is such that these restrictions would not function as they did before *Griswold*, and such legislation is likely to be counterproductive now.[52]

Similarly, I do not advocate restoring the *Hicklin* test. Such a standard is so divorced from reality that it would only be greeted with laughter now. Even the *Roth* standard will seem severe to a sizable percentage of Americans. (Yet I can understand why *some* persons would say that the *Hicklin* test is the obscenity standard that comes closest to the principle of "equal concern and respect." I can even imagine some liberals saying as much, if they reflected at length on the vulnerability of children.) For the record, however, the *Roth* standard strikes me as far more defensible than the *Miller* standard.

My concessions do not mean that the interests of children have lost their legitimacy. The concessions simply take account of vast changes in the moral and social environment in the United States. The new moral environment precludes certain kinds of legislation once widely used. The judiciary has done much to transform the moral environment, a transformation that we should lament, not celebrate.

"The Constitution of the United States: Contemporary Ratification," *South Texas Law Review* 27 (1986): 433.

[52] As explained in Rousseau's *Social Contract*, changes in a society's moral environment might make legislation that previously served public purposes useless—and, if enacted in the new environment, even inimical to the public welfare. Aquinas made a similar though slightly different point in *Summa Theologiae* I–II, q. 96, a. 1.

A BETTER WAY FORWARD?

To conclude, I offer a few more thoughts on public policy. My views might be better understood by considering a current scholarly debate. The debate was alluded to in Chapter Two, but I want to explore it more fully now.

Consider again the notion of "lexical priority." Today, giving a certain value lexical priority in a political or legal theory is likely to be characterized as a "monistic" impulse. We saw two examples of this: (1) the special status that Dworkin gives to freedom in the negative sense (as embodied in the principle of "equal concern and respect"); and (2) the priority Rawls extends to the "basic liberties" in *A Theory of Justice* and *Political Liberalism*. Ranking goods hierarchically or giving a specific good or value lexical priority is one definition of monism, and this is the definition used here.[53]

Political theorists often contrast monistic theories with pluralistic ones. For my purposes, "pluralism" refers to the view that there is a multiplicity of objective goods or values in our moral world, none of which ought to have lexical priority. According to this viewpoint, the reality of plural values should be evident to anyone who closely observes different societies.[54]

We can further describe the pluralist viewpoint. Pluralism is not relativism, and the pluralist may at once affirm the existence of both culturally specific and universal values. Furthermore, values are not infinite in number, and one may say that certain ideals, cultural practices, and traditions are *not* values. No one, for example, says that human sacrifice is a political or religious value in the United States, even though the practice figured prominently in a few societies in the past.

Although citizens and scholars alike might disagree about the criteria by which something is designated a value or a fundamental good, we can identify some shared political values in countries such as the United Kingdom or the United States. In "Two Concepts of Liberty," Isaiah Berlin singled out individual freedom, democracy, equality, and association. More recently, William Galston presented a list of seven goods endorsed by all liberal-democratic regimes: life; freedom; society [or association]; rationality; subjective satisfaction; the fulfillment of interests and purposes; and the normal development of basic capacities.[55] Liberal democracies promote

[53] "Monism" can also refer to the reduction of all goods in a theory to a common measure (as in utilitarianism) or to the view that all goods in a moral or social theory are compatible and perhaps even entail one another (Isaiah Berlin's definition).

[54] The account of pluralism offered here is indebted to Isaiah Berlin's writings on the subject as well as to more recent works, including John Gray's *Two Faces of Liberalism*, and William A. Galston's *Liberal Pluralism: The Implications of Value Pluralism for Political Theory and Practice* (Cambridge: Cambridge University Press, 2002).

[55] William A. Galston, *Liberal Purposes* (Cambridge: Cambridge University Press, 1991), 174–177.

and actualize these goods through laws, policies, and public pronouncements. Different institutions in civil society also help to realize these goods. Galston observes that different liberal democracies adopt different allocations of these goods, and that none has lexical priority.

The writings of Berlin and Galston help us to understand why value pluralists reject Dworkin's repeated attempts to fuse liberalism and democracy into a single conception of democracy (i.e., the "constitutional" conception of democracy). For the value pluralist, personal freedom and democracy are distinct political goods, sometimes in tension. Dworkin, however, evidently thinks he can develop a highly attractive conception of democracy (a "true" democracy?) in which this recurring tension dissolves. Trying to fuse the two is reminiscent of Rousseau, though saying as much might unnerve Dworkin.[56]

Why should we reject Dworkin's attempts to redescribe democracy in this manner? The reasons are both historical and theoretical. First, history shows that democracy and individual freedom can exist apart from each other (a central point in Constant's famous essay). Second, there is no logical connection between the two values (which might be thought to exist independent of history).

For similar reasons, most value pluralists would reject Dworkin's account of the majoritarian conception of democracy. The problem with the "majoritarian premise" is that it distorts an important truth: that most people in the West simultaneously esteem individual freedom and representative democracy. Each is now a basic political value, and, contrary to the majoritarian premise, people do not generally regard democracy as somehow being more fundamental to political morality. (This fact may help to explain why Dworkin fails to identify—in a straightforward way—those scholars and public figures who espouse the majoritarian premises.)

At its core, value pluralism implies a large number of morally valid ways for people to live. Men and women can flourish in many different ways, and no single way of life is right for everyone. Because different ways of life honor different things and realize different goods, they cannot all be combined in a single life. From the standpoint of value pluralism, it therefore makes little sense to speak of "a perfect life." Values present in one way of life may be absent in another, yet both ways of life might be attractive and worth leading.

Furthermore, if value pluralism is true, we will not find any "master virtue" in political, moral, or legal theory, and we should expect to see

---

[56] Besides the "Introduction" to *Freedom's Law,* see Dworkin's essay "Do Liberal Values Conflict?" in *The Legacy of Isaiah Berlin,* ed. Ronald Dworkin, Mark Lilla, and Robert Silvers (New York: New York Review Books, 2001).

some trade-offs among political goods. The trade-offs can be difficult, reminding us that politics sometimes evokes an acute sense of sacrifice.[57]

What, then, is the relationship between value pluralism and liberal democracy? On the one hand, since value pluralists see many different ways in which human beings can flourish, they consider it unreasonable for a state to prescribe one way of life as the model for all citizens. (So no value pluralist wants to live in North Korea or Saudi Arabia.) On the other hand, precisely because human beings can flourish in disparate circumstances, liberal democracy cannot be considered the only morally valid political system.

Which political systems are morally legitimate? Which are not? And are there criteria allowing us to distinguish the former from the latter? Such questions make for a lively debate.[58]

Readers who reflect upon the content of this book might understand why I regard its orientation as pluralist (or at least quasi-pluralist). But let me go further and explain why its arguments help to vindicate certain tenets of value pluralism.

The legal controversies described in Chapters Three and Four illustrate a similar point. However much contemporary liberals want to defend rights to contraception and abortion and something like the *Miller* test (or an even more permissive obscenity standard), the erstwhile restrictions on contraceptives and the obscenity standard embodied in the *Hicklin* rule promoted the realization of genuine goods. Value pluralism can help us to articulate what the legislation was meant to achieve. Most liberals today will object to the means used to promote those goods, but the goods themselves should be recognized as genuine.[59]

Because of his monistic tendencies, Ronald Dworkin might not grant this point. Recall that the principle of equal concern and respect aims to promote greater acceptance of the closely related ideas of negative freedom, moral independence, and ethical individualism. In promoting these ideas, however, Dworkin goes too far. Value pluralism suggests the folly of trying to develop a political and legal theory so heavily dependent on freedom in the negative sense. A more realistic perspective would recognize the need to include different, and even rival, notions of freedom in a political or legal theory.

---

[57] By contrast, I argue that Dworkin gives lexical priority to the notion of "equal concern and respect." For further evidence that this notion of equality functions like a "master virtue" in Dworkin's thought, see his book *Sovereign Virtue*.

[58] The debate is seen in articles and books by John Gray and William Galston, among others. See, for example, Gray's *Two Faces of Liberalism* and chapter 5 of Galston's *Liberal Pluralism*. A longer version of this chapter by Galston was published as "Value Pluralism and Liberal Political Theory," *American Political Science* Review 93 (December 1999): 769.

[59] See Galston, *Liberal Pluralism*, 3–11.

The need to integrate competing ideas of freedom arises because not all human beings are the fully rational and reflective adults presupposed by Dworkin's theory. Furthermore, even when achieved to a high degree—and we must remember that they are *achievements*—rationality and reflectiveness can be impaired or permanently lost. Political and legal theorists ought to take account of those possibilities and the circumstances that might lead to impairment. This is also a task for everyday politics, traditionally performed by legislators.[60]

As explained in Chapter One, different public policies are linked to different ideas of freedom, and the idea of positive freedom finds expression in a range of morally legitimate policies. In *Democracy and Disagreement,* Amy Gutmann and Dennis Thompson present a list of such policies, including

> safety laws and regulations (mandating seat belts, ignition interlocks, and air bags, or requiring motorcyclists to wear helmets); health regulations (requiring prescriptions for drugs, and banning certain drugs such as laetrile); criminal law (criminalizing suicide, and disallowing consent as a murder defense); and general social policy (restrictions on gambling, prevention of high risk recreational activities such as swimming in a local quarry, and licensing of professionals).[61]

Again, I do not mean to say that each of these policies is consciously based on the idea of freedom in the positive sense. But that idea helps us to understand key dimensions of them.

Would Dworkin accept most of these policies as both constitutionally and morally legitimate? It is an important question, because if he accepts them (or some of them), we should ask why he rejects the legitimacy of other policies based on the idea of positive freedom. I do not aim to resolve this matter, but only to direct the reader's attention to it.

As we have seen, liberal wariness of public policies resting on the idea of positive freedom is related to the abuse of certain notions of freedom under totalitarian regimes. Dworkin joins other liberals in invoking that specter. But as William Galston notes, "Generalized ideological claims based on positive freedom have all but vanished."[62] We might therefore ask when American liberal theorists will begin to question the preferred status of negative freedom, especially since different interests of children are unlikely to receive sufficient attention until the idea of positive freedom has been revived or rehabilitated.

---

[60] In this connection, see the views expressed by John Gray at 14–16 and throughout chapter 3 of *Two Faces of Liberalism.*

[61] Amy Gutmann and Dennis Thompson, *Democracy and Disagreement* (Cambridge, Mass.: Harvard University Press, 1996), 262. This passage is discussed in Galston, *Liberal Pluralism,* 85–86.

[62] See Galston, "Value Pluralism and Liberal Political Theory," 769.

These remarks suggest that value pluralism has implications for civil-liberties jurisprudence. If value pluralism were well understood by judges, it might make them a bit more reflective when confronted with legislation whose purposes are not immediately discernible. (One thinks of Justice David Souter's mistaken view that the Connecticut laws invalidated in *Griswold* were "purposeless restraints."[63]) Value pluralism might also spur judges to think about whether any political value in our constitutional system deserves lexical priority.

The emergence of a value-pluralism movement within liberalism is significant. It suggests the possibility of a reformed liberalism that still recognizes the importance of personal freedom and individual rights, while acknowledging the need sometimes to restrict adult rights for the sake of protecting minors. Such a reformed liberalism would broadly permit legislators—rather than judges—to decide how competing political and social goods should be allocated in public policies.

To judge from its growing importance in political science, value pluralism might soon make inroads in legal scholarship. How might this occur? A perhaps underappreciated point about value pluralism is its anti-utopian thrust, because it inflicts great damage on the ideas of a perfect life and the perfect polity. It may have a similar effect on some legal theories.

Value pluralism does not say that every decision in politics produces angst, regret, or a sense of loss, but it should induce a healthy skepticism, especially when a theory or political program promises an abundance of good things. It reminds us of the folly of trying to imagine a world without sacrifice or loss. So when we assess the goods in a political or legal theory, we should expect the theorist to acknowledge some competing goods and the costs of achieving and maintaining the goods in question. Failure to do so should put us on guard.

This point can be applied to Dworkin's "moral reading" of the Constitution. In his defense of the moral reading, Dworkin tries to show some of the unsatisfactory results originalism yields. For Dworkin, the two cases that best reveal the problems with originalism are *Brown v. Board of Education* and *Griswold v. Connecticut*. In his eyes, both cases were correctly decided, but the decisions would have been different on originalist grounds.[64]

---

[63] See his concurring opinion in *Washington v. Glucksberg*, 521 U.S. 702 (1997).

[64] Dworkin mentions other Supreme Court cases that in his judgment would have been decided differently if the tenets of originalism had been followed. His comments on these cases reveal his confidence about the correctness of the rulings. See *Freedom's Law*, 53. I am less confident, and in Chapter Three, I analyzed a few of the cases he mentions. In any event, *Brown* and *Griswold* do a tremendous amount of work in Dworkin's theory. For further evidence, see Dworkin's essay, "The Strange Case of Judge Alito," *New York Review of Books*, 23 February 2006.

While disagreeing with Dworkin about the correctness of the ruling in *Griswold,* I granted that *Brown* may present a significant problem for originalism. Leading proponents of originalism are aware of this and other problems with the theory. Justice Antonin Scalia, for example, identified several of them in an essay published in 1989. They include the need to complete the rigorous historical research sometimes required by the originalist method and possibly having to accept some morally unattractive outcomes as constitutionally valid.[65]

What does *Brown* mean for originalism? Because hard cases are said to make bad law, we may also ask about their effects on legal theory. That is, originalism could still be a defensible interpretative theory even if Dworkin is right in supposing that *Brown* cannot be justified on originalist grounds.

In places, however, Dworkin's opposition to originalism borders on the irrational. He has described Robert Bork's judicial philosophy as "no theory at all . . . no . . . jurisprudence, but only right-wing dogma."[66] In reviewing Bork's book *The Tempting of America,* Dworkin also (wrongly) predicted the rapid disappearance of originalism as an interpretative approach.[67] These and other comments on Bork suggest that Dworkin regards originalism as a grave threat, and he will go to great lengths, not all of them honorable, to discredit it. (To be fair, though, one should note that Dworkin was more respectful toward Antonin Scalia in an essay written after the attacks on Bork.[68])

Notice, however, this asymmetry: while Dworkin cites cases that present problems for originalism, he never tells his reader about cases that present difficulties for the moral reading. There is no crabgrass on Dworkin's lawn. He never cites a case whose outcome is congenial to him in which the judge may have abused his or her authority according to the tenets of the moral reading. It seems hard to believe that there are no such cases, and Dworkin's failure to mention any should make us suspicious.

Dworkin also fails to furnish meaningful criteria so that his readers can identify the judicial abuse of the moral reading in future cases. Are there such criteria? If so, they cannot be found in *Freedom's Law,* save for the

[65] See Scalia, "Originalism: The Lesser Evil." Near the end of this essay, Scalia asks (hypothetically) whether a judge who espouses originalism would need to accept as constitutionally valid a state law mandating public flogging for certain crimes (a punishment used in different states when the Constitution was ratified). In assessing this matter, one needs to think about the likelihood of any state legislature enacting such a policy today.

[66] Dworkin, *Freedom's Law,* 275.

[67] Ibid., 290; Robert Bork, *The Tempting of America: The Political Seduction of the Law* (New York: Macmillan, 1990).

[68] See the essay by Dworkin in *A Matter of Interpretation: Federal Courts and the Law,* by Antonin Scalia, ed. Amy Gutmann (Princeton: Princeton University Press, 1997).

essentially pointless concession that our federal judges cannot mandate Soviet-style ownership of the means of production.[69] (Dworkin's admission that judges who espouse the moral reading may act in bad faith has little value, since he says that *any* judge may act in bad faith, including judges who espouse originalism.)

Suppose a critic reminds Dworkin that the moral reading is supposed to take structure and precedent very seriously. On that basis, the critic might say that the decision in *Griswold* is very hard to justify. (The same considerations apply even more to the decisions in *Eisenstadt* and *Roe*). Dworkin would likely respond by saying that the critic overlooks the role that "fresh moral judgment" plays in the moral reading. But such a response would be unsatisfactory. If Dworkin took this line, we could conclude that his attention to structure and precedent was merely cosmetic and that he would ignore them whenever convenient.

Some might say that this is a harsh judgment on my part. In response, I would point out the following: if even a scholar such as Susan Moller Okin can see that *Eisenstadt* is "something of a leap from precedent," Dworkin should be able to do the same.

No one, however, should expect that to happen. Dworkin is not only pleased with the course of American civil-liberties jurisprudence in the contemporary era, he wants to export it.[70] Such eagerness is another sign of Dworkin's monistic tendencies, and though the impulse to share elements of the American political tradition is not blameworthy, some of us will be reluctant to join the project as conceived in *Freedom's Law* and elsewhere. Other scholars, including John Gray, find Dworkin's thinking on this subject arrogant, and we may ask whether the whole world is now supposed to take its bearings on fundamental matters of political morality from jurists such as William Brennan, Anthony Kennedy, and Dworkin himself. The indifference of these men to some vital interests of children is one reason that thoughtful persons—including thoughtful liberals, both here and abroad—may not be rejoicing at that prospect.

[69] Dworkin, *Freedom's Law*, 11.
[70] See, for example, ibid., 71 and 81.

Index

Paul Edward Gottfried, *After Liberalism:*
Mass Democracy in the Managerial State

Peter Berkowitz, *Virtue and the Making of Modern Liberalism*

John E. Coons and Patrick M. Brennan, *By Nature Equal:*
The Anatomy of a Western Insight

David Novak, *Covenantal Rights: A Study in Jewish Political Theory*

Charles L. Glenn, *The Ambiguous Embrace:*
Government and Faith-Based Schools and Social Agencies

Peter Bauer, *From Subsistence to Exchange and Other Essays*

Robert P. George, ed., *Great Cases in Constitutional Law*

Amitai Etzioni, *The Monochrome Society*

Daniel N. Robinson, *Praise and Blame:*
Moral Realism and Its Applications

Timothy P. Jackson, *The Priority of Love:*
Christian Charity and Social Justice

Sotirios A. Barber, *Welfare and the Constitution*

Jeffrey Stout, *Democracy and Tradition*

James Hitchcock, *The Supreme Court and Religion in American Life:*
Volume 1, The Odyssey of the Religion Clauses; Volume 2,
From "Higher Law" to "Sectarian Scruples"

Christopher Wolfe, ed., *That Eminent Tribunal:*
Judicial Supremacy and the Constitution

Patrick Deneen, *Democratic Faith*

David Novak, *The Jewish Social Contract:*
An Essay in Political Theology

Neil M. Gorsuch, *The Future of Assisted Suicide and Euthanasia*

David L. Tubbs, *Freedom's Orphans:*
Contemporary Liberalism and the Fate of American Children